Teaching English Language Learners in Secondary Subject Matter Classes

(2nd Edition)

Teaching English Language Learners in Secondary Subject Matter Classes

(2nd Edition)

By

Yu Ren Dong

INFORMATION AGE PUBLISHING, INC.
Charlotte, NC • www.infoagepub.com

Library of Congress Cataloging-In-Publication Data

Names: Dong, Yu Ren, author.
Title: Teaching English language learners in secondary subject matter
   classes / Yu Ren Dong.
Description: 2nd Edition. | Charlotte : Information Age Publishing Inc.,
   2020. | Includes bibliographical references. | Summary: "This book is
   for secondary subject matter teachers and administrators who work with
   English language learners (ELLs) in subject matter classes. It is also
   for college professors who prepare pre-service teachers to work with
   those students. The book brings together insights from linguistic,
   socio-cultural, educational, cognitive, developmental perspectives of
   what it means for ELLs to learn both English and subject matter
   knowledge in English as a second language. It delineates unique
   challenges that ELLs experience, offers ELLs' learning stories, and
   suggests concrete strategies with classroom teaching examples across
   academic disciplines. The 2nd edition broadens the scope of the 1st
   edition in several aspects. Specifically, it includes two chapters about
   secondary ELLs' previous educational experiences in their home
   countries, a chapter on subject matter lesson planning with ELLs in mind
   with teacher collaborative strategies, and more principle-based and
   field-tested effective instructional and assessment strategies for
   working with ELLs"-- Provided by publisher.
Identifiers: LCCN 2019029410 (print) | LCCN 2019029411 (ebook) | ISBN
   9781641137744 (paperback) | ISBN 9781641137751 (hardcover) | ISBN
   9781641137768 (ebook)
Subjects: LCSH: English language--Study and teaching (Secondary)--Foreign
   speakers. | Second language acquisition--Study and teaching--Foreign
   speakers. | Interdisciplinary approach in education.
Classification: LCC PE1128.A2 D623 2020 (print) | LCC PE1128.A2 (ebook) |
   DDC 428.0071--dc23
LC record available at https://lccn.loc.gov/2019029410
LC ebook record available at https://lccn.loc.gov/2019029411

Printed in the United States of America

CONTENTS

10. Preparing ELLs for Evaluation and Standardized Tests 201

     Conclusion... 217

     Bibliography 219

     Index 239

DEDICATION

In memory of my father, Ke Chang Dong
A historian, educator, poet, and story-teller

ACKNOWLEDGEMENTS

This book was developed over the years with the help of so many people. I owe a debt of gratitude to many classroom teachers and assistant principals at Flushing International High School, John Bowne High School, Long Island City High School, and Newtown High School. Those teachers and administrators shared with me their insights and ESL teaching examples across subject matter areas. Thanks to many ELLs at these schools who participated early and whose journeys to a new culture have provided insights into our understanding of second language acquisition for academic success. Also, part of the research findings reported in this book was sponsored by a CUNY PSC research grant and my thanks to their support.

I have taught Language, Literacy, and Culture in Education and Reading and Writing for Diverse Learners courses to mainstream subject matter teachers cross academic disciplines. Many of them responded to the courses enthusiastically, and many of their teaching ideas and strategies have contributed to our teaching subject matter knowledge to ELLs.

My special thanks go to several colleagues who read and edited parts of my manuscript for the 2nd edition. They are Suzanne Abruzzo, Frances Curcio, John Walsh, and Myra Zarnowski. Finally, thanks to my husband and son, who constantly keep me grounded and supported me throughout the writing process.

Teaching English Language Learners in Secondary Subject Matter Classes, pages ix–xi.
Copyright © 2019 by Information Age Publishing

COPYRIGHT ACKNOWLEDGEMENTS

From "Unlock their lonely hearts" by D. L. Fu, 1998. *Voices from the Middle, 6*(1), 3–10. Copyright by NCTE. Reprinted with permission.

From "Tapping into English language learners' (ELLs') prior knowledge in social studies instruction" by Y. R. Dong, 2017. *The Social Studies, 108*(4), 1–9. Copyright by NCSS. Reprinted with permission.

From "Promoting ELL students' participation in mainstream subject matter classes" by Y R. Dong, 2005a, *Thresholds in Education, 16* (1 & 2), 33–40. Copyright by Missouri State University, the Academy for Educational Studies. Reprinted with permission

INTRODUCTION

When asked about her childhood back in China, Qian Wen, a Chinese English language learner (ELL) newly arrived in a New York City high school as a 9th grader, revealed her love for nature back home:

> When I was young back home in my country in Mainland China, I would go out in the park close to my house, catching grasshoppers, butterflies, dragonflies, and lady bugs with my friends during the summer break. We collected these bugs and took them home and put them in different jars. We fed them with leaves and water and observed them. I don't remember what we found out but I do remember the excitement that I had over collecting those colorful dragonflies. Once I found a blue-tailed dragonfly. It took me quite a while to follow her and finally I caught her. That made a hit among my friends and also created several fascinating questions: How come dragonflies fly so fast? Why can dragonflies catch things to eat while flying? Why does a dragonfly have a small body but two large eyes?
> *— by Qian Wen, a 9th grade ELL*

Qian Wen wants to major in biology in college and become a doctor in the future. Over the years as I traveled from school to school, from class to class, watching and listening to these students, I have found that Qian Wen's love and dream were also shared by many ELLs. As ELLs are the fastest growing student population in the US public schools (NCES, 2019) in general and New York City where I work in particular, many subject matter teachers find themselves teaching either an ESL subject matter class that contains all ELLs at different levels of English proficiency or a mainstreamed subject matter class with a mixture of students of English proficient students and ELLs.). According to New York City Department of Education (2016), one out of every seven public school students is an ELL. Many of these ELLs spend a significant amount of time during the day in those subject matter classes to learn both academic English and subject matter knowledge and the rest day in ESL language classes to improve their English language skills.

Facing this new teaching reality, in recent years, we have made big strides in expanding the scope of ESL education to go beyond the ESL language class taught by the certified ESL teacher to the mainstream subject matter classes. For example, in New York City that I work many college teacher education programs have required an ESL teacher education course for all teacher candidates. Recently, New York State mandates all teachers to pass the Education for All Students (EAS) exam as a part of the teaching certification requirements. One key section of this exam is about educating ELLs in subject matter classes. As more and more subject matter teachers have become aware of ELLs in their classrooms, there is an increased need for preservice teachers and inservice teachers to develop knowledge and strategies in order to tailor their instruction toward those students' language levels and needs. More needs to be done; especially facing the increased graduation standards and standardized tests required for all graduating high school students including ELLs. A most recent report (Taylor, 2017) showed that while general New York City public high school English proficient students' graduation rate increased from 67.2% in 2015 to 69.6% in the 2016; however, the graduation rate for ELLs decreased to 26.6% in 2016 from 33.3% in 2015.

In addition to a big discrepancy in the graduation rate when comparing ELLs with English proficient students, many subject matter teachers find themselves teaching in a new instructional setting in secondary schools. In New York City schools, for example, many ESL teachers are no longer working alone to provide ESL instruction separate from mainstream subject matter teachers. Rather, they work in an ENL (English as a New Language) or a push-in instructional setting where an ESL teacher teaches side by side with a mainstream subject matter teacher in the same classroom. The new instructional set up offers new opportunities for both the ESL and mainstream subject matter teachers to work together toward the goal of facilitating and promoting ELLs' academic subject matter, language, and social success. This requires both the ESL teacher and mainstream subject matter teacher to work together on lesson planning, team teaching and providing instructional and assessment support. All this calls for secondary subject matter teachers to increase their knowledge of ESL language instruction, culturally responsive teaching in order to collaborate successfully with their ESL counterparts in planning instruction, modifying curriculum, and assessing ELLs' language and subject matter progress.

Although there has been a growing need for a while for a book like this to prepare all subject matter teachers for ELLs at the secondary level, however, there has been a gap in teacher education textbooks. On the one hand, we have seen many books preparing secondary subject matter teachers for teaching their respective subject matter to English proficient students, giving little recognition to ELLs, who are often mentioned in passing. There have been limited resources and a death of appropriate textbooks that deal in a systematic way with how to integrate ESL pedagogy into subject matter instruction. Therefore, it is long overdue to combine the strengths of the two fields: ESL education and subject matter teacher education and take a serious look at the discipline specific curriculum, instruction, and assessment in order to design teaching practices that are both subject matter challenging and relevant and linguistically and culturally responsive for ELLs.

My purpose for writing this book is to discuss what constitutes effective curriculum, instruction, and assessment for ELLs in secondary subject matter classrooms. As an English as a second language educator who prepares prospective teachers for their work with a diverse student body, including non-native English speaking students, I hope this book will provide one point of departure for bridging the gulf between subjects and provoking conversations among all teachers as they reflect on their practices and as their classrooms become more linguistically and culturally diverse.

Over the years I have been fortunate to work with a group of young and dedicated secondary subject matter teachers who saw diversity in their classroom as a resource and who tried out different methods and techniques to reach their ELLs and promote those students' second language learning and academic success. Also influential in my work were a few supportive assistant principals who welcomed my research with open arms and shared with me both their successes and problems in dealing with a diverse student population. Many ELLs in those classrooms taught by those teachers and in those schools were flourished. They talked, responded, and wrote. They touched, felt, smelled in addition to watching, reading, and listening. They sought, explored, imagined, and inquired. Many subject matters, such as biology, mathematics, and social studies, etc. though tough subjects, their teacher presented them in such a stimulating, relevant, and comprehensible way and provided these students with many exciting, meaningful, and challenging experiences and language support. All that made these students feel that they had a chance of success. Those experiences have enabled me to see culturally relevant and linguistically responsive teaching in action.

This book is intended for middle and high school subject matter teachers, preservice subject matter teachers, and school administrators, college faculty involved in both pre-service and in-service teacher preparation programs, curriculum developers, and policy makers. In this book they will find both research-based teaching principles and field-tests concrete ideas for teaching subject matter knowledge to ELLs. Although biology, earth science, chemistry, physics, US history, global history, English language arts, and mathematics are used as key subject matter examples for illustration, many ideas and strategies described in the book can be also applied to other subject matter area teaching contexts.

HOW THE SECOND EDITION DIFFERS FROM THE FIRST

My second edition has the following major changes and updates:

1. I updated the information in the 2004 book with data from the most re-
    cent statistics from the New York City Department of Education (DOE)
    as in Chapter One. I also included more ELLs' portraits as in Chapter
    Two to reflect diverse ELLs in secondary schools. I updated the New
    York State standardized test examples for high school graduation and
    accommodation information in Chapter Ten.
2. Based on the recent research findings to reflect the unique academic and
    cross-cultural literacy backgrounds of secondary ELLs, I broadened the
    theoretical framework. The theoretical framework adds to this edition re-
    flects research in 1) biliteracy education 2) culturally responsive teaching
    and 3) academic language and literacy education at the secondary levels.
3. Drawn on the expanded theoretical framework, I wrote two new chap-
    ters: Chapter Five: Previous literacy education for ELLs from Asian
    countries: China, South Korea, and Bangladesh; and Chapter Six: Previ-
    ous literacy education for ELLs from South American and Latin Ameri-
    can countries: Mexico, and the Dominican Republic. Those countries
    were selected because of a high percentage of ELLs in New York City
    public schools coming from those countries.
4. To address the recent teacher certification requirements and teaching re-
    ality, I expanded a section in the 2004 book to separate chapter on lesson
    planning for ESL oriented subject matter instruction. Using examples
    from various academic disciplines at the secondary level, I illustrated
    what and how to plan a language integrated subject matter instruction by
    applying ESL teaching principles, responding to ELLs' language levels,
    and tapping into ELLs' previous literacy and cultural backgrounds.
5. Based on the changing graduation demands and new instructional struc-
    tures, I combined some chapters in the first edition to make them more
    coherent and reflective of the current teaching realities in secondary lit-
    eracy and subject matter instruction for ELLs. They are Chapter Seven:
    ESL vocabulary and reading instruction, Chapter Eight: ESL vocabulary
    and writing instruction, and Chapter Nine: Promoting language learning
    through class discussions.

ORGANIZATION OF THE SECOND EDITION

This book is organized into ten chapters. Chapter 1, Principles and Methods in
Teaching ELLs lays out a theoretical framework for understanding adolescent
second language learners' second language, literacy, and culture acquisition and
learning. It reviews research in the field of second language acquisition and bilingual education and discusses social, cultural, language, cognitive, and psy-

chological factors that influence those students' learning of academic English in American schools. Focusing on school based second language acquisition and learning, the chapter discusses critical issues facing public school subject matter teachers today.

Chapter 2, Who Are Our ELLs? provides updated information about diverse ELLs in terms of their English language proficiency levels, previous literacy backgrounds, and learning needs. The chapter also gives an overall discussion of how those students are identified, screened, placed, and exit the ESL services and various ESL services offered in New York City schools. The chapter contains ten portraits of secondary ELLs and their subject matter teachers' success in working with them either along side of ESL teachers or on their own to promote their academic and language development in their classes.

Chapters 3 and 4, Asian ELLs Previous Literacy Experiences and Latino ELLs' Previous Literacy Experiences offer a detailed and in-depth review of what literacy education looks like in elementary and secondary schools in those countries, how it is structured, and why it differs from literacy education in the U.S.

Chapter 5, Planning for ESL Oriented Subject Matter Instruction offers ideas for subject matter lesson planning with ELLs in mind. Using discipline-specific subject matter topics, the chapter illustrates various examples of how to plan an ESL oriented lesson to provide language integrated subject matter instruction.

Chapter 6, Assessing ELLs in Subject Matter Classes discusses language assessment issues and offers effective tools and strategies for subject matter teachers to use in order to adjust their teaching expectations and differentiate instruction and assessment. The chapter provides both guidelines and examples for assessing English language learners' academic and language performance in daily instruction according to their English language proficiency levels and developmental sequences and needs.

Chapters 7, 8, and 9 cover a range of curricular and instructional methods and techniques used to teach discipline-specific vocabulary, language, reading, writing, and oral language. Each chapter pairs up two or three language and literacy focuses and addresses how to develop ELLs' skills in vocabulary, reading, writing, and classroom participation. For example, Chapter 7 focuses on ESL vocabulary and reading instruction in subject matter areas, Chapter 8 on ESL vocabulary and writing instruction in subject matter areas, and Chapter 9 on promoting language learning through class discussions in subject matter areas. Each of these three chapters contains relevant ESL teaching principles and language skill specific teaching strategies as well as actual classroom examples. Subject matter areas used for illustration include English language arts, social studies, mathematics, sciences, etc.

Chapter 10 focuses on the challenges of high school graduation requirements for ELLs and additional language and cultural issues embedded in the standardized tests. The chapter includes a series of critical reviews of sample New York State Regents Exams in major subject matter areas to highlight those ESL difficulties. The chapter also introduces updated state guidelines for ELL accommodations on the standardized testing and suggests ideas for how to prepare those students for those tests. Finally, the chapter suggests alternative ways of doing evaluation for ELLs.

CHAPTER 1

PRINCIPLES OF SECOND LANGUAGE LEARNING FOR ADOLESCENTS

How Do Adolescent English Language Learners (ELLs) Learn English as A Second Language?

As native English speakers, we acquired English, oral English in our childhood. Using English is such a natural part of our everyday lives that we seldom pause and examine how we became fluent with English. We listen, speak, read, and write in English with such ease that it is hard to imagine anyone having difficulty with it. We take language for granted until we start to learn a second language, or travel abroad, or witness ELLs in our own classrooms who struggle with the language that we have acquired so easily, automatically, and unconsciously. Why is second language acquisition so difficult, time consuming, and involving such conscious efforts?

How does an adolescent acquire a second language? Researchers have been asking this question for many years. Research has shown that while second language acquisition shares many similarities with first language acquisition, it also differs in significant ways. Generally speaking, adolescent ELLs undergo the

Teaching English Language Learners in Secondary Subject Matter Classes, pages 7–28.
Copyright © 2019 by Information Age Publishing

process of learning English as a second language through the following marked stages:

- Silent Period
- Acquiring Basic Interpersonal Communication Skills (BICS)
- Acquiring Cognitive Academic Language Proficiency (CALP)

Silent Period. Similar to first language acquisition, second language acquisition involves the language learner, whether a child or a teen or an adult, interacting frequently with people who speak that language in a meaningful way. In second language acquisition, as in the first, the learner is often silent at the very beginning (Krashen, 1982). However, that Silence Period does not mean that s/he is tuned off or acting dumb or giving little effort; rather it is a time when s/he is making active meaning of the new language through listening and observing. Gradually, the learner utters a sound or a word in the new language. Then, s/he begins to produce phrases and sentences. Research in both first and second language has shown that second language learners go through similar stages in their language development, specifically their learning of sounds and grammatical structures.

How long does it take for an adolescent to pass the Silent Period and speak in the new language? Generally speaking, the Silent period can last from a couple of weeks to a year. It depends on many factors, including the student's motivation, the new language learning environment and culture, teachers' way of making both spoken and written language comprehensible to the student, and many more. I'll be talking about those factors throughout this chapter.

Many people often think that the younger second language learner, the faster and the better outcome the second language acquisition. Age does play a critical role in second language learning. According to Critical Period Hypothesis (Lenneberg, 1967) there is a critical period of time roughly before puberty when the child's brain and vocal muscles are still developing and flexible for a child to acquire a second language with ease and fast and to achieve native like pronunciation and gaining an intuitive sense of grammaticality and oral fluency. After that period of time is past, for young adults and adults to learn second language, it often takes painstaking efforts, more time, and tremendous and conscious rule learning and practice. Still, the result may not be as successful as younger learners in achieving native like pronunciation and grammatical and oral fluency. However in recent years as more and more immigrant students come to the U.S. schools facing the challenges of the learning standards and graduation demands, research and teaching reality have argued that unlike younger ELLs secondary ELLs have more urgent needs for developing and achieving academic language and subject matter knowledge to meet the graduation demands.

Distinction between BICS and CALP. The distinction between the BICS and CALP is important in raising our awareness of acquisition of different types of second language, which very often is not so obvious. In first language acquisition, by the time a child reaches school age, six years old, s/he has already acquired a complex oral language for communication purposes. During the years of elementary school, middle school, and high school, the child's native language acquisition continues and expands to the acquisition of the written language (reading and writing), and to learning to use the language to think in the complex academic subject matter areas, such as mathematics, science, English language arts, social studies, etc.

Cummins (1979a) made a distinction in these two types of language acquisition: one is the acquisition of Basic Interpersonal Communication Skills (BICS) and the other is the acquisition of Cognitive Academic Language Proficiency (CALP). Young children or older adult learners of a second language for communication purposes might want to acquire BICS only. BICS are often called social language, everyday English, conversational English, or playground language, etc. Examples include using language for various social purposes, such as saying greetings and goodbyes, going shopping, making phone calls, giving introductions to get to know people, ordering a pizza, asking for direction, calling for help, etc. Fortunately, for young children at the early elementary level, they still have some time to improve their BICS before they encounter challenging CALP.

In comparison, CALP, often called academic English or discipline-specific language or written language includes

- General academic vocabulary used in the classroom and lab, to analyze, argue, compare and contrast,
- Discipline-specific vocabulary, such as photosynthesis, imperialism, Pythagorean theorem, thesis,
- Discipline-specific academic language structures, such as the nominal sentence structure in science, causal and effect sentence structure in social studies, conditional sentence structure to write the proof in mathematics, etc.
- Discipline-specific reading and writing genres such as lab reports, comparative essays, DBQ (Document Based Question) essays

Collier (1987, 1989) used scores obtained from the standardized tests and school records of thousands of ELLs, ranging from elementary to high school to find out how long it would take for an ELL to acquire grade level appropriate CALP. She found that ELLs who had schooling back in their home countries and were motivated to acquire a second language would take probably 5–7 years to acquire CALP and catch up with their native English-speaking peers.

However, most secondary ELLs who come to the U.S. to attend middle and high schools do not have the luxury of time as young children to acquire the oral language or BICS first and then the written language or CALP. Rather, they face a situation where they have to acquire both oral and written language simultaneously and quickly in order to meet graduation requirements. Many ELLs at secondary schools are placed in ESL classes two or three periods a day and spend the rest of their school day in the subject matter classes which demand they use the language they are trying to acquire to learn academic content. A 14-year-old ELL who has just arrived in the U.S. faces the enormous challenges of gaining proficiency in a second language and completing, in the new language, content area courses needed to graduate from high school all within four years. Therefore, subject matter teachers must teach both language and subject matter simultaneously in order to speed up ELLs' process of learning (Genesee, 1993; Slavit & Slavit, 2007; Snow, Met, & Genesee, 1989; Swain, 1996).

Keep in mind although in general BICS takes a shorter time to acquire, it also varies from learner to learner. When the language environment is not rich or the learner does not seek out and interact with native English-speaking peers, BICS might take a longer time to acquire, and the same is true to acquisition of CALP. Leki (1992) cited the example of international students who had developed high proficiency of CALP, but could not carry on daily conversations in English. In inner city public schools, students who live in a home environment where English is not the dominant language and where daily communicative activities are conducted using their native language these learners' acquisition of BICS or CALP may be seriously delayed due to those factors.

Teaching Implications for the BICS and CALP in Subject Matter Classes. There are several implications for teaching based on the above research findings. BICS and CALP are two kinds of language skills and take the learner different amounts of time and levels of cognition, skills, and contexts to acquire fluency. Folk knowledge often assumes that students need to have acquired BICS before learning CALP. However, this is flawed based on the fact that if ELLs cannot participate in the subject matter class or communicate adequately in English and then they are not eligible for the acquisition of CALP. The reverse may also be the case in that even if ELLs have shown the ability to communicate adequately in English, still it does not mean that they have caught up with their native peers in CALP on standardized tests. Achieving CALP requires far more intensive, time consuming, cognitively challenging, and involves abstract and complex thinking and learning.

In New York City secondary schools, the majority (74.3%) of secondary ELLs come to the U.S. with the grade level equivalent of education, native language and literacy skills learned in their native countries. Those adolescent ELLs cannot afford waiting until they have developed BICS before they start to acquire CALP. For secondary ELLs who enter American schools in grade nine for example, time is not on their side as they will run out of time to learn CALP before they leave high school. Because of the length of time it takes for secondary ELLs to learn CALP, we cannot delay CALP instruction until they have mastered the BICS. As shown by research, despite their lack of English proficiency, many ELLs, especially those with previous schooling are very capable of learning CALP as long as the teacher is willing to uncover and tap into their prior knowledge and skills and provide language support. Therefore, subject matter teachers must not assume or place ELLs on hold but engage those students in learning academic language alongside subject matter and provide a meaningful context and opportunities for ELLs to learn and use both BICS and CALP at the same time.

Finally, providing secondary ELLs with academic and discipline-specific language instruction is the key for subject matter teachers to speed up ELLs' second language learning. Mohan (1986) argued that language is not just a medium of communication but a medium of learning across the curriculum. The goal of integration should be both language learning and content learning. ESL students need to acquire English, as well as learn difficult subject matter through English. There may have been little continuity in their educational experiences in their home country, yet at the end of their secondary education, their level of academic achievement in English and their level of subject matter knowledge will be judged in comparison with English speaking students. Therefore, there is an urgent need for all teachers to take the responsibility of educating ELLs by providing these students with access to the subject matter curriculum and the opportunity to acquire both BICS and CALP using ESL teaching principles and techniques.

WHAT CAN SUBJECT MATTER TEACHERS DO TO PROMOTE ELLS' SECOND LANGUAGE LEARNING IN SUBJECT MATTER CLASSES?

In recent years, we have seen a shift in focus of second language teaching from a traditional satellite type of ESL language instruction to an integrated language and subject matter instruction (Adamson, 1993; Carrasquillo & Rodriguez, 1996; Chamot & O'Malley, 1994; Mohan, 1986; Peitzman & Gadda, 1994; Richard-Amato & Snow, 1992). This shift is supported by two important second language acquisition principles proposed by Stephen Krashen (1982): One is called Input Principle and the other the Affective Filter Principle.

Krashen's Comprehensible Input Hypothesis. According to Krashen, (1982, 1985) second language acquisition becomes successful only when the learner is exposed to comprehensible input, the input that is meaningful, challenging, and relevant to the student at the level a little above the learner's current language and cognitive level or i+1. The "i" stands for the second language learner's current language or interlanguage (Selinker, 1972) that shows both features of English and the student's native language and "+1" is the next stage in his or her language acquisition. According to Krashen, it is essential for the teacher to provide comprehensible input in order to assist the language learner progress. Krashen's hypothesis parallels with Vygotsky's Zone of Proximal Development (Vygotsky, 1978) in that both acknowledge the rich learning context and the necessary challenge required to motivate the learner to acquire language.

Over the years, researchers have studied various input from the teacher and students in class and characterized the teacher's input as both oral, including teacher's questions, directions given in class and written, including teacher's board work, PowerPoint slides, homework assignments, reading and writing assignments, test questions, etc. Although Krashen's Comprehensible Input is easy to understand, it's not that easy to put into action. It requires the subject matter teacher to be vigilant about his or her language use, examine the lesson plan from an ELL's perspective, and be willing to modify and simplify both oral and written language use in class as well as in the assignments for ELLs.

Krashen's Affective Filter Hypothesis. According to Krashen (1982), an Affective Filter refers to the level of anxiety that the language learner has while learning a new language. The degree of the affective filter can be influenced by factors both from within the learner, such as the learner's motivation, self-confidence, attitude, and personality, and from the environment, such as classroom learning tasks, teacher input, peer influence, etc. For example, an introverted student or the student who has a negative attitude toward the new language and the new culture is not likely to participate in classroom discussions and make an active use of the new language. Also, if the teacher's input is too much above the student's level of language or it is not related to the student, it will induce much anxiety from the learner, thus, overwhelming or frustrating the learner. A classroom environment with optimal affective filter, not too high or too low, is conducive to learning. In this learning environment, the learner has some eager anticipation or low anxiety but is challenged and motivated to make sense of the input thus leading to active and positive learning and use of the new language.

Teaching Implications for Krashen's Second Language Teaching Principles. Traditionally, middle and high school subject matter is taught with the expectation that students have already learned about it in their early school years and have had appropriate cultural knowledge and vocabulary. For example, biology textbooks at the high school level are written based on the assumption that students have grown up in the American culture and will understand and learn the content which is presented in scientifically appropriate ways and written for students with appropriate grade reading levels. However, with the increasing diversity of the student population across the nation, these assumptions and expectations have to be re-examined.

Second language learning principles, such as Krashen's Input principle and Affective Filter principle, indicate that in order to promote subject matter learning for all students, textbook designers, administrators, and subject matter teachers need to address the issues of language and ELLs' English proficiency levels and reading levels and needs. In order to help ELLs to catch up or keep up with their native English-speaking peers, all teachers must teach both subject matter and language at the same time by creating comprehensible input and an optimal affective filter. Both teacher input and affective filter can go hand in hand. Without care taken for these ELLs' current level of language proficiency and language difficulties they are dealing with, the input will not be comprehensible, thus increasing the level of classroom affective filter.

WHAT ROLE DOES ADOLESCENT ELLS' NATIVE CULTURE PLAY IN THEIR SECOND LANGUAGE LEARNING?

One of my student teachers at the student teaching seminar wrote about this incident which occurred in her ESL class:

> Eliza had only been here for a few months and was doing wonderfully. However, some days she just put her head down on the desk and started crying. Although I asked her, she did not wish to talk about what was wrong. But I learned from her aunt that she was here with her aunt's family and her parents were still back home in Dominican. One day students were asked what they would buy if they had $1,000. As I was going around the room helping students, I saw most of them writing about things like cars, clothes, houses, etc. But when I came to Eliza, her paper had only one sentence: "I would buy an airplane ticket to Dominican Republic and never come back."

Eliza's writing gives us a glimpse of an acculturation process in second language acquisition for adolescents. The process of second language acquisition is also a process of acculturation, a gradual adaptation to the new culture in behaving, communicating, and thinking. Unlike first language learners acquiring a language in the native culture, second language learners are acquiring a new language away from their native culture. Many immigrant students come to the U.S. with relatives or siblings and are separated from their parents as in Eliza's case. Very often this uprooting and confusing situation adds to the difficulty in their second language acquisition and acculturation. Different from first language learners, second language learners especially teenagers and adults have already acquired their first language, a set of cultural values and beliefs, and literacy skills. Therefore, they come to learn a second language by constantly comparing and contrasting their native language with the new language and their prior cultural and educational experiences with the new experiences.

Acculturation Process for Adolescent ELLs. On the whole, second language learners go through four stages of acculturation paralleling their second language acquisition process. Acton and Felix (1986) labeled the four stages as tourist, survivor, immigrant, and citizen. In the first two stages of acculturation process, second language learners first experience the excitement and newness of just being in a new country, seeing different people and things. During these two stages, second language learners acquire their BICS. However, that newness and excitement wear off quickly when the second language learners experience overwhelming differences and confusions in the new language and the new culture. Their affective filter goes up and culture shock comes in, which is characterized by extreme homesickness, loneliness, anger, frustration, sadness, and even some physical discomfort as shown in Eliza's case. At this point, they view the new culture with dissatisfaction or even hostility and they tend to withdraw to their inner self or to their fellow country students for comfort and solace. According to second language researchers, this is called the acculturation threshold, in that students either progress into the next stage of acculturation and language acquisition or remain in the same stage and fail to move on to the next stage. Eliza is obviously suffering from cultural shock, the survivor stage in the acculturation process.

Language learning is also culture learning. For many adolescents and young adult ELLs, their home cultures and life experiences often are not shared by their American teacher (Dong, 2009, 2013–2014; Freeman & Freeman, 2009; Weisman & Hansen, 2007). In addition, what they are asked to read, write, and discuss in class is routinely foreign to them if not against their previous cultural and/or religious beliefs, traditions, and expectations (Marino, 2011). These cultural differences or even clashes compound their difficulty in learning English and put them in a disadvantaged position, often leading to their negativity toward and limited success with English and academic learning.

Acculturation for ELLs is a Two-Way Street. The role that sociocultural factors play in second language acquisition was first articulated by Schumann (1978) in his Acculturation Model using a case study method. Schumann observed the second language and culture acquisition of Alberto, an adult immigrant from Costa Rica for a period of ten months. Schumann found that second language acquisition to a large degree depended on the learner's social and psychological distance from the new culture. Social distance is defined by Schumann as how much the second language learner can identify with people in the new culture, which can be related to the difference between the learner's native culture and the new culture. The psychological distance is defined as whether the second language learner can feel comfortable in learning the new language in the new environment, which can be determined by the degree of willingness or motivation or risk-taking on the part of the learner to learn the new language.

Alberto, as Schumann noted, learned English just to get by for his basic survival needs. Being in the U.S. as a manual worker, he interacted only with his Spanish speaking friends. He found comfort and solace in his Spanish speaking community and had no motivation for learning English or for acculturating into the American mainstream culture, even though there were English classes and English TV programs available to him. As a result, Alberto's English remained minimal and showed no progress. Studying Alberto's language acquisition and acculturation process led Schumann to believe that the acculturation process was vital in second language acquisition. When the social and psychological distance was large, the learner would be less likely to pass the early stages in second language acquisition.

An ideal second language and culture acquisition environment, as described by Schumann, has the characteristics of a shorter social and psychological distance between the learner's native culture and the new culture; a sincere desire and motivation for both the second language learner and the people in the new culture to acculturate. Meeting each other at least halfway required a new culture to be open and positive toward immigrants and immigrant children from other cultures. Schumann emphasized the importance of a two-way street for both the teacher and ELLs to reach out to each other in order for these students to have bigger gains in second language acquisition and learning and academic success.

Culturally Relevant Pedagogy. In recent years, second language teaching and learning has extended Schumann's acculturation principle to call for the culturally and linguistically responsive teaching approach. Culturally relevant pedagogy (Gay, 2010; Lee, 2010) was originated from research on educational disparities of racial minority students in the 1990s. It argued for the importance of inclusive education to learning experiences relevant and meaningful to those minority students. Defined as a teaching approach to recognize, tap into, and build on those students' home cultural knowledge, prior learning, and familiar points of reference, culturally relevant pedagogy delineated three major teaching applications:

1. Teachers' investigation of students' prior knowledge
2. Teachers' recognition and inclusion of students' prior knowledge and voices in their curriculum and instruction; and
3. Teachers' adjustment made during the teaching process to engage and motivate students to participate in the learning process

Research findings have shown that when teachers use culturally relevant pedagogy, students respond positively and engage actively in the learning process (Choi, 2013; Irizarry, 2007; Ladson-Billings, 1995; Moll et al., 1992).

Linguistically Responsive Teaching. The linguistically responsive teaching research literature overlaps and complements the Culturally Relevant Pedagogy research in a significant and meaningful way. Faced with an increasing number of ELLs coming to American schools in recent years, the culturally relevant pedagogy has expanded its application to educating ELLs to promote their academic success (An, 2009; Choi, 2013; Choi, Lim, & An, 2011; Duff, 2001; Irizarry, 2011; Ramirez & Jaffee, 2016). Drawing on the principles and processes second language acquisition and effective ESL teaching methods and techniques, researchers have identified the following key ingredients of culturally relevant pedagogy and linguistic responsive teaching, for example in social studies, are:

- Sending a clear message that what ELLs bring to the social studies class is not only a valid but an important resource for learning
- Providing language support and being knowledgeable about those students' second language developmental stages, characteristics, and needs
- Building disciplinary language and literacy skills into the lesson by explicitly teaching the language functions, vocabulary, discourse patterns used in the social studies texts
- Tapping into ELLs' native language, culture, literacy skills, and styles of learning and allowing ELLs to use their native language when they are limited in using English to express their intelligence and thoughts
- Learning about ELLs' cultural backgrounds and culturally familiar referents and using them to bridge the social studies content presented in class

- Using comparisons and contrasts to analyze different historical narratives, perspectives and enrich the social studies curriculum and develop critical learners (Dong, 2017, pp. 2–3)

Teaching Implications for the Cultural Theories. Subject matter teachers must be aware of possible cultural differences or even cultural clashes in their daily teaching. For example, a Bangladeshi ELL's struggles with learning about human sexual functions in her biology class may be the result of the cultural differences on the topic.

> Sexual reproduction is difficult to learn because in my country, in high school, we were not allowed to talk about the sexual stuff until the students have become 18... I don't know how to approach these kinds of things. My parents have never given a mention to me about this. I was so stressed out during those days of biology classes.
> — *Jasmine, a 9th grade Bangladeshi ELL*

Jasmine's teacher was initially unaware of her struggle and was puzzled by her lack of performance, interpreting it as a lack of effort and motivation. Also, the education that the biology teacher received and the way biology curriculum is set up is based on the dominant culture, taking a Eurocentric perspective, lacking ethnic and cultural diversity. Thus, the teacher needs to be trained and be aware of possible cultural differences or even clashes going on in the classroom and adjust the curriculum and instruction to decrease the social distance, and facilitate the acculturation and language acquisition process.

Acton and Felix's acculturation stages and Schumann's acculturation hypothesis have implications for teaching ELLs in public schools. Knowing the four stages of the acculturation process will help teachers who work with second language learners to understand and assess some of the early behaviors and attitudes that these students exhibit and how to strategize to ease the difficulty in the students' acculturation. Also, knowing the best environment in which acculturation and second language acquisition takes place, teachers can create a classroom environment that is open, non-threatening, and positive for both native English speaking students and non-native English speaking students (Harklau, 1994; Rubinstein-Avilla, 2003; Watkins-Hoffman & Cummins, 1997). As a two-way street, the acculturation process takes place not only through the second language learner's active interaction with the target culture, but also by people from the target culture embracing the people from other cultures and offering opportunities and resources for them to learn and use the new language and be a part of the target culture. It is incumbent upon teachers who work with a diverse student body to create classroom environments conducive to language and culture acquisition.

WHAT ROLE DOES ELLS' NATIVE LANGUAGE AND PREVIOUS LITERACY EXPERIENCE PLAY IN THEIR SECOND LANGUAGE LEARNING?

My second period is the mathematics class. I didn't understand what the teacher was talking about, but those signs and numbers are familiar to me. My brain could not translate the word "Trigonometry" into my own language even though I knew I have studied it before in my country. By Angela, a 10th grade ELL (Dong, 2016, p. 536)

Angela's frustration is not alone. Many ELLs come into the secondary subject matter class with a grade-level equivalent subject matter learning history and language and literacy skills gained in their native language. What can subject matter teachers do to support students like Angela especially when learning that she does have a prior knowledge on the teaching topic even though it is learned in her native language?

Cummins' Interdependence Hypothesis (Iceberg Theory). Based on his research on bilingualism and biliteracy education, Jim Cummins proposed that despite differences among languages on the surface, there is a Common Underlying Proficiency (CUP) across languages, especially for cognitively challenging language and learning tasks, such as CALP (Cummins, 1979b, 1984). Cummins illustrated his hypothesis in Figure 1.1.

According to Cummins, the tips of the iceberg show two distinctively different languages at the surface level. However, deep down below of those differences is the shared CUP at the CALP level featuring academically and high order thinking skills between the two languages. Cummins argued that the linguistic and cognitive interdependence between L1 and L2 facilitates rather than impedes ELLs learning of English in general and academic English in particular. Cummins' lin-

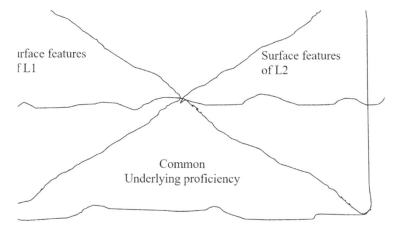

Surface features of L1

Surface features of L2

Common Underlying proficiency

FIGURE 1.1. Cummins' Iceberg Model of Language Interdependence

guistically interdependence theory has taken a new look at second language acquisition for school aged students and opened new possibilities for teachers to use ELLs' native language and literacy skills to support and speed up their language learning in English while teaching subject matter knowledge.

Research since then has shown repeatedly a positive correlation in ELLs' academic language and literacy skills and subject matter knowledge learning between their native language and English (Carson, 1992; Dong, 2013–2014; Esquinca, 2011; Rodriguez, 2001). The higher the ELLs' grade level, the stronger that interdependence is (August et al., 2005). For ELLs who have learned the subject matter concepts and literacy skills in their native language country, they will learn the English word more easily and faster if the subject matter teacher recognizes and taps into that prior knowledge. Through systematic analysis, research has shown that students from Romance language backgrounds in particular, including French, Portuguese, Spanish, Haitian Creole, Italian, etc. have an advantage through the use of cognates to learn English and subject matter concepts. Cognates are the words with similar sounds and spelling and have the same meaning between languages. Even for students from non-Romance language backgrounds, such as Chinese, Korean, Bangladesh, and Urdu, a translated version of academic concepts will trigger the activation of the cognitive academic language base in their native language and provide a meaningful and quick entry into learning the subject matter concept in English. Below are examples of this strong sharing at the CUP level in discipline-specific vocabulary across languages.

Teaching Implications for Cummins' Iceberg Theory. Subject matter teachers don't have to be multilingual in order to use ELLs' native language for instruction. They can either use websites, such as the Google translation (see http://

TABLE 1.1. Multilingual Glossary Across Subject Matters

Mathematics

English	Spanish	French	Portuguese	Chinese	Korean	Urdu
Exponent	exponente	exposant	expoente	指数	멱지수	ماتیادک

Science

English	Spanish	French	Portuguese	Chinese	Korean	Urdu
Pollen	polen	pollen	pólen	花粉	화분	جرگ

Social studies

English	French	Portuguese	Spanish	Chinese	Korean	Urdu
Imperialism	impérialisme	Imperialismo	imperialismo	帝国主义	제정	سامراجیت

English

English	French	Portuguese	Spanish	Chinese	Korean	Urdu
Simile	métaphore	metáfora	metáfora	隐喻	은유	استعاره

translate.google.com/) or ask the ESL or Bilingual or foreign language teacher who speaks ELLs' native languages in their school to assist. They can even ask their bilingual students to help with the translation. In a mainstream subject matter class with both English proficient students and ELLs, subject matter teachers can prepare a multilingual glossary handout as above and give it to their ELLs who are newcomers needing the language support. By doing so, ELLs like Angela won't be lost during the lesson rather they will have something familiar to help with their comprehension, concept transfer between languages, and even participation.

In addition, when mainstream subject matter teachers show a sincere interest in their ELLs' funds of knowledge and use that knowledge in their instruction, ELLs will have an anchor for the new words and concepts learned in English and see the possibility for cross language, culture, and literacy skill transfers. In doing so, the teacher easies the anxiety and provides a meaningful and comprehensible context for both second language and subject matter knowledge learning.

Whorfian Hypothesis. According to Benjamin Lee Whorf, an anthropologist and linguist, Language is shaped by and reflective of the culture and thought patterns in that culture (Carroll, 1956). An intriguing discussion of the interrelationship among language, culture, and thought patterns can be traced back to the Whorfian Hypothesis. Based on their study the linguist Edward Sapir and his student Benjamin Lee Whorf concluded that language and culture and thought patterns were closely interrelated, shaping and being shaped by one another. Language reflects culturally specific ways of looking at the world and making sense of the world and thinking about the world. One of the well-known the Whorfian Hypothesis examples is a large number of words for "snow" in the Inuit language for Eskimos. According to Whorf, those fine-grained semantic distinctions are not random or for no reason, rather it reflects how people in those cultures perceive the world and express their surroundings and thinking.

In working with ELLs or in learning English, teachers have become aware of the fact that different languages have different sound systems and words and ways to describe, explain, and express their meanings and thoughts. These experiences lead us to ask, what role does native language play in second language acquisition? Look at the following examples:

Hebrew:	kaniti bair / et hagluya
Non-native English:	I bought downtown the postcard.
English:	I bought the postcard downtown.
Spanish:	se habla espanol?
Non-native English:	He speaks Spanish?
English:	Does he speak Spanish?
Chinese:	wo kanjian na ge mai dong xi de nu ren.
Non-native English:	I saw the buy stuff woman.
English:	I saw the woman who bought the stuff.

Arabic:	Baytuhu qadimun.
Non-native English:	his house old
English:	His house is old.

What do these examples tell us about the impact that ELLs' native language has on the second language learner's production of English? Look closely at non-English examples and we can easily trace the ways of forming sentences back to that language. The above examples illustrate how native language and thought patterns influence the acquisition of a second language for ELLs.

Besides the positive use of the ELL's native language, as shown in Cummins' Iceberg theory, confusions and mistakes often arise to make second language acquisition difficult and the learner frustrated (Brown, 1987; Lightbown & Spada, 2013). This is especially the case when the sounds, spellings, or the sentence structures in ELLs' native language differ widely from English, or when certain English sounds, words, or the sentence structures do not exist in the ELL's native language. Research comparing and contrasting second language learners' native language and literacy learning has shown that transfers in those situations between languages, though may not lead to immediate positive results, can still reveal deep and subtle culturally mediated ways of thinking and should not be dismissed or ignored.

One interesting English word which I couldn't find the Chinese equivalent is the word "privacy" as I began my journey of learning of English and American culture. The closest Chinese translation of the English word "privacy" is "secrecy" in Chinese, carrying the negative connotation. In the Chinese culture, there is nothing private, and everything is in the public domain and controlled by the government and social and cultural norms. I still remember cracking my brain to figure out why Americans often say, "Oh, this is a private matter or let's respect her privacy" and would wonder what those Americans were trying to hide from me. It was not until after I learned more about American culture and its orientation toward individualism before I could understand this concept.

Another example to illustrate the Whorfian Hypothesis is the difference in kinship terms comparing English and Chinese. The English word for "uncle" can refer to either the father's brother or the mother's brother, while the Chinese often use different words to differentiate which side the uncle belongs to the father's brother or the mother's brother. The same is true for the terms used to describe other human relationships.

English	Chinese
aunt	da yi (mother's older sister)
	xiao yi (mother's younger sister)
	da gu (father's older sister)
	xiao gu (father's younger sister)
cousin	biao jie (mother's sister's daughter older than the speaker)
	biao mei (mother's sister's daughter younger than the speaker)

English   **Chinese**
        tang jie (father's sister's daughter older than the speaker)
        tang mei (father's sister's daughter younger than the speaker)
        biao ge (mother's sister's son older than the speaker)
        biao di (mother's sister's son younger than the speaker)
        tang ge (father's sister's son older than the speaker)
        tang di (father's sister's son younger than the speaker)

While there are no English equivalent translations, there are different terms used in Chinese to refer to the following relationships:

a. Mother's sister's daughter's son
b. Mother's brother's son's daughter
c. Mother's mother's brother's son
d. Mother's father's sister's daughter's son

While a native Chinese speaker will learn early the close and tight kinship organizations through learning the kinship terminology, however, these detailed break-downs of the relationships may baffle a native English speaker, whose language does not have such as an elaborate terminology for the kinship system, and as a result, it might make the Chinese kinship terms more difficult to learn for a native English speaker.

Even some of the prototypical examples used in American classrooms, such as blue jay or gray fish in biology, are very much culture bound too. For instance, in high school biology textbooks in China, the prototypical example used for this topic is a woodpecker and the Chinese students would have no clue of what a blue jay is unless the biology teacher is aware of this difference and use culturally familiar examples to connect it with students' prior knowledge or teach ELLs what a blue jay is (Dong, 2002). Furthermore, Lakoff and Johnson (1980) argued that metaphorical thinking is culturally specific and shaped by cultural conventions and values and beliefs. Dong (2004a) emphasized the importance of teaching ELLs' figurative language, its cultural context and history. She illustrated effective instructional strategies used to promote second language and cultural learning in subject matter classes.

Kaplan's Contrastive Rhetoric Hypothesis. Research on the culturally mediated ways of thinking and their impact on adolescents' and adults' second language learning in academic settings was expanded by Kaplan's ground-breaking study in 1966, entitled "Cultural Thought Patterns in Intercultural Education." Kaplan was concerned with the fact that "Foreign students who have mastered syntactic structures have still demonstrated inability to compose adequate themes, term papers, theses, and dissertations" (Kaplan, 1966, p. 3). Influenced by the Whorfian Hypothesis and after analyzing hundreds of non-native English-speaking and native English-speaking college students' expository essays in English, Kaplan proposed the Contrastive Rhetoric Hypothesis. He argued that different

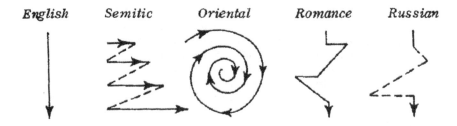

FIGURE 1.2. Kaplan'S Culturally Varied Ways of Organization in Academic Writing.

cultures have different ways of thinking, thus, have different ways of organizing their thoughts through writing. Therefore, the 'foreignness' in foreign students' writing in English is the result of not only language problems but also a revelation of their native thinking patterns. Kaplan doodled or diagramed those organizational patterns of an academic expositive essay written in different languages (see Figure 1.2).

According to Kaplan, an American English essay is organized in a direct, linear, and deductive fashion, which has grown out of Platonic-Aristotelian philosophical and rhetorical traditions. The Semitic essay organization, referring to Arabic and Hebrew languages, is characterized as parallelism, favoring coordination over subordination. The diagram of the organization writing of Romance language, referring to Spanish and French, is marked by digressions from time to time but going back to the main point at the end of the essay. The diagram for the Russian writing pattern even allows for bigger digressions from the main point but always returns to its original point near the end. The organizational pattern for Asian language writing, referring to Chinese, Japanese, and Korean, is characterized by an indirect and circular organization to address the main topic, illustrated by an obliqueness of the main point until the very end of an essay.

Yum (1988) analyzed the interpersonal communication patterns between the East and the West, such as North American and European cultures. He traced those communication patterns to the fundamental philosophies and ideologies that are deeply rooted in those cultures. He noted the following key differences between the two and characterized them as collectivistic cultures and individualistic cultures (see Table 1.2).

In her year of teaching college students how to write in English in Mainland China, Matalene (1985) attributed the Chinese way of writing to the cultural values that were deeply rooted in Confucian and Marxist philosophies. She argued that, as the Chinese culture values uniformity and social harmony, children who grow up in that culture have already internalized those ways of thinking into their ways of writing. They had acquired a different set of reader expectations, and they transferred what they learned so well in Chinese into their writing in English.

TABLE 1.2. Cross-Cultural Communication Style Comparisons

Communication	East Asian Cultures	American Mainstream Culture
Orientation	• "We" identity and promoting selfless and being considerate for others	• "I" identity and promoting thinking for yourself
Norms	• Conformity and unity, performing your part in the family and society	• Emphasizing laws and individual human rights
Expectations	• Inter-dependence, indebtedness, reciprocity, filial piety, politeness, and social/family connections • Striving for group success	• Independence and self- reliance • Striving for individual short-term and symmetrical success
Interpersonal relationship	• Long-term and asymmetrical reciprocity and hieratical	• Short-term and symmetrical
Linguistic codes and patterns	• Indirect and subtle, different linguistic codes according to the hierarchy • Emphasizing listening, seeing, observing and respect for social orders and elders	• Direct, linear, and less differentiation • Emphasizing doing, producing • Focusing on individual thoughts, originality and creativity

Therefore, it was natural to express one's views by referring to the traditional and culturally accepted patterns and echoing the Party line. Matalene's reflection on her students' writing and her own way of writing shed light on what is logical or illogical, direct or indirect in thinking and writing:

> Our own rhetorical values are profoundly affected by the fact that we are post-Romantic Westerners, teaching and writing in the humanities. As such, we value originality and individuality, what we call the "Authentic Voice." We encourage self-expression and stylistic innovation. In persuasive discourse, we subscribe to Aristotle's dictum, "State your case and prove it," and we expect to be provided with premises and conclusions connected by inductive or deductive reasoning. We call this a "logical" argument.... But Western rhetoric is only Western. As we commit ourselves to reinventing our own rhetorical tradition, we need to understand the limits as well as the virtues of that tradition. And as our world becomes a global village in which ethnocentrism is a less and less appropriate response, we need to understand and appreciate rhetorical systems that are different from our own. (p. 790)

Teaching Implications of Culturally Varied Ways of Thinking, Communicating, and Writing. The above discussion on the impact of culture on language, thought, and literacy learning adds to our understanding of ELLs' reading and writing difficulties and why those difficulties exist in our classrooms. Since many secondary second language learners come to our classrooms have already trained in some of the approaches and strategies used in reading and writing in their native language, they may not be aware of American academic ways of reading and writing and thinking. Instead of assuming that those students should understand standard ways of communicating in class and doing academic writing, teachers need to be aware of possible mismatches of cultural values and different ways of thinking, communicating, and writing.

In dealing with academic writing tasks, such as research writing in science, argumentative essays in English, comparative writing and document-based writing in social studies, norms and conventions have to be taught explicitly. For example, the norm of backing up one's claim with citations is an obvious academic practice to many American teachers. However, it is not that obvious to many students from cultures, such as China, where more emphasis is placed on using the works of others to learn and on imitation rather than on citing others' works in students' written work. Also, for some students from cultures where a critical reading is not encouraged or taught at all, the students may simply summarize or memorize others' words or even commit plagiarism.

Finally, the style of classroom talks is not universal. In Chinese, Korean, and Japanese cultures for example, the teacher is an authority and teacher talk is the only talk in the classroom. Students are taught to be silent (Hasegawa & Gundykunst, 1998; Jones, 1999; Sullivan, 1996) and silence is valued rather than an indication of lack of motivation or efforts or ignorance. Therefore, only demanding those students to participate may not be effective, rather, subject matter teachers need to show those students how different cultures and schools have different ways of teaching and learning (see Chapters 3 and 4 for an in-depth review of literacy education in Asian and Latin American countries). Knowing about the students' cultures will sensitize all teachers to those differences in order to teach both the subject matter knowledge and language and literacy skills effectively to their ELLs.

WHAT ROLE DOES DEVELOPMENTAL PSYCHOLOGY PLAY IN ADOLESCENTS' SECOND LANGUAGE ACQUISITION?

Despite differences in ELLs' cultural and language backgrounds, those students do share one thing in common with their English proficient peers. That is, they are all teenagers going through similar biological and cognitive development. As Piaget's (1947, 1972) child's intellectual development theory noted, a teenager of 14, 15, or 16 years of age is undergoing a cognitive change moving from the concrete operational stage to the formal operational stage and then to the abstraction and formal thinking stage. Students at this age are eager to learn new things, to attempt to define their identity, to experiment with new possibilities, to discover contradictions, and to question the authority. Their physical and cognitive maturation can facilitate their language acquisition. One major development in their language use is marked by their use of language ranging from literal and affective oriented responses to interpretive and abstract thinking related responses. In second language acquisition, researchers such as Lightbown and Spada (2013) documented several studies to argue that adolescents are better language learners than younger children, especially in CALP learning.

Comparing Adolescent ELLs with Children ELLs. Although it is true that younger children ELLs in elementary grades acquire a second language with ease and speed and achieve native-like pronunciation and intuitive sense of grammar (Lenneberg, 1967; Johnson & Newport, 1989), however, when the CALP is concerned, teenage ELLs demonstrate their strengths and have an edge over younger children (Lightbown, 2012; Snow & Hoefnagel-Hohle, 1978). Teenage ELLs have already acquired many concepts in their native language. In learning the second language, they don't need to learn each concept all over again; instead, they only need to learn a different name or phrase for the concept that they know through actively drawing on their previous language, cultural, and educational experiences. Also, since teenagers have already developed their cognitive abilities through formal education or through life experience, they are much better in making generalizations, applying abstract concepts to suitable exemplars, and solving problems.

Some researchers such as Genesee (1976) have found that there is a positive correlation between intelligence and the development of second language literacy skills such as reading, grammar, writing, and vocabulary, even though intelligence may not always be related to oral communication skills. In all these situations, teenagers are better academic second language learners in comparison to younger children. Even though those students may speak broken or accented English, which makes them look childish or ignorant, still, normally their cognitive level is at the similar stage as their native English-speaking peers, moving from the concrete level to the abstract level of cognitive development. On the one hand, their cognitive ability to function abstractly and think critically can be transferable between languages as long as the teacher allows and encourages that transfer. These transferable elements can be enhanced by using visual aids, graphics, by making a connection between the task at hand and students' lives, and by concrete and culturally familiar examples of the abstraction from the student's perspective. Chamot and O'Malley (1994) gave an example of a high school ELL encountering a task in science. Although in the beginning the student was overwhelmed by the task, after some probing questions asked by the teacher, the student realized that she had already learned about this in her native country, even though she had learned it in Spanish. The teacher's probing questions triggered the student's transfer of her knowledge and skills in Spanish to the learning environment in English.

On the other hand, this emerging self and increasing thinking power for many adolescents can also hinder their language acquisition because of their being highly self-conscious about themselves, feeling inferior to English proficient peers, lack of social skills to be part of a group, and their intolerance of ambiguities, differences, and contradictions (Derwing, DeCorby, & Ichikawa, 1999). They might even try to hide their language deficiency at all costs. All that can result in their hesitation to venture out to actively seek language learning opportunities and participate in class.

Similar to their native English-speaking peers, teens at this age also go through the period of "imaginary audience," and agonizing over what others perceive them to be both physically and mentally and speech wise. All this requires the classroom teacher and school to establish early in their school and classroom positive and culturally respective and inclusive environment. In addition, both ESL/Bilingual and subject matter teachers should be vigilant about peer bullying and language discrimination and educate their students accordingly. The following is an example of a Pakistani teen's account of his embarrassing moment in his first year in the new school:

> There I was in America at the age of thirteen in the middle of my 8th grade. I was the only person in that middle school who couldn't say a single word in English. I found it as an insult, and a disappointment. Soon I was admitted to Bryant Cullen High School as a freshman. I had to walk home every day because the school did not support school buses. Well, one day I was walking behind some students who looked like thugs or bad people. By accident, I stepped onto one guy's foot. The apology was right on my tongue, but I was unable to spit it out quickly. Before I could say anything, somebody stepped on my foot. When I turned and looked, I realized that he was the guy whose foot I stepped on. He talked really fast and I could not make out what he was saying. But judging by his facial expressions and body language I knew that he was pretty angry at what I did and especially at that I did not apologize to him. One of the boys said something like "Are you blind?" I understood "Are you" but I did not know the word "blind," so I murmured "yes." All of a sudden, they all started laughing and clapping their hands. I did not know what was going on, but I sensed that they were making fun of me. I was so mad. The next day I could still feel everyone at school was laughing at my inability to speak English.
>
> *— by a Pakistani ELL student*

Obviously, the over self-consciousness about speaking English by the ELL and a lack of tolerance on the part of his American teenagers can make language acquisition especially challenging for these students. It is especially true for ELLs who feel they are being constantly judged and discriminated against because of their outsider status and language barrier.

Many adolescent ELLs whom I interviewed over the years are concerned about their future and feel stigmatized being labeled as an ELL, a common theme in their reflections. The following comments of ELLs illustrate this kind of dissatisfaction and concern:

> Everything [I take] is ESL. That's why I am very sad... I like to go to the regular class. A lot of students make fun of me because of my failure to test out of ESL classes. Also, by testing out I can go into a good college, I heard... A lot of people who are here for a shorter period of time, such as a year and a half were able to go to the regular class. But I couldn't, and that made me very upset. —by a Bangladeshi ELL

Back in the Philippines, I took Tagalog, my native language. But English was my subject language. I have learned English since Kindergarten. But I am still placed in ESL classes. I don't know why. What is more is that we are treated like we don't have any intelligence. What we learned in ESL is like what we learned in kindergarten. Teachers here don't know that what we had learned back home was far more and far advanced in science and math than American students in the same grade. I was very insulted by all this.

— by a Philippine ELL

It was hard to make friends here because each class has different people in it. In my school back in Poland, all the students have all their classes together for all four years of high school. It's easier to make friends that way. Also, we don't need to run around to find our classrooms between breaks because we have the same classroom all day and the teacher comes to us to teach. So, all this chaos between breaks really threw me off the first few weeks when I came here.

— by a Polish ELL

The above collection of ELLs' reflection on the cultural, language, and educational differences comparing schooling back in their native countries and the U.S. points to the need for a change in the mainstream subject matter teachers' attitudes and teaching methods in instruction. Below is an example of a Bosnia student's telling of how he was spotlighted by the teacher to share with the class his trauma due to the war in his home country.

I remember my first social studies class in which my well-meaning teacher took me in front of my class to explain what was happening in Bosnia. I did not know where to start. It seems that she asked too much. Where do I start? The firing line? The concentration camp? What do I tell them about me? Even when I finally figured that I should explain the history of the conflict, I did not have linguistic skill to do it. Finally, I decided to draw on the chalkboard a picture of the city encircled by Serbian soldiers. But since I did not know how to say "surrounded" I just repeated, "Serbs around, Serbs around and then boom, boom." I used my whole body to try to explain. Even though my teacher constantly smiled to indicate that she understood, I was sure that the students had no idea what I meant. I could see their confused faces, wide eyes and open mouths. I just remembered that I was in a sweat after this class, and even though I was extremely frustrated, I still smiled. Inside, I was ready to cry. Perhaps I felt this way because this was the first time I ever looked back at my experiences during the war or perhaps because I had an uncomfortable feeling of being different. Maybe I just did not want to be put on the spot and made to talk. Or maybe I just wanted to keep my memory of the horrors inside of me. (Garrod & Davis, 1999, pp. 181–182)

In dealing with teenage second language learners, even a good intention on the part of the teacher may not always lead to a good outcome because of many factors coming into play in learning the new language and new culture as discussed in this chapter. All this reveals a complex task for the teacher today in dealing with teenage second language students. Teachers must be sensitive toward those students' needs, tailor their instruction to the ELLs' levels and expand their teaching repertoire in order to meet the challenges of the profession in the 21st century.

SUMMARY

This chapter has discussed what it means to learn English as a second language for adolescent learners who face a unique set of academic demands and who come into the subject matter classroom with previous cultural, educational, and linguistic backgrounds. Besides the motivation and efforts on the part of the learner various linguistic, cultural, cognitive, individual, and educational factors come into play when a secondary ELL tries to learn the subject matter in a language they are still learning and meet the learning standards and graduation demands in a timely fashion. Major theories and principles discussed in this chapter have important teaching implications for subject matter teachers. The complexity of second language acquisition and time it takes for a learner to master not only BICS but also CALP for graduation purposes requires all teachers to have awareness and willingness as well as knowledge and skills to provide comprehensible input, build on those students' prior knowledge, and give ample opportunities for those students to learn in a supportive and meaningful learning environment.

CHAPTER 2

WHO ARE THESE DIVERSE ELLS?

In the previous chapter we discussed major principles of second language acquisition for adolescents. Now it is time to take a closer look at those ELLs and familiarize ourselves with their unique characteristics, previous educational history, native language and cultural backgrounds, and their learning experiences in American schools. According to National Center for Education Statistics (2018), there were 4.85 million ELLs in U.S. schools composing about 10% of all public school students in 2015. As a fast-growing student population, there has been a steady increase (60%) in ELLs across the nation.

As one of the states serving a large number of ELLs, New York State has seen a steady increase in recent years. One in every six students is an ELL and provided with the ESL/ENL services in New York City public high schools (New York City Department of Education, 2018). There is often a misconception that ELLs are all similar in that they all lack English language proficiency. However, in teaching reality and when subject matter teachers look beyond those students' English proficiency status, they will see that ELLs are very diverse with unique individual characteristics and learning needs. For subject matter teachers, the more you know about your ELLs, the better you will serve them.

Teaching English Language Learners in Secondary Subject Matter Classes, pages 29–53.

HOW ARE ELLS IDENTIFIED, SCREENED, AND PLACED FOR ESL SERVICE?

For students who come from overseas, they undergo a series of screening measures to evaluate their English language proficiency and then are placed in the ESL Service if needed.

First, both the students and parents receive handouts and view an informational video in multiple languages at the Enrollment Center in each borough of New York City. The Enrollment Center assigns the new student and his or her parents to the school where they are given both the Home Language Questionnaire (HLQ) (translated into multiple languages and completed by the parent) and a quick oral interview by an ESL coordinator in the school with an interpreter using two languages: English and the student's native language.

If the home language is identified as other than English in the Home Language Questionnaire and the oral interviewer deems necessary, the student is given the New York State Initial Test for English Language Learners (NYSITELL). The NYSITELL tests students' grade level appropriate English skills in listening, speaking, reading, and writing in English. It serves dual purposes: 1) to determine the student's level of English proficiency and 2) to use that determination to place the student for appropriate ESL service (New York State Department of Education, 2018).

In 2015, the New York State Department of Education revised the ELLs' English performance levels to reflect more accurately ELLs' baseline proficiency and progression in five levels of an ELLs language proficiency continuum (Commissioner's Regulation Part 154, 2015), including:

Entering (formerly Beginning)

A student at the Entering level has great dependence on supports and structures to advance his or her academic language skills. As measured by the NYSESLAT, a student at this level has yet to meet the linguistic demands necessary to demonstrate proficiency in a variety of academic contexts within this grade level.

Emerging (formerly Low Intermediate)

A student at the Emerging level has some dependence on supports and structures to advance his or her academic language skills. As measured by the NYSESLAT, a student at this level has yet to meet the linguistic demands necessary to demonstrate proficiency in a variety of academic contexts within this grade level.

Transitioning (formerly Intermediate)

A student at the Transitioning level shows some independence in advancing his or her academic language skills. As measured by the NYSESLAT, a student at this level has yet to meet the linguistic demands necessary to demonstrate proficiency in a variety of academic contexts within this grade level.

Expanding (formerly Advanced)

A student at the Expanding level shows great independence in advancing his or her academic language skills. As measured by the NYSESLAT, a student at this level is approaching the linguistic demands necessary to demonstrate proficiency in a variety of academic contexts within this grade level.

Commanding (formerly Proficient)

A student at the Commanding level is now designated as a Former ELL, and entitled to receive two years of continued ELL services. As measured by the NYSESLAT, a student at this level has met the linguistic demands necessary to demonstrate proficiency in a variety of academic contexts within this grade level. (Commissioner's Regulation Part 154, 2015, pp. 7–8)

ELLs' Subject Matter Class Placement. For ELLs who come to the U.S. with some or grade level appropriate literacy and subject matter education in their native countries, their transcripts are translated and reviewed by the school to decide whether they are better served Bilingual subject matter instruction or ESL or ENL (English as a New Language) subject matter instruction upon parental approval.

MAJOR TYPES OF SERVICES FOR ELLS IN NEW YORK CITY PUBLIC SCHOOLS

Currently there are two major program models for ELLs. Besides the required ESL language support service, ELLs have options of either attending the Bilingual Education Program in the subject matter instruction using both English and their native language, or English as a New Language (ENL) Education Program. For the Bilingual Education Program, students who come from the same home language background are grouped together and taught by a subject matter teacher who is certified in both the subject matter and Bilingual Education in the same language spoken as students (New York City Department of Education, 2017).

Bilingual Education Programs. There are two types of Bilingual Education Program: one is called the Transitional Bilingual Education (TBE) Program where ELLs are receiving instruction in both English and their native language. Taken into consideration of ELLs' English proficiency levels, the certified subject matter teacher with the Bilingual Education Extension initially uses a developmental approach to gradually increase their use of English while using the student's native language as support. Mostly, the TBE program is offered in secondary schools (New York City Department of Education, 2017, p. 40).

The other bilingual education program is called Two-way or Dual Language Program which supports both the student's native language and their English and aims to achieve bilingualism and biliteracy in two languages. In order to accomplish this, the subject matter teacher certified in Bilingual Education alternates their language instruction between English and the student's native language in either the half and half model (half day in English and the other half in another language) or alternating language use during the days the week (Monday, Wed. in English and Tues. and Thurs. in another language). The Dual Language program is mostly offered in the lower grade levels, such as elementary schools (New York City Department of Education, 2017, p. 44).

English as a Second or New Language Program. Formerly known as ESL programs (English as a second language), the ENL (English as a new language) programs have a focus on English language acquisition. The program is in the form of either a push-in model or an integrated ESL and subject matter class where ELLs receive instruction by both the ESL language teacher and their subject matter teacher, teaching side by side in the same classroom. This requires collaboration between the two teachers to share expertise, plan, assess, and deliver instruction in a coherent manner so that students get to use ample and comprehensible English to support their subject matter learning.

Another ENL program class is called a stand-alone or pull-out ENL class where the ESL certified teacher teaches language skills by focusing on different language areas, such as listening, speaking, vocabulary, reading, writing, and grammar. Those classes contain students from different home language backgrounds but with the similar English proficiency levels, such as entering or advancing (New York City Department of Education, 2017, p. 45).

For ELLs whose native language is not offered by school's bilingual education program, the ENL program is the program for them to learn both English and subject matter knowledge in English. Besides attending those ENL classes, those students also receive ESL language classes and ESL subject matter classes taught by the subject matter teacher who has received training in ESL in a class of ELLs with different English proficiency levels.

WHO ARE THESE ELLS IN THE SUBJECT MATTER CLASSES?

By the definition given by the New York City Department of Education, an ELL is a student who is limited in English language skills and needs support learning English. Those students can be both native born and non-native born students as long as they have been identified and served by the ESL service. According to the demographic report by the New York City Department of Education (2016), a little over half of ELLs were born within the U.S., and the rest were born outside of the U.S. coming from 187 countries. The top ten countries where ELLs are from are: the U.S., the Dominican Republic, Mainland China, Bangladesh, Yemen, Ecuador, Uzbekistan, Haiti, Honduras, and Pakistan. The top ten home languages spoken by ELLs are Spanish, Chinese, Arabic, Bengali, Russian, Urdu, Haitian Creole, French, Uzbek, and Punjabi.

Besides their varied English proficiency levels, ELLs have diverse backgrounds and needs. There are five major subgroups of ELLs: newcomer ELLs, developing ELLs, long-term ELLs, SIFE ELLs, and ELLs with disabilities.

Newcomer ELLs. Newcomer ELLs are ELLs and have been in the U.S. school for between 0 and 3 years who receive the ESL service. A little over 61% of all

ELLs were newcomer ELLs in the 2015–16 school year (New York City Department of Education, 2016). Some were at the very initial stage of English language acquisition, such as Entering and Emerging, while others may have made great progress functioning at a high level of English proficiency, such as Transitioning and Expanding. In New York City, we have a few secondary schools that contain only the newcomer ELLs. All teachers in those schools are required to have solid training in ESL teaching and learning and teach subject matter knowledge using ESL methodology and techniques.

Developing ELLs. Developing ELLs are the ELLs who have received ESL service and ESL/Bilingual instruction for between four to six school years. Many of those students have developed the BICS; however, they may have difficulty with the CALP, thus are unable to pass the ESL exit exam NYSESLAT, New York State English as a Second Language (New York State Department of Education, 2017) and be mainstreamed.

Long-Term ELLs. Long-term ELLs are the ELLs who have been receiving ESL instruction for more than six years but still are unable to exit the ESL program. Some of those students may be native born but have extra language and literacy issues that prevent them from passing the ESL exit test: NYSESLAT. They are often proficient in BICS, speaking native like oral English and bilingual, however, they suffer from inadequate literacy skills in English and often additional learning and motivational issues. Some of those students may be transnational students who have been sent back and forth by their families between the U.S. and their home countries, and as a result, the education that they received in the U.S. is inconsistent with significant knowledge gaps in subject matter learning. They often perform below grade level in reading and writing, presenting an extra challenge for subject matter teachers to address.

SIFE ELLs (ELLs with Interrupted Formal Education). SIFE students range from newcomer ELLs to long-term ELLs, performing at two or more years below grade level in subject matter due to interrupted schooling prior to their arrival in the U.S. Although SIFE students can be identified early when they are given an oral interview and NYSITELL test, still, some may not be identified until later due to missing paperwork or transcripts from their previous schools back in their home countries and their gaps in their previous education. There are various reasons for SIFE students' interrupting schooling, including war, family crises, economic hardship, etc. Because of their limited schooling, those students may appear on par with grade level students, however, their CALP is seriously delayed in both native language and English, thus hindering their understanding of the basic academic concepts and learning of grade level appropriate subject matter.

ELLs with Disabilities. ELLs with disabilities are the ELLs who are served by an Individualized Education Program (IEP) due to their disabilities, such as physical, psychological, or learning, in addition to their English deficiencies. In order to prevent a situation where an ELL is misplaced for a special needs student because of his or her language issues, in New York City schools, an ELL is first screened for the ESL service to allow for some time (a year) to develop and demonstrate their language skills before they are considered for special education evaluation (RTI: Response to Intervention). Once the identification and evaluation is completed, the ELL is served by both ESL and special education services.

Now we have learned different types of ELLs and major ESL/bilingual programs as well as ELLs' screening, identification, and placement process, we are going to listen to ten secondary ELLs' stories and to learn about their characteristics, previous cultural and literacy experiences, English language proficiency levels, and learning needs. We are also going to read about how their subject matter teachers adjusted their teaching to accommodate those learners' backgrounds and needs. These ten students emerged from over 80 case studies conducted by me and graduate students who are either in-service or pre-service subject matter teachers across all academic disciplines. Many of them did the case studies in my course, entitled Language, Literacy, and Culture in Education, a required teacher certification course for ESL teaching and learning by New York State. Those studies revealed ELLs' real struggles and successes, pains and joys in their odysseys of second language and second culture acquisition. The case studies also captured successful ESL oriented teaching in various mainstream subject matter classes. As you will see, each teacher's attempt and effort to listen to and observe these students' language and culture knowledge and use it to inform their subject matter instruction is commendable. These case studies have demonstrated that ESL teaching is not just the ESL teacher's responsibility only. Rather, all teachers have an important role to play in better understanding ELLs, guiding, and educating them through language and academic subject matter learning as well (Genesee, 1993).

Nargis. Nargis is a 13-year-old girl, who came to the U.S. from Bangladesh nine months ago with her aunt and sister. Her parents are still living in Bangladesh and she misses them very much. Nargis loves school. She still remembers she was too excited to go to sleep when her mother told her that she was going to start school the next day when she was six years old. Bangladesh was her favorite school subject and she enjoys reading and speaking her native language. She was placed in both an ESL class and several 7th grade mainstreamed subject matter classes. In all her ESL and content classes, she was very quiet and reserved in class, living in her own silent world.

Her social studies teacher complained that she was extremely quiet and never raised her hand, and she did not complete her assignment correctly. Half of what she handed in was written in Bengali and the other in English. A closer look of her written work shows that she copied all the questions in English, but her answers to the questions were all written in Bengali. Her English teacher also noticed a similar pattern in her writing portfolio that is she never responded to the assignment. For example, the assignment asked her to use figurative language to write, however, she turned in a paper on how much she missed her family.

Nargis is a student still going through her "Silent Period" (Krashen, 1982). Silent Period is one of the characteristics many ELLs share in their second language acquisition. They may appear silent, passive, and even physically withdrawn. This period can be very short for some students (a few months) and longer for others (a year or two). However, a student who is in silent period does not necessarily mean s/he is not learning anything or not involved in the lesson. Even though s/he is not actively participating, s/he is busy absorbing and processing the new language, observing the world around her or him. In Nargis's case, her trying very hard to do her assignments was a strong indication that she was eager to join in class activities, but her language skills held her back. As Nargis's teacher, it was important to read into her silence and recognize her effort by providing her with opportunities to break that silence.

Several things that Nargis's social studies teacher and English teacher did next helped her tremendously. First, her English teacher decided to set aside time after class each day to check on Nargis' understanding of the class and the assignment. She told Nargis to make marks on her notes to let her know which part of the lesson she did not understand. Also finding that Nargis was more comfortable with writing than speaking and eager to share anything about home with others, the teacher allowed Nargis to write down some of the words that she wanted to say first and used writing to communicate with each other in their conversations after class. These "conversations" proved to be helpful not only to ease her fear and anxiety of living in a new culture without her family but also for her teacher to learn about her needs.

Her social studies teacher examined and adjusted his ways of questioning when he called on Nargis to participate. He used yes or no questions to make sure that Nargis would have something to say and then built upon that gradually. Also, he paired Nargis with her native language speaking peer to help out with her understanding of the assignment. Both Nargis' English and social studies teachers noted the sparks in her eyes when Nargis was able to say a word or two in class and her homework answers shifted quickly from only Bengali to half Bengali and half English to finally all English within a semester. When they were studying Asia as part of their social studies curriculum, the social studies teacher invited her to share her firsthand knowledge with the class. Nargis happily accepted the task and went out her way of bringing clothes, souvenirs, and pictures from her home country to class and did a wonderful presentation using Bengali first and then having her peer translate it into English. The class was amazed, asking many interesting questions. Even though Nargis could not understand some of the questions, still in the eyes of her classmates, she knew she earned a new respect. That excitement spilled over to the English class, Nargis' English teacher launched a unit on world folktales, inviting her students to not only read the folktales but also to write their own. Nargis was involved actively in group preparation and then presentation of their folktales.

Assar. Assar came to the U.S. from Pakistan with his family two years ago, speaking Urdu only. He progressed quickly and moved from ESL level 1 entering to level 3 transitioning. After entering high school in the 9th grade, his performance in subject matter classes in comparison did not show the same pace of progression. He liked biology and wanted to make it his major in college. However, biology was the subject that gave him the most difficulty. Even though Assar's biology class was an ESL self-contained biology class, the class was using the same textbook as their native English-speaking peers. The textbook language was filled with jargon and so many complex and abstract "big words" that he had no way of comprehending all of them at once. Even though he took general science back home in junior high school, still the depth of the subject matter and the amount of biology vocabulary threw him off. Although Assar kept good class notes, they often did not make sense when he reviewed them after class due to the teacher's frequent use of abbreviations, acronyms, and sentence fragments. He said that he missed a lot and was unable to make connections between what the teacher discussed in class and what he read in the textbook. Assar worked very hard sometimes without lunch breaks, however, his test scores did not reflect his hard work. In desperation, Assar resorted to his old learning habit: memorizing his textbook section by section.

Assar's difficulty with biology content and language was also shared by many ELLs, even those who exited ESL and were mainstreamed. The reading demands in subject matter classes, such as biology can be very challenging for those students who just progressed from basic understanding of everyday language. In addition, facing the graduation standards, the amount of subject matter specific vocabulary covered in these classes and in the reading can be overwhelming. Fortunately, Assar's biology teacher quickly learned about his situation and needs. Three things that he did eased Assar's anxiety and helped Assar's biology learning. First, the biology teacher changed his way of board work by giving out complete sentences rather than just phrases or key vocabulary items. He also highlighted key topics and words on the board by putting simplified words or synonyms in the brackets on the side of the new topic and words to smooth the transition and help with comprehension. Next, after talking to the chair of the department, the students were given two sets of textbooks: one, a simplified version with a lower reading level and rich visuals, and the other a regular biology textbook used by all students. Students could refer back to the simplified version in class quickly to keep up with the lesson, but they could also use the regular version for enrichment and details back home when they had more time to do the reading. The teacher put on the board the lesson and the corresponding pages of the textbook reading for the day. Finally, with the help of his departmental chair, the teacher gave out copies of biology glossaries in both English and in some of the languages that his students spoke at home. Assar confided that what his biology teacher did help him and other students like him tremendously. His biology test score improved drastically.

Fatima. Fatima is a 12-year-old girl who came to this country from Nicaragua eight months earlier with her parents. Due to frequent family moves, she had an interrupted schooling, spending several weeks and even months at a time out of school. Fatima's mother stayed at home taking care of children, while her father worked as a commercial painter of houses. As a 6th grader, while attending ESL classes three periods a day, Fatima spent the rest of her day in an English language arts class. The English teacher had a tutor work with her on her lessons once a week. In class Fatima sat in the rear of the classroom behind her Spanish-speaking friend. It was an arrangement her English teacher made to make sure that her Spanish-speaking peer helped with her comprehension. Recently, the teacher had doubts about this peer help arrangement, wondering whether they abused this privilege as the two became too chatty in Spanish, and Fatima did not take risks by speaking English. Even when asked a factual question, Fatima often blushed and said with a thick accent, "I don't remember." Because of all this, she removed Fatima from her peer. Was there any other way that the English teacher could get through to her?

To learn about how to work with Fatima, the English teacher went to visit Fatima's ESL class. From the ESL teacher, she learned that Fatima was still in her silent period, struggling with listening and reading comprehension in English. The rule in the ESL classroom was that all students speak in English. Fatima was grouped with a Korean student and an Israeli student playing monopoly, applying the vocabulary they newly learned. The English teacher sat on the side eavesdropping to see Fatima's performance in the group. The Korean student went to get some extra money out of the monopoly bank when the other girls were busy counting their own. Fatima noticed this and said, louder than she usually spoke, "Hey, you are cheating!" Later she said to the Korean student, "No, it is my turn. You just had a turn." The English teacher was pleasantly surprised to see Fatima's correct use of the language, but also being assertive and involved in a real communication. From this observation, she had a different view toward Fatima and ideas for engaging students like Fatima in her own class.

A real breakthrough happened when Fatima's tutor used bilingual books to get her to open up. The tutor used the anthology *The Adventures of Connie and Diego* (Las Adenturas de Connie Y Diego) by Maria Garcia (1997). The book is about a third-grade reading level with colorful pictures, and with an English version of the story on one side of the page and Spanish on the other. They took turns reading the Spanish version of the story and then retelling it in English, recording new words learned. After the first few pages, she refused to use the Spanish, saying that was "cheating." She then focused on only the picture and the English version of the story to do her retelling. The tutor noted "I had not heard so much English come out of this girl's mouth since we met!"

Gina. Gina is a 9th grader who came to the country with her parents and brother from Colombia a year and a half prior, did not want to be American. Reluctant to leave her home country because she had bonded strongly with her peers and friends, Gina claimed that if she could, she would go back to her native land. Gina's negative attitude toward America was also triggered by her brother's quick "Americanization." "He eats fast food." Gina scorned. "He talks back to Mother, and when he pauses in between his sentences, he would say those umms, uhhs... We always say what we mean, we don't say umms and uhhs and we don't have the American style of sitting with legs on the table." Gina revealed that when her brother doesn't do his chores, her mother calls him a "lazy American."

To her English teacher's surprise, Gina's attitude was shared by quite a few students in her class. One day after their reading Richter's *the light in the forest* (2004), a novel about a Native American boy's struggle with his identity, the English teacher asked the class a sentence completion question: "I consider myself _____ (American)." To her surprise, many of her students considered themselves Chinese, Greek, Puerto Rican, etc. They did not consider themselves American or Chinese American after being in the country for several years. The English teacher was dismayed. She could not understand why these students were here if they did not like to be American. When she asked them the reason, several students complained about how they were discriminated against by some of their American peers, such as being laughed at during the presentation by their ways of speaking or being shunned from friendships because of their accents and ethnicity. Gina and two other girls talked about how they were harassed verbally by American boys and were not able to talk back, and dared not to report them. Still others talked about how they had to fight stereotypes and prejudices about who they were on a daily basis.

This open discussion made Gina's English teacher realize the difficulty with acculturation and how marginalized her students were even though they appeared to be well adjusted academically and linguistically. She decided to do something about it. Taking advantage of their next reading *Death of a Salesman* (Miller, 1976), the English teacher conducted a unit on the American dream. She first assigned the class a writing topic on their journeys of coming over to the U.S. and their dreams and goals. Many of her students noted that they were pretty much told by their parents with short notice that they would be moving to another country. For many the announcement was made the night before or a week before. This uprooting experience was very traumatic giving no time for the students to mentally prepare for a new way of life. Separation from friends and family members led to fear and resentment toward the new culture. Furthermore, some students came only with relatives or siblings, leaving their parents behind, precipitating the new responsibilities and anxieties over the journey. All these mixed feelings were compounded by the initial adjustment to a new culture, and the language and demands posed by the new school and the teacher.

Student writing also revealed their family's dreams and goals and reasons for coming to America. A shared goal among her students was to have academic and social opportunities in the new culture. Many of the students listed their career goals, such as doctor, lawyer, engineer, fashion designer, teacher, etc. Her students' writings gave the English teacher more clues about what about being in America which was different from what she had presumed. Learning about her students' backgrounds and interests helped the English teacher make a decision to include *The House on Mango Street* by Sandra Cisneros (1991) in their unit of American dream. Results were phenomenal. Many of her students related their experience with the protagonist's experience in *The House on Mango Street* and they responded by comparing and contrasting the two literature works and debated about various issues that they struggled with. The English teacher came to fully realize the impact of literature like *The House on Mango Street* when a mother came to her at the parent-teacher conference asking for permission to let her child keep the book *The House on Mango Street* a few more days so that she could finish reading it.

Finally, with the help of the school guidance counselor, the English teacher arranged several extra-curricular student club presidents and music or sport team captains to come to her class to talk about their activities and invite students to join and try out. This opened up her ELLs' eyes because many of them did not even know these extra-curricular activities existed or could enrich their lives. As ELLs, they were often told language learning and their grades were their priority; this was especially true to some who came from a culture whose students only focused on and valued academic performance. The English teacher's eyes lit up when a few days later Gina told her that she joined Spanish club and made some new friends.

Julieta. Julieta is a 10th grader from Argentina came with her family a year prior, was placed in an ESL self-contained social studies class called "World History for Foreigners" and other subject matter classes, while attending three periods of ESL classes during the day. According to Julieta, life back in Argentina was often very trying for her family. After a failed small business attempt, Julieta's family decided to pull up roots and move to Queens, New York City, to join her uncle and his family, exploring economic opportunities.

Julieta was determined to learn English. She said, "I want to have command of my English. I want to be able to ask a teacher a question that he is able to understand. I want to be able to answer and express my views in English." Julieta's Silent Period only lasted for a month. After that she assumed a more active role in group work and showed a particular interest in a unit on the Ancient Egyptians. However, Julieta's determination to learn was challenged by heavy use of disciplinary words and the amount of information covered in her social studies class. Even though she had a dictionary handy, which she called her lifeline, still, the new words were just too many to look up in the dictionary, such as "settled along the Nile River" "acclaimed" and "at the height of power." She became exhausted in each class as she orchestrated multiple tasks all at once, including listening to the teacher's lecture, checking the dictionary for unknown words, copying notes on the board, and reading the handouts. Both the textbook and the document handouts were beyond Julieta's language proficiency level. Because of all this, Julieta seldom had time to enjoy and participate in the class. Facing the upcoming Regents exam in World History, both Julieta and her teacher felt pressured. Her social studies teacher's question was: How can I encourage Julieta to learn, but at the same time make the learning process more manageable and meaningful to her?

One of the avenues that her social studies teacher and Julieta explored was the internet. Learning that Julieta is fascinated by the web, spending most of her afternoons after school surfing the web, they explored several ESL and social studies websites. He made a list for Julieta's website adventure, paralleling the search with the topics covered in the social studies curriculum. The ESL websites got Julieta started with listening and writing exercises, offering instant feedback. The social studies websites provided rich visuals and simpler ways of communication, compared to their textbook. Also, the teacher invited Julieta to communicate with him through email reporting on what she has found on the internet and asking questions. Gradually their communication expanded to other members of the class. Julieta paired up with a student from Cambodia and they sent email messages to each other, discussing topics that they had learned in their social studies class. Also, inspired by Julieta's desire to learn, the social studies teacher made it part of his daily planning to include a glossary list to cover the key words and phrases that he sensed would be difficult for his ESL learners. Now he could see more hands shooting up when he asked questions and enjoyed seeing the sparks in Julieta's eyes.

Alex. Alex is a 13-year-old 8th grader, attending a Junior High School. He moved from China with his family four years ago. Due to his schooling back home and basic English skills he learned in China, he was faring very well. Alex considered himself a Chinese American, a sign of acculturation that is not often shown in immigrant students who have been living in this country for a short period of time. An American, according to Alex is "someone who lives in this country and takes advantage of all the different things it has to offer."

Alex's favorite subject was mathematics. He participated by coming to the board to put his answers, and was successful getting hundreds on the tests. He even tutored his classmates during his lunch break. When asked, Alex noted that sometimes even in mathematics words in English were new and hard to understand. He often got a little confused when he was not sure about the word use in English, even though he knew that he had already learned some of the mathematics topics back in China. He always had his electronic English-Chinese dictionary out on his desk, constantly punching in words. Once he found out the Chinese equivalents of these words, he understood everything immediately. Alex's parents supported their son's language acquisition and acculturation. They even established a no Chinese rule between 3:00 p.m. to 8:00 p.m. after school from Monday to Friday. The only person in the house to whom they could speak in Chinese was Alex's grandmother. All this motivated Alex to learn and excel. He was just tested out ESL program and was really proud of being placed in a mainstream English class.

While Alex was doing beautifully in other subject matter classes, in his mainstream English class he would raise his hand to answer some factual questions, but he was shied from answering those questions that did not have right or wrong questions, thus requiring his own opinion. He revealed to his English teacher, "They can't be right or wrong. Then I don't know what you want me to say." Even though his English teacher explained to him that those questions have to be answered with his feelings or opinions on the topic, still he said that he preferred when the teacher asked more direct questions where there was a right or wrong answer. Alex recalled that teachers in Chinese schools were authority figures, having all the right answers. Or their questions primarily required a single answer that was either right or wrong.

Intrigued by his response and troubled by Alex and many of her Asian students' lack of participation, Alex's English teacher decided to read about the educational system and cultural values in mainland China. The two articles that she read were Matalene's article entitled "Contrastive rhetoric: American writing teacher in China" (1985) and Carson's article "Becoming biliterate" (1992). She learned that unlike American culture valuing individuality and originality, Chinese culture values collective wisdom and conformity. Children learn from an early age how to behave properly in school and how to respect the teacher as an authority figure. Lectures are a predominant form of instruction and the teacher is the one who has knowledge and passes it on to the students. Questions are not often asked, let alone the questions without right or wrong answers. Even if the teacher asks a question, that is for an evaluative purpose to see whether the student has mastered the content, rather than for the student's feelings and opinions. Therefore, even though Chinese students may have a strong foundation of schooling and get ahead in subject matter knowledge, they often are not prepared for the independent, creative, and critical thinking skills that American teachers ask for.

Knowing about culturally varied ways of teaching and learning helped Alex's English teacher change her view toward Alex's and other Asian students' inability to respond to her critical thinking questions. She realized a need to raise the issue and compare and contrast different ways of schooling and cultural values. She used class participation as a writing assignment to engage students in writing about appropriate classroom behaviors in American schools and in schools of their native countries or in their previous schooling. This led students to identify the differences and similarities. Based on their writing, the class had a discussion on the issue.

Noticing many of her students really did not know how to answer a question without a right or wrong answer, the English teacher even modeled her ways of thinking to show how she came up with her views critically and expressed her feelings openly. The open discussion also got Alex's English teacher to reflect on her ways of questioning. She realized that her wait time for critical thinking questions was the same in length as her factual questions, as she fired a question and expected students to answer it right away. After modeling, she found that even she needed some time to process the question, organize her thoughts, and find ways to express her views. This discovery led to a change in Alex's teacher's questioning technique. She still asked questions without right or wrong answers, but she would allow the class to first write down what they thought about the question or to pair up to talk about the question and the responses before she demanded an answer. After several weeks, she heard with delight from Alex responding to one of her questions with his own opinion.

Andrew. Andrew is a 10th grader who came from Mexico with his family at the age of eight. He went through all the ESL levels and finally was tested out of the ESL program and mainstreamed in the beginning of his sophomore year in high school. Andrew recalled being put into ESL and all the ESL self-contained subject matter classes which made him feel like an outcast and prevented him from interacting with mainstream students. Andrew was dying to get out of ESL, however, each time he took the ESL exit test, his mind "drew a blank," and he failed to pass it, despite the fact he could speak English like a native speaker by his middle school year. So, testing out of the ESL and being with mainstream students gave Andrew a new-found excitement, confidence, and motivation to learn. Andrew's guidance counselor informed his subject matter teachers about Andrew's coming, in an effort to make his transition from the ESL to mainstream classes go smoothly.

Andrew's English class was reading *The Lord of the Flies* by William Golding (2013). The English teacher was really impressed by his keen sense of understanding and active participation. He revealed that judging by Andrew's speaking and participation in class he had no idea that Andrew had come from ESL, if the guidance counselor did not tell him about it. In comparison to Andrew's fluent oral language, his written language was less fluent, displaying a few non-native English markers. Most of his mistakes were problems with following a steady stream of thought, being specific, spelling, subject-verb agreement problems, etc. Noticing that these weaknesses were also weaknesses found in many of his immigrant students' writing and to prepare them for the English Regents exam in their junior year, the English teacher wondered how he should go about helping his students with their writing.

The English teacher decided to tackle the comparison and contrast essay, which newly mainstreamed ELLs had most difficulty with. First, he gave students two pieces of literature to read both Wylie's "Puritan Sonnet" (2016) and an excerpt from *Ethan Frome* (Wharton, 2018).

PURITAN SONNET
Elinor Wylie (1921)

Down to the Puritan marrow of my bones
There's something in this richness that I hate.
I love the look, austere, immaculate,
Of landscapes drawn in pearly monotones.
There's something in my very blood that owns
Bare hills, cold silver on a sky of slate,
A thread of water, churned to milky spate
Streaming through pastures fenced with stones.

I love those skies, thin blue or snowy gray,
Those fields sparse-planted, rendering meager sheaves;
That spring, briefer than apple-blossom's breather,
Summer, so much too beautiful to stay,
Swift autumn, like a bonfire of leaves,
And sleepy winter, like the sleep of death.

During the early part of my stay I had been struck by the contrast between the vitality of the climate and the deadness of the community. Day by day, after the December snows were over, a blazing blue sky poured down torrents of light and air on the white landscape, which gave them back in an intenser glitter. One would have supposed that such an atmosphere must quicken the emotions as well as the blood; but it seemed to produce no change except that of retarding still more the sluggish pulse of Starkfield. When I had been there a little longer, an seen this phase of crystal clearness followed by long stretches of sunless cold; when the storms of February had pitched their white tents about the devoted village and the wild cavalry of march winds had charged down to their support; I began to understand why Starkfield emerged from its six months' siege like a starved garrison capitulating without quarter.

About a mile farther, on a road I had never traveled, we came to an orchard of starved apple trees writhing over a hillside among outcroppings of slate that nuzzled up through the snow like animals pushing out their noses to breathe. Beyond the orchard lay a field or two, their boundaries lost under drifts; and above the fields, huddled against the white immensities of land and sky, one of those lonely New England farmhouse that make the landscape lonelier. (Wharton, 2018, pp. 7, 15)

Then the students worked in groups to generate as many similarities and differences as possible according to literary elements of the writing. Based on their findings, students selected two literary aspects to write about. Afterwards, they came up with two main patterns to organize their comparisons and contrasts. They had to also decide on what the purpose of the comparison and contrast was, that is the attitude of the essay. Even though students were quick to compare and contrast two works, they had trouble in understanding that the comparison and contrast essay was more than listing similarities and differences. There was a purpose to persuade and to inform the reader also. That was the overall emphasis that the writer placed. The English teacher helped the students come up with their thesis statement and two organizational patterns as shown below.

Organizational Pattern One (point by point)
Thesis Statement: The speaker in the Puritan Sonnet has the intense and fearless attitude toward the New England winter in contrast to the speaker in *Ethan Frome.* The attitude was conveyed through the tone of the speaker and the figurative language used.

Paragraph One
A. The tone of the speaker in the Puritan Sonnet: warm and fearless and positive
B. The tone of the speaker in Ethan Frome: cold and depressing and negative

Paragraph Two
A. The figurative language use in the Puritan Sonnet: sky, seasons, water
B. The figurative language use in Ethan Frome: field, community, road

Organizational Pattern Two (all in one/all of the other)
Thesis Statement: The speaker in the Puritan Sonnet has the intense and fearless attitude toward the New England winter in contrast to the speaker in *Ethan Frome*. The attitude was conveyed through the tone of the speaker and the figurative language use.

Paragraph One
A. The tone of the speaker in the Puritan Sonnet: warm and fearless and positive
B. The figurative language use in the Puritan Sonnet: sky, seasons, water

Paragraph Two
A. The tone of the speaker in Ethan Frome: cold and depressing and negative
B. The figurative language use in Ethan Frome: field, community, road

Taking into consideration that many of his students are like Andrew newly exited ESL, he decided to add transitional expressions to his mini-lesson. Once the thesis statement and the organizational patterns were on the paper, Andrew's English teacher engaged the class into generating transitional words used for comparison and contrast. These expressions helped to organize ideas in a coherent way and to add a flow to the essay. The following is a list generated by his students:

Transitional expressions to show comparison and contrast:
in contrast to
in comparison to
whereas
while
unlike
on the other hand
on the contrary
but
yet
similarly
likewise
conversely
however
different from
just as

Transitional expressions to show emphasis:
in addition
moreover
also
besides
even though
although

Armed with the framework of the essay and language support, students were ready to produce their group comparison and contrast essay. Once the group essay was written, the teacher made multiple copies of the group essays for peer review. Each group would get a different group's essay to read and critique. Students were instructed to make comments and correct errors, pointing out at least two positive aspects of the essay and two constructive criticisms. Finally, they put their essays on a poster on the wall around the classroom. The English teacher's face lit up when he saw Andrew was among the peers who were critiquing the use of the subject and verb agreement of one group's essay.

George. George is an 11th grader who came from Haiti three years ago with his mother, brother, and sister. Raised by his grandmother who was a retired teacher back in Haiti, George had respect for education and had learned the importance of discipline and hard work. He revealed that he had a dream to become a lawyer someday. While working at a supermarket after school, George attended ESL classes two periods a day and other periods in mainstream subject matter classes. George liked his ESL class the best. He sat right up front, almost under the nose of his ESL teacher. He was most vocal in that class, talking with the teacher and his peers with all smiles. His hand was up whenever the teacher asked a question.

However, in his subject matter classes, such as mathematics (Sequential III) class, George behaved like a different person. The mathematics teacher asked the students to come to the front of the classroom to write their homework answers on the board and then to explain how they arrived at these answers. George sat in the back of the room with his head down most of the time, preoccupied by his work without any interactions with his peers or his teacher or volunteering any answers. George revealed that he had difficulty with advanced mathematical concepts and was not able to keep up with his homework. As a result, he could not go up to the board to do the homework demonstration. Even if he had an answer, he was embarrassed to talk because of his accent. George recalled that mathematics was one of his favorite subjects when he first came to America. He was good at calculations back in his elementary and middle schools. However, as the subject matter content progressed and more and more thinking and language use were involved, he gradually fell behind and struggled in class. George was disappointed in himself for letting his mother down. George's mathematics teacher was aware of his silence and poor test scores, wondering what happened to him.

One day after class George approached the mathematics teacher to ask for help. He was totally confused about the concept of functions. While he could understand $f(x) = x^2$, he could not understand $f(x+y) = (x+y)^2$, x^2+y or x^2+y^2. George's cry for help was a wake-up call for his mathematics teacher. The teacher realized that his students had not learned the basic concept of representation in Haiti. Knowing that the majority of his students were ELLs, he decided to use a language approach to re-teach the concept of functions.

The next day in class the mathematics teacher first asked the class what they have learned so far in their ESL classes about the English word order. Students gave him the basic word order: subject + verb + object. Then he asked the students to think about the relationship between the subject and the verb, that is what happens to the verb if the subject is the first-person plural like "we" or the subject is the third person singular, like "she." Students who had learned English syntax had no difficulty in coming up with the sentences like:

> We play basketball in gym every day.
> She plays basketball in gym every day.

Why did you change the verb by adding "s" to its ending in the second sentence? The mathematics teacher asked. Many hands rose, "Because the subject is a third person singular and you have to put "s" to it." "It is one of those English language rules." "So, there is a relationship between the two." The mathematics teacher probed. "The verb has to be in an agreement with the subject. In my native language, not only the verb but also the adjective has to agree with the subject." "Then does it seem that the verb form in English is dependent on the subject?" "Sure." The mathematics teacher put a diagram on the board:

$$S \quad + \quad V$$

Independent Dependent

"So, we call the subject independent variable and the verb a dependent variable." "What is a variable?" Some student asked. "A variable is an unknown value that can change." The mathematics teacher continued, "Similar to language sentence structure we just discussed, in talking about functions in mathematics, we also talk about the relationship between two variables: one is an independent variable and the other the dependent variable as in the expression:

$$f(x) = x^2$$

In this expression, x represents an independent variable and $f(x)$ represents a dependent variable. In other words, x like the subject in a sentence can change, and $f(x)$ will follow in agreement with the value of x. Think about the following two examples:

> Celsius = (5/9) Fahrenheit − 32
> Distance = time × rate

How do we use functional expression to represent these two commonly used formulas?

> $f(x)$= (5/9) F − 32
> $f(x)$= $t \times r$

"How do we say it in English?"

Function of *x* equals five-ninth of Fahrenheit and minus 32.

Function of *x* equals time multiplies rate.

"So, what is the *x*?" "*x*" represents Celsius temperature and distance." "Very well, these Xs are variables. They can be either the temperature value or the distance. So, *f(x)* represents a relationship between the two variables, one depending on the other.

f(x)	*x*
dependent variable	independent variable

The mathematics teacher knew George understood it when he walked over to George and saw the answer in his notebook (Figure 2.1).

John. John is from Ecuador where he grew up in the mountains with his grandmother. John's parents left him when he was two, so he often felt unimportant and unloved. He didn't have much schooling back in Ecuador because the school was so far away and often, he had to leave school to help out his grandmother at home. John was very excited to come to America and loved to learn. He was fascinated about the internet and had a great memory and could recall everything that happened in class. John liked music and took guitar lessons after school.

John's ESL teacher, Joan saw more talent and desire in John than what he lacked. To work with students like John who were "new to print" with scarce

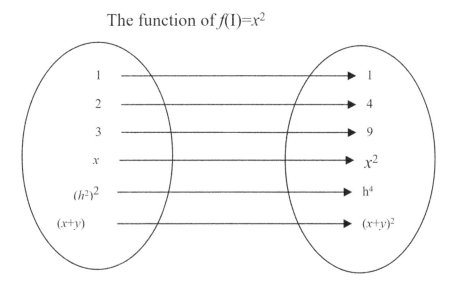

FIGURE 2.1. Function Diagram

formal education Joan focuses on bringing those students to the basic academic literacy level by using their oral Spanish and life experiences while teaching them basic communication skills in English.

Learning that most of her SIFE students had phones and internet access, Joan did most of her teaching through pictures, drawings, physical movements, internet videos, students' native languages, and music. Besides Joan's ESL, John took world history, living environment, and geometry. It was a big challenge both for John and his mainstream subject matter teachers. Joan reached out to John's subject matter teachers to inform them of John's background, strengths, and weaknesses. During the school's weekly staff development meetings, Joan would answer their questions and help them with resources, such as adjusted reading materials according to ELLs' English proficiency levels, using bilingual glossaries, maps of her students' home countries, different ways of teaching vocabulary, etc.

Joan was delighted to hear one day when John came to her class telling her "Miss! I saw my country in my book and my social studies teacher mentioned my country!" She emailed John's social studies teacher, Sam, immediately and teamed up to plan lessons and design key assessment strategies. Working with Joan, Sam quickly found out that despite John's serious lack of grade level academic experience and English skills, his life experiences went well beyond his age. John knew well how to care for his grandmother, was knowledgeable about fishing, hunting, storytelling about the Civil Wars in his country. Since his coming to the U.S., John got hooked by rap music, which was shared by many of his students. Using that as a way in, Sam brought a hip-hop artist to the class to show how to use hip hop songs to learn complex social studies concepts and develop ELLs' language skills as well as writing and performance skills.

By the end of the year, Joan was pleasantly surprised to read one of John's hip hop songs about imperialism and to hear from Sam that John had won him over with his motivation for learning. There was a marked improvement in his social studies class despite his initial concerns and questions about whether John was going to make it in his class.

Jayson. Jayson is a 17-year- old special education ELL coming from Mexico three years ago with a hearing impairment and behavioral issues. He came from a large family with a rich cultural background in music and soccer. His parents spoke Spanglish and were big on music and cars. They participated in the music competition held both in Long Island and California and won quite a few 1st place trophies. Their family SUV was loaded with loud speakers with the output from 8X subwoofers that produced about 16,000 watts of power and about 167 dB (a jet plane take-off generates 140dB). When the music was played, you can feel the whole SUV vibrate.

To cultivate their love for music, his father subscribed to iTunes and had access to all the latest music. His father's passion for cars and music made Jayson interested in physics which he claimed to be his favorite subject in school back in Mexico. According to his father, Jayson was good at fixing cars and sound systems and wanted to work on cars like his father and own a retail store that customized in vehicles with sound system for music competitions.

Despite Jayson's interest in music and cars, he was seriously lacking progress in the written language of Spanish and English as well as subject matter knowledge. He was unable to read or write despite of his prior secondary schooling and being in the U.S. for over a year. As a native Spanish speaker, Jayson's ESL teacher was able to speak with him in Spanish and ascertain that his errors in completing his work were not simply due to his lack of comprehension of instruction. It became obvious in his second year that Jayson was having trouble learning both languages and was recommended for testing for IEP services. After being evaluated, Jayson was given services in both ESL and special education while taking regular living environments, Spanish, English, mathematics, social studies, and other classes due to his hearing and behavioral issues.

Jayson's ESL and special education teachers contacted his subject matter teachers on a weekly basis to discuss ways to connect and engage Jayson in various ways and letting them know his learning needs and progresses. A home visit by his science teacher was eye-opening as he discovered that Jayson and his family's had extensive experience with cars, music, and sound systems. Based on his findings, the science teacher decided to use Jayson's strength to teach science to him.

After learning more about the sound system from his colleagues, the science teacher started the unit on the sound system, hearing, and biology by inviting Jayson's father to the class to show and talk about the power of sound and music. That unit was a hit. Encouraged by his students' responses and interests, the science teacher assigned the class to do a research project by interviewing their parents in various professions about science topics in their work and daily life and write a report afterwards. Motivated by his interest and success in science, Jayson worked hard with his ESL and special education teachers and made a marked improvement in his reading and writing skills on the topics of sound, hearing, and biology. Based on the recommendations from his ESL and special education colleagues, Jayson's science teacher developed a few strategies as well. For example, he now is more aware of his directions given in class and on the test and is willing to differentiate and offer vocabulary and reading support. He learned the benefits of teaching science by breaking down the long and complex sentences into short sentences to ease reading difficulties for his ELLs.

WHAT DO THOSE SUCCESS STORIES TELL US ABOUT ESL INSTRUCTION IN SUBJECT MATTER CLASSES?

Secondary ELLs face the increasingly high academic demands across subject matter areas and tough high school graduation standards. The challenge is extremely overwhelming for those students who have not mastered the English language skills yet. Teachers of these students also face a tremendous challenge of having to teach rigorous academic content while simultaneously needing to help these students develop their language skills. Several themes running through the success stories of those ten students illustrated in the above are:

Subject matter teachers must become good listeners and observers of the changing student body in their classrooms. As illustrated in the above cases, ELLs come to our classroom with their own unique personal, literacy, and cultural experiences which can be explored, identified, and built upon. All teachers who worked with those learners sought necessary information about their students through ESL teachers, other subject matter teachers, and school staff. They also actively sought information from their students, parents, after class talks, home visits, email communication, writing assignments, and tutorial opportunities to connect to those students. They used that knowledge about the students to inform and adjust their teaching as shown in Nargis' case. In the situation where a mismatch was identified as in Alex's case, the teacher was willing to read scholarly journals to find out more about students' prior education and preferred ways of learning. As one of the teacher said, "These students are silently trying hard to be heard, and mainstream teachers must open up their ears to the voices of these students."

Subject matter teachers must make the academic content accessible to all learners including ELLs. Even though all the teachers in the above ten cases faced rigorous subject matter curriculum, they were still able to make changes to accommodate those students' needs. Sometimes these needs can be simplifying difficult academic language by adding a synonym to the key word as shown in Assar's case. Other times the textbook or the reading materials may need to be modified and extra resources sought out as shown in Julieta's case. Still other times ways of teaching have to be adjusted to these students' needs as shown in Gina's case and George's case. As one of the teachers reflected on her changing ways of teaching:

> You can see for example, the crayfish, for students who may never see crayfish or know crayfish. If a textbook never supplements the picture of crayfish, I, the teacher have to first to define a crayfish: What does it look like? What's the color?... So, there are certain things that we take for granted, for example, we would say a blue jay and a sparrow, like common things that children would see on the curb when they grow up here. But for these children they may never see these things before since they are new to this country. So, you really have to think backwards. If the child never saw the item, let alone the internal structure before, the first thing you have to introduce what it is and how it is and then you can teach biology. (Dong, 2002, p. 45)

A preservice teacher reflected on her tutorial experience like this:

> (The tutorial) episode really opened my eyes a great deal. Math is usually a subject that most people would think that an ESL student would have the least trouble as far as language is concerned. I found that there was so much terminology in the math book and so many concepts, such as "fair" and random." This clearly demonstrates

why content area teachers have to adapt materials in order to address the needs of the ESL student.

— By Jean, a mathematics pre-service teacher

Subject matter teachers must expand their areas of competence to include knowledge about the English language, second language acquisition, and strategies for teaching second language learners while working together with ESL professionals. Traditionally, secondary education has been often fragmented and departmentalized. Even though many ELLs spend a large amount of time in mainstream subject matter classes, those teachers do not interact or even know about their ESL status or their ESL teachers and ESL teachers often teach in isolation of the academic demands of the content curriculum. Working with ELLs challenges subject matter teachers to seek support and assistance from ESL teachers and to extend their competencies to include some of the skills and practices that are the specialty of ESL teachers, as we saw in Nargis', Fatima's, and George's cases here. George's mathematics teacher in particular demonstrated to us the best integration of language and content in that he was willing and able to make use of the English language structures that ELLs are familiar with in order to teach complex concepts of functions. In recent years, New York State has adopted teacher certification guidelines that require all teachers to have some training in language, literacy and education in order to work effectively with an increasing number of ELLs in their classrooms. These teachers as shown in the above ten cases can and should serve as models for subject matter teachers.

In working with ELLs, subject matter teachers must use more enrichment and elaboration of subject matter knowledge and provide ample opportunities for students to collaboratively work with the materials. Extra readings, more student-student interactions, and internet and multi-media resources as demonstrated here are both promoting language development and providing the intellectual challenge. As shown in the above cases, Julieta's social studies teacher invited her to do internet searches for appropriate materials to learn and communicate; Andrew's English teacher used a series of group work to generate sufficient amount of subject matter knowledge and language assistance to prepare students before writing; and Fatima's tutor and teacher used bilingual literature and group work to get Fatima actively involved in the language learning process. These activities provided the students with ample opportunities and rich contexts for active language use and language and literacy skills development.

Subject matter teachers must keep in mind that no matter how limited their students' English language skills are and/or what kind of learning disabilities they may have, still every ELL has strengths and background to be capitalized on. Even dealing with ELLs who have additional learning challenges, such as John with interrupted schooling and Jayson with special education needs, if we look hard enough, we will find their strengths and ways into their academic subject matter learning. Also, working with support systems, teachers who have ESL and special education expertise can open our eyes and ears to see those students from a new perspective and tailor subject matter instruction to their levels and needs.

In working with ELLs, subject matter teachers must also recognize the powerful impact of culture and attitudes on language and subject matter learning. As shown in Gina's and Alex's cases, an acculturation process is a two-way street. It involves both second language learners, the outsiders to the culture, actively immersing in the new culture. It also requires insiders of the target culture actively reaching out to accept and understand the differences, withholding their judgment, and introducing their culture to the newcomers. Simply being placed in the new culture does not guarantee acculturation especially for teenagers who might not have chosen to leave their home country, friends, and family to begin with. What seems normal and natural for students growing up in this culture may come as a culture shock to ELLs as illustrated in Gina's case. Instead of demanding a positive attitude, Gina's English teacher engaged her students writing and reflecting on their journey to America. She included literature that ELLs could identify with and introduced students to the wider school culture. In Alex's case, rather than blaming the student for his lack of expected American classroom behavior, his English teacher went out of her way to read about how schooling operates in Chinese culture, trying to understand her student's class participation behavior. Mainstream teachers need to have empathy for ELLs in order to work with these students effectively. The following are a few preservice and in-service mainstream teachers' reflections after working with ELLs:

> Reflecting back on my own cross-cultural experiences of visiting Croatia and working in a job that involved communicating with people whose native language is not English has helped me to understand the needs of ESL students. I know how frustrating it is when I want to communicate in Croatian but due to the fact of my limited proficiency, I am not able to. People might perceive me to be less intelligent, but the truth of the matter is that the language is the barrier and not my intelligence. Similarly, in my job and dealing with people from many different countries I have seen the same frustration with these people. This is the same situation that the ESL student is in.
>
> — *By a social studies teacher*

> This experience has taught me the value of what immigrants go through when they come to our country. I take the language for granted and often find myself at a loss to explain why we use certain words in certain situation -I don't know- we just do is often my explanation. When a young individual comes to the United States and enters our school system as an English Language Learner, the difficulties s/he faces are enormous. It takes an extremely strong individual to conquer the fear and criticism of learning everything from scratch. As an educator the experience has taught me to be more patient with the student. ELLs students will not get "it" on the first try or second try, might not get "it" on the third or fourth try, but after a number of times tasks will begin to sink in, and that is when I know I have accomplished my goal.
>
> — *By an English language arts teacher*

I always regretted not speaking another language or spending a prolonged period of time in another country. In the past three semesters working with ESL students I have truly been made aware of what an incredible experience these people have. The small and large successes that they have made are all the more remarkable considering the adjustments they have to make.

— By an English language arts teacher

I used to interpret silence from the ELLs as a lack of enthusiasm; however, I have come to understand that there can be many reasons for silence. It could mean embarrassment, lack of understanding, discomfort, respect, etc.

— By a biology teacher

One of my true loves of New York as the place I call home is in its awesome ethnic diversity. I have always admired the bravery of someone who was willing to take a chance on the "American Dream." The ability to grab one's family and brave along their trip to the unknown shores of fate and destiny in search of a better life is, in my estimation, nothing short of true heroism. As we have seen, one of the most difficult transitions to this new life is mastery of language. I have been continuously impressed with the tenacity and desire of some of my ESL students and I praise them for accomplishing goals that I doubt that I myself could reach. I feel I have become infinitely more appreciative of the ESL learners' vulnerabilities, needs, and strengths and I will try, with a more experienced set of educational tools, to implement many of the lessons and techniques I have learned this year into my work, next year.

— By a social studies teacher

CHAPTER 3

ASIAN ELLS' PREVIOUS EDUCATIONAL EXPERIENCES

Secondary ELLs who enter American schools bring with them not only their native languages, literacy and subject matter knowledge and skills but also learning beliefs, traditions, and expectations gained from their schooling back in their home countries. Familiarizing with ELLs' prior learning experiences and cultural beliefs and expectations and making those connections in teaching can not only ease those students' subject matter and language learning difficulties but also promote motivation, meaning, and critical thinking for those students.

Although basic demographic information about the ELLs in their classroom can be readily available from the school or district or via online, it takes time and effort for subject matter teachers to gain knowledge about ELLs' prior learning experiences and cultural beliefs, traditions, and expectations. Research has shown some serious cultural differences or even clashes in learning beliefs, traditions, and expectations between the teachers and students (Cummins, 1986; Dong, 2009, 2013–2014; Gaytan, Carhill, & Suarez-Orozzo, 2007; Lucas & Villegas, 2010). Educated and trained according to the US cultural beliefs, traditions, and expectations, often subject matter teachers do not share or are not aware of many ELLs' cultural beliefs, traditions, and expectations gained through their schooling in their home countries. If those differences are not adequately addressed by the

Teaching English Language Learners in Secondary Subject Matter Classes, pages 55–71.
Copyright © 2019 by Information Age Publishing

subject matter teachers, ELLs can be disoriented and confused to say the least and silenced and disengaged during the learning process.

In this chapter I give an overview of what different educational systems in Asia and Latin/Caribbean America, including China, Bangladesh, Mexico, and the Dominican Republic. Those are the top places where ELLs came from between the 2015 and 2016 school year (New York City Department of Education, 2016). For each country, I discuss the structure of basic education, social/cultural contexts of schooling, language and literacy and subject matter curriculum and instruction. I also offer teaching implications for subject matter teachers in order to provide meaningful, relevant, and effective instruction.

CHINESE EDUCATIONAL SYSTEM

Chinese students are the second largest ELL/bilingual student population in the New York City public schools. According to the 2015–2016 NYC Department of Education's report (New York City Department of Education, 2016), most Chinese ELLs came to the U.S. secondary schools with grade level appropriate literacy and subject matter education in their native language. In recent years as the Chinese economy makes strides on the world stage, we have seen more and more Chinese students come to the U.S. from all parts of China, including those from small cities and rural areas whose educational background and Chinese language literacy skills are not as strong as students from big cities, such as Beijing and Shanghai. Therefore, it is important for the subject matter teacher not to paint the Chinese ELLs with a broad brush but to make a concerted effort to get to know individual Chinese students, including what native language literacy skills and educational background that they bring with them to the subject matter classroom.

How is the Chinese Educational System Different from the American One? In 2015, the literacy rate in China was 96.4% (List of countries by literacy rate, 2017). Literacy rate refers to achieving reading and writing skills of the 9th grade level. In China, students are required to have nine years of compulsory education. The educational system, curricular guidelines, standardized tests are all controlled by the Department of Education. There are 200 school days in a year with two semesters: spring semester starts in March and ends in July and fall in September and ends in early Jan.

As the Chinese New Year often falls either in late January or in early February, Chinese schools have a longer fall semester. A typical school day starts at 7:30 a.m. and ends by 5:30 p.m. Children begin their elementary education at the age of 6 and elementary school is between grade 1 and grade 6. In elementary schools, students learn Chinese, mathematics, physical education, art/music, history and party history. By grade three, students begin learning a foreign language. The popular choices are English, Russian, Japanese, and Spanish. They also begin learning general science at grade three.

After elementary school, students go on to junior high school for three years. In junior high school, students learn physics in their first year, then chemistry, and finally biology. After nine years of compulsory education, students go through a standardized test to determine which and what kind of senior high school they will go to. After junior high school, students take the local senior high school entrance exam to get into high school. Senior high schools are ranked, and good senior high schools require a very high score on those entrance exams in order to get in. Also, this is the time for students and their parents to decide on whether to go to senior high school or vocational school. Students with a very low score on the high school entrance exam often go to vocational schools.

By their second year of senior high school, students are asked to choose a concentration field between humanities/social sciences and mathematics/natural science so their curriculum at the senior high school will be tailored to their concentrations. For example, while all senior high school students learn Chinese and the party history, students concentrating on the humanities and social science will spend more time studying history and Chinese language arts, while students concentrating on mathematics /natural sciences will spend more time in those subjects as well. Once the concentration is made, students will be placed in a class emphasizing in that concentration and stay with it throughout their senior high school years. The curricular objectives of the senior high school are to prepare students for the challenging college entrance exam, called Gao Kao.

Each year for three days in June, senior high school graduating students undergo the annual nationwide college entrance exam for two and half days in June, called Gao Kao. Students are tested on their knowledge and skills about the Chinese language, foreign language, mathematics, physics, chemistry, biology, geography, history, and party history. Only the exam score determines college admission and admission into a top-ranked college or university. The percentage of senior high school graduates going on to college/university has increased over the years from only 5% in the early 80s (Carson, 1992) to 75% in 2000 (Education in China, n.d.).

Chang came to the U.S. when she was in the seventh grade. When asked about her schooling back in China, Chang noted the following differences:

> It is very, very different. The desks are different, not like here one person for one desk. We have two students sharing one desk. There is no group work, everybody works alone. In Chinese schools, the teacher travels from class to class to teach while students stay in the same classroom throughout the day, semester, and year. We have a heavier workload. It would take me about 3–4 hours each day to complete my homework.
>
> — *By Chang, a 9th grade ELL*

Chang's remarks of differences between American schools and Chinese schools can be also extended to other aspects of a typical school day. There are three daily rituals in the Chinese school: At the beginning of each class students will all stand up to greet the teacher by saying: Lao shi ni hao (How are you teacher?). Twice a day, one in the morning and the other in the afternoon, students will have a break to do eye exercises by following the music and directions in the intercom. Based on the traditional Chinese medicine, eye exercises, which contain a series of massages around the eyes to promote blood circulation and relax muscles. Also, twice a day, students will go out in the playground, lining up by grades and classes and following the music to do a set of physical exercises (Education in China, n.d.).

The average size of the Chinese class is a lot bigger than the average American class with about 50–60 students in each class. Because of the large size and limited space, students all sit in rows with each pair sharing a desk. In this tight space with a large number of students, each class has an elaborate hierarchical structure set up, such as the class president, who communicates directly to the teacher and holds the whole class meetings on the weekly basis, learning monitor, who is responsible for communicating back and forth between subject matter teachers and the class on learning activities, subject matter representatives for each subject, communication monitor, who is responsible for publishing the class bulletin board each month, on homework monitor who collects and helps the teacher check the homework, hygiene monitor, who checks on both the classroom environment and the students' hygiene, organizational monitor, who works with the president and teachers to organize various social activities both in and outside the school, and even group monitors (students sitting in the same row are grouped together), with a student in charge of the row and is responsible for delegating tasks of cleaning the classroom, and a politeness monitor who reports and assists the teacher on disciplinary issues. There is no custodial staff to clean the classroom; instead, groups take turns cleaning the classroom each day.

Class ground rules are posted on the wall and students have class meetings weekly to go over those rules. Those who break the rules will be singled out by the teacher and/or peers and given either an oral or written reprimand first. If the offence is severe, parents will be called in to meet the teacher and develop a plan on how to prevent such an offense in the future. As the Chinese school is based on Confucius' philosophy, respecting the elder, teacher, parents, authority, disciplinary issues are often not as severe or frequent as we see in American classrooms. In addition, influenced by the Confucius teachings, parents often believe and communicate to their children that they listen to their parents at home and listen to the teacher in school. The fact that both the teacher and parents are on the same page in most of the cases, the full control and authority of the teacher plus the hierarchical order of the class makes the classroom management easy to handle.

Why Do Schools in China Operate Differently? To gain a deeper understanding of the Chinese educational system, we need to look at the foundations of Chinese education. Different from the American educational system, the Chinese educational system is based on the Confucian philosophy and the Chinese Communist Party's principles of maintaining social order, conformity, and harmony. Confucius, a philosopher and educator in ancient China, used his teachings to pass on educational values and principles of how to become an educated and social person. Confucianism is often characterized by four key principles which are taught early in Chinese schools through Chinese literature readings, social studies lessons, and explicit civic instruction daily. Besides schools, daily conversations at home, and news in the media constantly instill those principles using examples and patriotic slogans (Biggs, 1999; On, 1999; Yum, 1988). The Confucius four principles are:

Li (礼) refers to ways to become a proper person in the society following social norms, orders, and traditions. According to Confucius, it is only when students learn early on about Li that the society can maintain its harmony. Based on Li, students in China start to learn his or her place in the family, school, and society and what is expected of them by their parents, teachers, and society and how to behave accordingly and communicate properly both at home and in a social setting. Exemplary behaviors of Li and consequences of a lack of it are constantly reinforced by all teachers in the classroom using modeling, lecturing, positive and negative reinforcements.

Ren (仁) refers to humanness in the Chinese culture, meaning taking care of the elderly and parents and protecting children. According to Ren, there is a life-long and asymmetrical relationship between parents and children. Once being born, children are indebted to their parents all their lives. Both at home and in schools as well as at work, and in social media, students are taught to be filial to their parents, modest about themselves, and loyal to their family and country.

Yi (义) refers to respect and loyalty. Rather than having their own thoughts, placing self at the center, and taking care of their personal interests and needs, students are taught to behave for the betterment of the other, family, group, and society. To follow Confucius teachings, students are taught to respect and listen to their elders, including parents, teachers in order to maintain the social hierarchical order. Schools play an important role of teaching and cultivating Yi during its civics education and moral teachings. A proverb goes "Once my teacher, forever my parent" shows high regard that the Chinese culture places on the authority and power of teacher. The concept of Yi is reflected in all school curricular materials, readings, etc.

Zhi (智) refers to knowledge. As an educator by profession, Confucius emphasizes the importance of cultivating knowledge and using that knowledge to communicate effectively and maintain the social order. According to Confucius teachings, education is for social mobility. Only those who have achieved high learning should be promoted to the position of power. In the Chinese language and history curriculum for example, extensive attention is given to learning not only the linguistic codes, registers, and modes, but also elaborate and systematic lessons on the importance of keeping the social stratification systems and hierarchical structure using language and knowledge. The concept and ways of indirect communication to save face, and avoid at all costs of the embarrassment and disagreements in social settings are paramount to the Chinese being and behaving.

Those four Confucian principles also overlap the Chinese Communist Party's doctrine taught explicitly in schools and in the media. Every classroom has those four party doctrines posted on the wall as Carson (1992) listed:

- Love for the country
- Service to others (the interests of the group and society always supersede individual's interests. Individual interests and thoughts and views are considered bad and have to be replaced by group and country's interests)
- Abide group/society rules
- Respect for authority (p. 43)

How Do Chinese Students Learn the Chinese Language? Unlike English and Romance languages that have an alphabet and phonetic system, Chinese is a language derived from the Sino-Tibetan language family spoken by 1.2 billion people about 16% of the world, and is an official language of China, Hong Kong, Taiwan, Singapore, and Macau (Chinese language, n.d.). Chinese written language is composed of characters developed by four major principles of formation and has different spatial orientations in writing (Chang et al., 2014; Hudson-Ross & Dong, 1990; Zhou et al., 2018). Those four major principles of character formation are:

Pictograms (象形): characters that have strong resemblances to the actual objects, such as 日for sun, 雨for rain. Many of the modern Chinese characters can still be traced back to those pictograms that those characters are originated.

Indicators (指事): characters that derived from early pictograms but are assigned to abstract meanings, such as上 up and下 down.

Ideograms (會意): characters that combine two or more indicators, such as 林, composed of two trees 木 to mean forest 林.

Phonograms (形聲): characters with a phonetic component that is added to a pictogram or indicator to give a pronunciation aid. For example, the character of missing someone: 想 combines the pictogram of heart 心and the phonogram 相.

Those four word-formation principles are the building blocks of the Chinese characters. Although some basic Chinese characters are formed using a single principle, such as a pictogram or indicator, most of the Chinese characters are formed using two or multiple principle combinations, such as a combination of a pictogram, indicator, and phonogram. Uniquely different from the word formation in English, the Chinese language lacks an explicit association between the sound and the character, making it extra difficult to learn. Children in Chinese elementary schools spend a lot more time during their early elementary school years just on learning those basic formations of the character and building a foundation of how to read and write using basic characters. Studies have shown that by grade 6 Chinese students will learn about 3,000 characters to form 50,000 phrases. Those

3,000 characters provide a foundation for students to continue their learning and to become independent readers and writers (Carson, 1992).

Although there are many regional and ethnic dialects (56 dialects in total) spoken in China, the standard Chinese language (汉语), also known as Mandarin or Putonghua is the language for Han, the majority of the Chinese ethnic groups that composed of 1.2 billion people. It is the language based on Beijing dialect and used in schools and media. In contrast to the oral language, there are only two written languages: One consists of the traditional Chinese writing system and the other the simplified Chinese writing system. Children who speak a regional dialect come to school to learn both the standard oral and written Chinese.

Chinese Language Reforms. In 1958 soon after the establishment of the People's Republic of China, the Chinese government launched two language reforms: 1) using Pinyin as an oral pronunciation aid and 2) simplifying the written language to promote literacy education and unify the nation (Liu, 2005).

Pinyin adopts the phonetic pronunciation system of Romance languages to give each Chinese character a sound to aid word recognition, standardize the pronunciation, which is called Putonghua or Mandarin as often referred to overseas. School children learn Pinyin first in their beginning Chinese language curriculum to build a foundation of the standardized pronunciation and use it to learn the Chinese character. One major difference between the Pinyin and the Romance language phonetic system is that Pinyin has four intonation marks for each character. They are rising tone, falling tone, turning tone, and flat tone. Throughout their elementary education, reading materials contain both Pinyin and the Chinese characters. Public literacy and education systems also underwent the reform later by including Pinyin in dictionaries and word processing and literacy reading materials. Pinyin is now used not only in Mainland China, but also in Taiwan, Macau, Hong Kong, and many other overseas Chinese communities (Chinese language, n.d.).

Simplification of the Chinese Character. One major difficulty for students to learn to write Chinese comes from its complex stroke order, sequence, numbers, and coordination. After the Pinyin reform, the Chinese government began simplifying each traditional Chinese character by reducing the number of strokes significantly. Although the traditional Chinese writing system is still seen in many classic literature works, used by some overseas Chinese communities, due to its strong associations and similarities between the two systems, many students can still read the traditional Chinese characters even though they learn the simplified Chinese characters in schools. The character simplification eased the language learning process and facilitates literacy development (Chinese language, n.d.).

How Do Chinese Students Learn to Read and Write? Based on the philosophy of education, the Chinese literacy education focuses on instilling the cultural knowledge and social values through reading and writing curriculum, instruction, and assessment. Curdt-Christiansen (2008) studied the cultural themes of how to become a good student and right person in a series of elementary Chinese language textbooks and found the recurring themes through grades 1 and 6, such as filial piety, obedience, conformity, patriotism, diligence, modesty, and perseverance. Those themes are derived from Confucius' teachings and Party principles running through both parental teachings at home and mass media propaganda to promote cultural knowledge, the Communist Party's expectations and views.

Chinese literacy instruction is mainly conducted in a lecture mode with the teacher imparting knowledge embedded in the reading for the students through choral readings, recitations, and memorization drills. I still remember vividly how my Chinese literature teacher assigned us to have a vocabulary notebook to document any idiomatic sayings, called Chenyu (a four-letter word expression) and use them in our writings. Whoever had the most sayings and used them appropriately in their essays would receive extra points on the exam. The essays with vivid expressions and proper language use would also be posted and read aloud in class.

Chinese students spend a lot of time learning to write. Because of the unique and complex formation of the Chinese characters, students in elementary school will first practice learning to write basic stroke for one hour a day besides taking a language arts class. The teacher teaches students how to hold the pen and/ or the Chinese calligraphy brush and have a correct posture when writing. Like American students doing coloring, the Chinese elementary students use the calligraphy brush to trace the line and learn how to first write strokes and then the whole character.

In contrast to American reading curriculum and instruction, the Chinese reading curriculum is more of a surrogate of the party indoctrination and transmission of Confucius' ideology. Most of the literature readings are selected by the Ministry of Education to align with the party's and Confucius' four principle and serve the political and ideological purposes. All Chinese literature readings both fiction and nonfiction have a moral and history lesson to be discussed by the teacher. Personal reader responses, views, and opinions are not allowed (Buley-Messiner, 1990).

Composition is emphasized. Throughout the elementary, middle, and high schools, students learn to write in multiple genres, including expository and descriptive writing. The commonly used American writing genres like argumentative essays and perspective writing are not part of the Chinese composition curriculum. While teaching writing, the teacher often provides a model essay and gives details and sentence frames for students to follow before composing on their own. A sample expositive essay would often begin with the Chinese current political events to be in line with the party line. Often famous sayings from Confucius and party leaders, such as Mao, Deng, and Xi are considered to be a good introduction.

Unlike American academic essays requiring students to support their opinions with details or readings, the Chinese essays require the party line to be used as an introduction. Throughout the essay, students are expected to cite those party leaders' sayings to support those views. No specific citation rules or requirements are given. Including others' words in the essay without giving credits is an expected practice for students in the learning process. A famous Chinese proverb goes "You cannot compose your own poem unless you have memorized 300 poems by poets in the Tang Dynasty" (a dynasty considered to be the Chinese literary Renaissance). That's why so many Chinese students commit the academic crime of plagiarism without knowing why. Also, without explicit instruction, those students don't know how to do citation and be vigilant about lifting others' words without giving credit where the credit is due (Matalene, 1985; Shen, 1989).

How Do Chinese Students Learn Subject Matter Knowledge? Mark, an earth science teacher, often surveyed his students, including ELLs for their prior knowledge about science. When asked how science classes in the United States are different from those in China, Sam, a 11th grader who came to the U.S. last year, responded,

> Back in China, we learned physics first, then chemistry, and finally biology. Students are not required to pass a standardized test on it like Regents here; instead, they are required to learn each subject for one year and complete all the three subjects by the end of senior high school. I love science and read 10,000 whys, a popular science series in my spare time. That is a series of books on popular science topics. Each chapter opens up with a why question. It asks the reader to think about the topic and solve common problems using science. For example, "Why does the bike have two wheels?" "Why does cement become hardened after having contact with water?" It then provides us with a detailed explanation and scientific reasoning behind it. I like to read those books because they tell me something that I don't know before. —by Sam, an 11th grade ELL

Thanks to his science teacher's sincere interest in his prior science learning experience, Sam's strengths and interests were connected to science learning in a meaningful way. The subject matter curriculum and instruction in Chinese schools are all centralized. The Ministry of Education determines the sequence, content coverage, and learning standards. There is a clear focus and more time is given to Chinese language arts and mathematics, while other subject matter areas, such as science and history gain more attention in secondary schools. Starting from junior high school, many Chinese parents send their children to Gao Kao prep schools at nights and on the weekends. Instruction in senior high school is designed to prepare students for Gao Kao.

In early grades of the elementary school, science is not taught as a separate subject, rather a general education course in health and nature. By grade 4 or 5 students start learning science as a separate subject like general science. By junior high school, general science becomes a separate and focused scientific-discipline study. Students first learn physics, then chemistry, and finally biology. By senior high school, students follow the same sequence of physics in the first year, chemistry the second, and biology the third. In comparison to those subjects that students learned in the junior high school, the subject matter becomes more in-depth and broadened. As Sam mentioned, there is no standardized exam given on the subject by the end of the year (Wang, 2015; Wang et al., 1996).

The social studies curriculum in both junior and senior high schools is divided into four major domains: Chinese Communist Party history, Chinese history, world history, philosophy and economics. Marxism, Leninism, and Maoism are the three major philosophical theories taught throughout schooling, especially in senior high school. Students read both primary source documents, such as *Manifesto of the Communist Party* by Marx, *On Contradiction* by Mao, etc. and textbooks on the major philosophical and economic principles of those major figures. In recent years, students also read about Xiao Ping Deng's economic policies and selected essays by Xi Jinping, current President of China.

What Does All This Mean to Teach Chinese ELLs? Having been educated in the Chinese schools, new Chinese ELLs need time, teachers' willingness, and effort to understand and participate in American ways of learning. Three implications for bridging those differences are:

Compare and Contrast Different Ways of Teaching and Learning. Coming from a previous learning environment characterized by the rigor, teacher-centered instruction, test-driven curriculum and instruction, and emphasis on digesting and memorizing of a large amount of abstract information and language system, Chinese students may be bewildered or confused by the experiential learning, group work, and inquiry and discovery learning methods, etc. Using comparisons and giving rationales and backgrounds for American teaching methods and teacher expectations is better for secondary Chinese ELLs to logically understand those different ways of learning. The ways they learned back home are not necessarily bad but just different. Engaging students in comparing and contrasting those differences between the two cultures in an analytical and critical manner can also promote cross-cultural understanding and higher order thinking skills.

Being aware of those differences can make subject matter teachers re-examine some taken for granted teaching practices, such as group work and inquiry-oriented teaching. Rather than assuming students should have already learned how to do them by secondary schools, the subject matter teacher should model the expected behavior during the group work and train these students to ask inquiry-oriented questions. This way Chinese ELLs can learn how to participate in the new ways of learning.

Build on Chinese ELLs' Prior Learning and Literacy and Family Strengths. As we have seen so far, secondary ELLs from China have unique strengths and family and cultural traditions of learning. Subject matter teachers should invite students to share their previous learning experiences and interests, such as Sam's interest in using popular science books to learn science. The Chinese ELLs' strong family structures and unique cultural traditions can be easily connected to various subject matter topics in social studies, English language arts, mathematics, and science. Chinese parents are very supportive of their children's education and want to be a part of their educational process. However, in America, many

Chinese parents are often handicapped because of their limited language skills and cultural knowledge. As a result, their support is often reduced to emotional and financial support. As an immigrant student's first contact in school, getting to know those students' background is vital. Also, having an interpreter and translating letters, report cards, and major assignments into their native language can be an effective first step to get parents involved. Considering the respect that the Chinese parents often have for teachers, those efforts and initiations will receive positive responses from the parents.

In addition, the U.S. teachers should be aware that many schools in Asian cultures have a different academic sequence. For example, in secondary Chinese schools, physics is taught first before chemistry and last biology. Therefore, they need to adjust their expectations. A newly arrived 9th grade Chinese ELL may have learned physics but not biology yet. Still, the student's prior learning of physics can be used to learn biology. Also, the student may need extra help with basic biological concept and vocabulary learning.

Mathematics teachers should be aware that many Chinese students may have advanced mathematical knowledge and strong mental mathematics skills built in their previous schooling back home in comparison to their U.S. grade level counterparts. This is probably due to not only the Chinese school culture, family culture's stress on teaching and learning mathematics and science, but also may be due to the in-depth teaching by their mathematics teacher who often has fewer students and classes to teach during the day but more time to increase their own mathematical knowledge and prepare for their lessons. A Chinese mathematics teacher only teaches two periods a day and spends the rest of the day on lesson planning, professional development, tutoring, and developing resources. As a result, Chinese mathematics teachers have a strong subject matter knowledge base and place a priority on conceptual understanding before problem solving.

BANGLADESHI EDUCATIONAL SYSTEM

In comparison to students from East Asian countries, such as China and South Korea, teachers often know little about Bangladeshi students, their native cultural, language, literacy backgrounds as well as their educational beliefs, traditions, and expectations. In recent years, New York City public schools have seen a huge wave of students from Bangladesh. Those students compose a sizable portion of the ELL body. There are many differences in educational systems as well as cultural beliefs and traditions comparing the Bangladeshi culture with American culture. Therefore, taking the time to learn about those students' backgrounds, strengths, and needs will enable subject matter teachers to connect with them and instruct those students effectively (Luna, 2015).

Bangladesh is located in the Southeast Asia on the Bay of Bengal with Burma and India as its neighbors. It has a population of about 165 million and Bengali as its official language. The country went through the British colonization from 1700s to 1947 and afterward the Pakistani colonization (1947–1971). It was not until 1972 that Bangladesh gained its independence and became a secular, social-istic, and democratic state governed by the parliamentary form of government (Bangladeshi culture, n.d.; Rahman et al., 2010). English is also used for legal and government purposes and in higher education.

How is the Bangladeshi Educational System Different from the U.S. System? In 2015, the literacy rate in Bangladesh was 61.5% (List of countries by lit-eracy rate, 2017). Public schools in Bangladesh consist of five years of compulso-ry and free elementary schools and seven years of secondary schools (Bangladesh education system, n.d.; Education in Bangladesh, n.d.). Children begin their el-ementary education at the age of six. The parents choose one of the two education systems for their children: general education and Madrasah education, the school focusing on the Islamic language and religion. After elementary schools, students and their parents will decide on whether to go into the vocational education track or continue with the general education track. Within the general education track, students and their parents will decide on whether to focus on humanities/social sciences or mathematics/natural sciences as their future career choices (Educa-tion system-Bangladesh, 2012; Secondary education, 2015). Secondary schools in Bangladesh consists of three years of junior secondary school (grades 6 through 8), secondary school (grades 9 and 10), and higher secondary school (grades 11 and 12). Higher Secondary Schools are also considered to be intermediate col-leges or degree colleges.

Ahnaf, a 15 years old who just came to the U.S. two months ago talked about his difficulty in making adjustment in the U.S.

> The academic calendar in Bangladesh is from January to December, so I had attend-ed almost three months of the ninth grade in Bangladesh before immigrating to the United States. I was close to finishing high school (Bangladeshi intermediate college starts at the 11th grade). However, I was placed in an 8th grade classroom in my cur-rent school, being held back one year and repeating one grade. I was very insulted by this. Back in Bangladesh I learned Algebra, Euclidean (coordinate) Geometry and basic trigonometry. I was a good student and even on the national cricket team.
> — *by Ahnaf, a 9th grade ELL*

Although the enrollment in elementary education was high about 95% in Bangladesh, the drop-out rate and repeat rate was also high. About 20.4% of the students dropped out from elementary schools in 2015 and 38.3% of students dropped out from secondary schools in 2016. It is not uncommon for a child to take 8.5 years to complete the five-year elementary education.

The standardized test by the end of secondary schools (grade 10) is adminis-tered by the Boards of Intermediate and Secondary Education to award students the Secondary School Certificate. Higher Secondary Education (grades 11 and 12) is provided by colleges, leading to Higher Secondary Education Certificate, which is required for higher education. Madrasah education system also has two certificate exams and students will be awarded by the end of the 10th grade and 12th grade (Secondary education, 2015).

College/university admission is based on the Higher Secondary Education Certificate, GPA, and individual college/university entrance exams. Currently only about 10% of graduating students from higher secondary education go on to colleges or universities (Education system Bangladesh, 2012).

Bangladeshi students go to school from Sunday to Thursday but not Friday as it is the Islamic Holy Day. Schools are challenged by a lack of resources as well as teachers. Ninety percent of the schools run on a double shift with one shift in the morning from 7:30 a.m. to 11 a.m. or 1:30 p.m. and the other in the afternoon from 11:30 a.m. to 4:30 p.m. or 2:30 p.m. to 5:30 p.m. Many elementary schools teach both Bengali and English simultaneously while Madrasah schools also teach Arabic (Bangladesh: Curriculum planning, 1998; Education in Bangladesh, n.d.; Education system-Bangladesh, 2012; Prodhan, 2016).

Similar to the Chinese schools, students in Bangladeshi schools remain in the same classroom throughout the day and semester while teachers travel from classroom to classroom to teach. Unlike the American school calendar, a Bangladeshi school year starts in Jan. and ends in Dec. The lecture style of teaching and memorization is predominant and considered to be the way of teaching and learning.

Why Do Bangladeshi Schools Operate Differently? As 85% of the Bangladeshi people are Muslims, the philosophy of Bangladeshi education is derived from the Islamic philosophy that emphasizes achieving a balance between sense, mind, and religious faith through education (Rayan, 2012; Schogar, 2014; Sultana, 2012). Instead of a separation of religion and education as in the U.S. public education system, Bangladeshi schools place religion, specifically, Islamic religion at the center of the education process. Unlike the Western educational goal to achieve free, critical, and independent thinking and develop individualistic and creative thoughts through education, Bangladeshi schools train students to be responsible moral beings and achieve harmony between sense, mind, and religious faith.

Similar to the Indian culture, a neighbor geographically and culturally, the class system and social stratification is also the norm of the Bangladeshi culture. Extended family is a valued tradition and a typical family consists of parents and grandparents with children and grandchildren. Obedience toward and respect for elders, higher classes, and conformity are taught both in schools and at home (Rahman, 2014). Work ethics, dedication, sacrifice, and commitment are key values instilled in children early at home in the Bangladeshi culture. Even for teenagers in the U.S., supporting the family often comes first before education, especially when the family is in need of help. It's not uncommon to see some Bangladeshi adolescents take on challenging work after school or even give up their education to support the family both in the U.S. and back in Bangladesh (Zhao, 2002).

As an agricultural country with a strict caste and class system, there is a great divide in the literacy rate between the urban and rural Bangladeshi communities.

In those rural communities, only about 75% of children attend elementary schools and graduation rate is only about 55%. About 85% of elementary graduates go onto secondary schools. With one-thirds of the Bangladeshi people are below the poverty line, in many rural communities, the attendance rate is even lower and drop-out rate is higher. When there is a natural disaster, short of labor, poverty, or family crises, such as ailing and elderly relatives, students are often pulled out of the school to help out (Sarkar & Corrigan, 2014).

There is a major gender discrepancy in literacy rate between the female students (58.5%) and male students (64.6%). As a pariah society, a preference for sons is still strong. Girls are considered inferior to boys. While sons are considered as an asset to take care of his parents in their old ages and continue the family lineage, the daughters are considered as a burden, vulnerable and in a constant need for protection from men. Her life is centered round domestic duties of her own family first and then her husband's family after she is married (Chowdbury, 2004; Scales, Benson, & Dershem, 2013). In rural and poverty-stricken villages, adolescent girls are not allowed to go to school but stay home to care for the family and get married at a very young age. So, it is only through marriage that her family can transfer this burden to her husband and his family.

Over the years despite improvement of women's social status and educational opportunities, the social and cultural belief is still that the woman does not need an education, instead, what she needs is a husband. In 2016, the dropout rate at the secondary level among female students was 42.19% while the dropout rate was 33.80% for male students (Mahadi, 2017).

How Do Bangladeshi Students Learn the Bengali Language and Reading and Writing Skills? Bengali is an Indo-Aryan language spoken by 230 million people including Bangladeshis and Indians in West Bengal. The Bengali script is derived from Brahmi script written from left to right. It has a Romanized pronunciation scheme with 29 consonants and 13 vowels to match the script letter and provide the sound-letter connection and ease the difficulty in the language acquisition and learning process. Bengali basic sentence structure follows the subject-object-verb word order. Like other Asian languages, such as Korean, Bengali has honorific referents used to address people according to their seniority, social status, kinship terms, and age (Bengali language, n.d.).

During the time of the British colonization (1757–1947), the English language was introduced and established as an official school language in schools. After the Liberation War in 1971 from Pakistan, Bengali was replaced English as an official national language. It was not until the 20th century, when the English language education again was institutionalized as a second language.

Teachers in Bangladeshi schools teach using a predominantly teacher-centered approach characterized by memorization drills, teaching to the test, and copying. The common classroom practice involves students coming to the front of the classroom to write what they have memorized on the board (Walters, 2011). Walters interviewed a group of Bangladeshi teachers at an urban school and found that, "[t]he teaching of Bengali was undertaken by the teacher, standing in front of the class, writing a letter from the Bengali alphabet on the board and saying the sound of the letter out loud, followed by the children repeating the sound and then writing the letter" (Cooke, 2013, p. 172). There is a focus on correct pronunciation and neatness of the written work. Students learn individually not in pairs or in groups.

At the secondary level, teachers provide students with the handouts and lecture notes to prepare them for the exam. Assessment and testing also reinforce this method of teaching and learning by asking students to repeat information on the test of what they have memorized in a predictable fashion. As a result, many Bangladeshi students have weak reading comprehension skills and limited experience with reading and writing skills or creative and critical thinking skills (Mirza & Mahmud, 2012).

Kenner et al. (2008) experimented with using family stories, folktales, and poetry as authentic literature to teach the 2nd and 3rd generations of Bengali speaking students to promote bilingual and bicultural learning in a British primary school. They found that this is helpful and not only increased engagement from the students but also from parents as well. Students' writing to compare and contrast lullabies and folktales in both English and Bengali led to an increased interest not only in their native culture and language but also enhanced cognitive skills and reading and writing skills.

How Do Bangladeshi Students Learn Subject Matter Knowledge? Rafig who came to the U.S. a year ago reflected on his secondary education in Bangladesh like this:

> We had classes five days a week about seven hours a day. The number of students varied depending on the subject. For example, we would have 20 students in an English class while 60 in a science class. I heard students in the village would often have one teacher teaching most of the subjects during the day in a crowded class about 60 students. I appreciate my Madrasah secondary education because it prepares me for my education today in the U.S., especially helps me become a trilingual: I can speak Arabic, Bengali, and English. Knowing three languages enables me to learn English fast. Also, having learned the history of Bangladesh and the Muslim religion, I can relate more to some of the topics in my social studies class here in the U.S.
>
> — *By Rafig, a 10th grade ELL*

Bangladeshi secondary education has gone through quite a few changes over the years in an effort to 1) unify three types of secondary schools: general education, vocational education, and Madrasah education and 2) modernize the school and teaching pedagogy and 3) provide equal education for all. The objectives of secondary education aims to equip students with new knowledge and skills to use modern science and technology, positive outlook and scientific attitude, skills for self-employment, and promote patriotism, religious, moral, cultural and social values (Secondary education, 2015). The curriculum of secondary schools in general education includes six required subjects: Bengali, English, mathematics, religious education, social science, and science. Electives include business education, Islamic studies, home economics/agriculture, etc. History classes focus more on the history of Bangladesh, such as the history under the British rule and then Pakistani rule. It is also oriented toward the teaching of the Muslim culture and religion (Bangladesh curriculum planning, n.d.; Secondary education, 2015).

Although Bangladeshi students learn science from grade three and continue on to study more broad and in-depth scientific disciplines, such as physics, chemistry, and biology in secondary schools, science classes are only taught in the classroom using a lecture mode due to a lack of science labs, equipment, and lab assistants (Miah, 2006). In comparison, in Madrasah schools (schools with a focus on the Islamic religion), science in general education schools covers more general science topics, including physics, chemistry, biology, and mathematics. Due to limited resources and teaching staff, science lessons are often taught in the classroom in a lecture format without lab classes.

Sartkar and Corrigan (2014) surveyed a group of 159 junior secondary science educators in Bangladesh to explore their views on scientific literacy and their instructional and assessment practices. They found that teachers varied in their perspectives toward scientific literacy and were limited by their own scientific education. Despite their efforts to connect scientific concepts to students' everyday experiences and application aspects of learning science, they were constrained by the standardized test which favors memorization and a surface understanding of concepts as well as a large class size and a lack of lab facilities (Tapan, 2010).

What Does All This Mean to Teach Bangladeshi ELLs? The review of the educational system, values, and practices in Bangladesh is an important first step to understand that not all Asian students are the same. Students from Southeastern Asian countries, such as Bangladesh have a unique set of educational backgrounds, challenges in second language and cultural learning, and rich native language, cultural and religious traditions. Knowing about those matters will enable the teacher to move beyond just providing vocabulary support, rather to looking for entry points and opportunities to create meaningful and effective subject matter instruction.

Listen to Bangladeshi ELLs' Previous Learning Stories. As shown in the above students' reflections on their schooling back home, those students want to share their previous learning with both the teacher and students in the classroom. Bangladeshi students' beliefs and values from their cultural and religious perspectives can be the key for the US teachers to bridge the differences and use them for critical learning. For example, Rafig came to the U.S. with basic trilingual education in Arabic and Bangladeshi and English, and all those backgrounds and experiences should be used at different points in various subject matter classes. A sincere interest in what he knows can be a motivating factor for Rafig to participate in the learning process. Conscious learning about what Bangladeshi students knew and learned back in their home country can also be a good opportunity for the teacher to integrate what students know into what they do not know and create a new pathway to teaching and learning.

Bridge the Bangladeshi Students' Literacy and Cultural Gap. Becoming a literate person in the U.S. culture is not the same as becoming a literate person in Bangladeshi culture because of the differences in learning context, objectives of education, cultural expectations and traditions, and teaching and learning practices. The U.S. teacher should investigate those differences first in order to bridge those differences and teach the U.S. cultural, educational values and goals meaningfully and effectively. Students from Bangladesh need to know those differences in order to gain a real understanding and see the logical purpose of learning what deemed to be different or even culturally and religiously forbidden in their previous educational experiences. That way they will realize what it means to be literate in the U.S. and become a willing participant in the classroom to practice those new values, thoughts, and views.

Finally, willingness to gain an understanding of Bangladeshi students' familiar ways of learning and cultural beliefs can also engage the teacher in critically examining their own beliefs and viewing the teaching topics from another perspective based on a different belief system. The ability to see another's belief and value can be a key in working with students from different language, cultural, and religious groups.

CHAPTER 4

LATINO ELLS' PREVIOUS EDUCATIONAL EXPERIENCES

In this chapter I discuss public educational systems in Mexico and the Dominican Republic. These two countries are among the top countries where Spanish-speaking ELLs come from between the 2015 and 2016 school year (New York City Department of Education, 2016). For each country, I discuss the structure of basic education, sociocultural contexts of schooling, language and literacy and subject matter curriculum and instruction. Using comparisons and contrasts between those educational systems and that of the U.S., I offer teaching implications for subject matter teachers.

MEXICAN PUBLIC EDUCATIONAL SYSTEM

Students from Mexico are one of the fastest growing ELLs in the nation, composing a significant portion of the ELL body. Although it is well known that many students from Mexico speak Spanish, there is diversity within Mexican ELLs in previous education, native language and literacy skills, and socioeconomic backgrounds. Below are Maria, Lucia, and John's accounts of their schooling back in Mexico:

I grew up in Puebla, Mexico. We started Kindergarten at 3 years old, then primary school until the 6th grade. In primary school we had one teacher covering all

Teaching English Language Learners in Secondary Subject Matter Classes, pages 73–85.

major subjects, such as grammar, dictation, math, Spanish, and history. Students mostly read as a whole class and then were assigned questions to answer in a workbook. In secondary school, we had different teachers for different subjects, but I liked Spanish literature the most because I was good at it. In secondary school, teachers gave exams to promote students to the next level. Also, in secondary school, we had a variety of electives, such as chorus, art, theater, dancing, and so on. I was pleasantly surprised that my talent for singing was discovered in chorus class here in America.

— By Maria, a 10ᵗʰ grade ELL

I was born in Sinaloa, Mexico. I only completed my primaria (primary school) before coming to the US two years ago. Back home not everyone got to go to middle school or high school. I came from a poor family, and I had to work to support my family after primary school. Now I'm in the U.S., I must go to school.

— By Lucia, a 7ᵗʰ grade ELL

I completed my 9ᵗʰ grade in Mexico. When I first came to this country, everything was so different. The school day here is very long. In Mexico, we go to school from 8 am–12 pm for kindergarten, 8 am–1 pm for primary school. I used to finish around 3:30 pm in high school. I felt overwhelmed with so many hours of studying and very little time for myself. Another difference, my lunch break here in the US is not the same as it is in Mexico. It was great to have free lunch here in the U.S., however American teachers are always watching us even during the lunch, so lunch time is not really free time as we had in school back in Mexico.

— By John, a 9ᵗʰ grade ELL

How is the Mexican Education System Different from the U.S. System?
An overall literacy rate in Mexico was 94.4% in 2015 (List of countries by literacy rate, 2017). Public schools in Mexico consist of six years of elementary schools for children between ages of 6 and 12, three years of lower-secondary school (grades 7–9); and three years of upper-secondary school (grades 10–12). In 1993 the Mexican government increased years of compulsory education from 6 years to 9 years. The curriculum of education is controlled by the Secretariat of Public Education and learning standards are set by the Ministry as well. There is a national exam at the end of each school year, and students who score less than 6 out of 10 on this exam repeat the grade. The grading scale is 1 to 10 in Mexican schools (Education in Mexico, n.d.).

The school year in Mexico starts in late August and ends in early July consisting of 200 days of classes. Elementary students spend about four hours a day, five days a week in school; while secondary students spend at least seven hours a day, five days a week in school. Secondary schools often run shifts: morning, afternoon, and evening. Although about 92% of children enroll in elementary school, the enrollment for the lower-secondary schools the percentage drops to 62%. Among the lower-secondary school students, only half of the graduating students continue to upper-secondary school, and only a quarter of the upper-secondary graduates go onto higher education (How are K–12 schools different in Mexico, n.d.).

A typical school day starts at either 8 or 9 a.m. with students singing the national anthem. In Mexico schools, teachers change classes after a period, while students stay in the same classroom throughout the day or even the semester. When the teacher comes to the class, every student stands up to show respect. There is no ability level tracking and every class is a mixed level class. Students have a mid-morning break for snacks and recess around 10 a.m. Students wear uniforms, and they only attend school for four hours a day in elementary school. Mexican classroom learning is more informal and interactive than learning in American classrooms. In class students are frequently involved in group work and they are encouraged to interact with each other (Howard, 2007; James, 2002).

Every Monday morning all students are gathered together in the "patio" or yard to watch the Mexican flag rise and sing the national anthem. Only the top students are selected by the teachers to be escorts to march along with the flag. Juan, an 8th grader, vividly remembers,

> When I was a student in Mexico, my parents wanted me to be part of the escort. That privilege is hard to earn because many students wanted to be part of it. It was an honor. I remember working harder than ever, even went for extra help with my teacher. The hard work paid off in the end when I was able to hold the Mexican flag. I still remember that day as yesterday when everyone was watching me and I was extremely proud and happy. My parents were very proud of me, too. I couldn't believe I had done this. This accomplishment showed me that everything in life is possible as long as you work hard and believe that you can do it.
>
> — *By Juan, a 9th grade ELL*

Mexican education is influenced by its religious values and its collective practices and beliefs shaped by many indigenous cultures and languages. About 82% of Mexicans are Catholic, and the Catholic Church has played an important role in Mexican education dated back to the Spanish colonization to the Independence of Mexico. Even though the church and the state are separate, many Catholic values overlap with the traditional Mexican cultural values and traditions, thus constituting the social and cultural context of Mexican education (French & Manzanarez, 2002; Zimmerman, 2015). Those key values are: social and family hierarchy, Machismo, and collectivism.

Hierarchy and Machismo. Machismo refers to a strong sense of masculinity. Mexican society values men and believes that men are protectors and breadwinners of the family. A popular saying is "A man is king in his home." Patriarchal tradition and hierarchy order in society and the family are valued by indigenous cultures and 60% of the Mexican population comes from indigenous cultures. Ethnic and family loyalty and kinship orientation often override the individual preferences and needs. Thus, respect for authority, loyalty, avoidance of conflict, and indirect communication are valued and practiced in school. Lowering the eyes in the presence of an elder and teacher is a sign of respect (Martinez-Miron & Rebolledo-Mendez, 2015).

Collectivism. An extended patriarchal family structure is a hallmark of Mexican society. Many Mexican homes include not just parents and children but also grandparents, aunts, uncles, cousins, and grandchildren. This extended family is where children receive their early education and are taught to be obedient and respectful. Children in an extended Mexican family often learn early to defer to authorities, such as parents and elders. A direct stare or eye contact has to be avoided at all costs, a sign of disrespect and bad raising. As the proverb "A tree that grows crooked cannot be straightened" shows the importance of the parental role in children's education. Group orientation and respect for elders are valued in the classroom as well as in the Mexican proverb goes, "Better to be a fool within the crowd than wise by oneself." Cooperative learning is very popular in the Mexican classroom and students do not want to show what they know for fear of embarrassing those who do not know (Culture of Mexico, n.d.; Hall, 2006; Mount-Cors, 2013).

Parental involvement in education is expected and valued in Mexican schools. Parents not only participate in the parent-teacher conference, but also involving in maintaining and repairing school facilities, celebrating major holidays together, and increasing social and cultural awareness of local communities (Mexico: Closing the Gap, 2007; Zarate, 2007). Juan recalled his early literacy education at home like this:

> My mother told me about those holidays when we were very, very young. She told us how and why we make the offerings and how important it is to honor our past families. Other times we tell consejos to help each other when times are hard, or to never give up. Life is not easy, like how to never be jealous of another person, because you don't know what they are going through. Or to how we should always be grateful for what we have, we don't know how hard others have it out there. Those memoriable consejos or dichos (proverbs and sayings) is a big part of being Mexican.
>
> — By Juan, a 9th grade ELL)

Urban vs. Rural Education. There is a huge difference in the educational experiences between urban and rural school students (Meyers, 2009, 2011). Urban schools have a convenient public transportation system that enables more students to attend schools. In rural areas, such as Pueblo, from which the majority of Mexican immigrants come to the U.S., there is a lack of public transportation. Furthermore, many secondary schools in those areas lack of financial support, resources, teachers, and even basic living necessities like running water and electricity, which prevent students from continuing their education after elementary school.

How Do Mexican Students Learn the Spanish Language and Reading and Writing Skills? Spanish is spoken by over 400 million people in the world, the official language for more than twenty countries. As a Romance language, Spanish shares many similarities with English. Both English and Spanish use the Roman alphabet and are built on the similar sound and letter system. About one-third of English words can be traced to Spanish, especially in academic language, thus producing sizable cognates, words with similar sounds and spelling and the same meanings, to assist Spanish speakers with learning English and vice versa. Finally, both Spanish and English have the same basic word order: Subject-Verb-Object.

Spanish has fewer consonants and fewer vowels compared with English. Because of this, Spanish speakers may have a hard time differentiating some of the English vowel sounds, such as *she* vs. *see*, *keep* vs. *lid*, and learning to pronounce consonant clusters and the words ending with a consonant like s*mart*, *but*, *scold*, *think*. Also, Spanish differs from English in that its nouns have gender, and adjectives are placed after the nouns. Since the phrase "ser" (to be) is expressed as "tener" (to have) Spanish speakers tend to confuse and misuse the expression (Spanish language, n.d.). For example, the Spanish translation of "I'm fifteen years old" is "Tengo quince enos de edad" which literally means "I have 15 years."

In Mexico, Spanish language and literacy education play an important role in students' schooling. In the elementary school, students have between six and nine hours a week to learn the Spanish language, the most time spent in one subject among all subjects. That focus stays the same throughout lower-secondary schools and upper-secondary schools even though students have more subjects to learn in high school (Herrara, 1996). In addition, in recent years there were more students entering the primary school with pre-school education becoming the emphasis of early literacy education (Miller, 2001).

The Spanish language arts curriculum aims at teaching students reading readiness and comprehension, vocabulary, oral expression, writing, and grammar. In early elementary Spanish language learning, the teacher focuses more on the sound-letter recognition and association, spelling, and vocabulary learning. Later, language arts teachers expand the focus to reading comprehension, oral expression, grammar, and writing. Some popular and unique Mexican language and literacy teaching practices are recitation, dictation, and oral literature (Miller, 2001).

> In many of the homes, stories relating to Mexican history were also told when children asked about topics that they were studying in school. For example, a child might ask a parent about the ninos heroes (child heroes) and the cadet who wrapped himself in the flag and jumped from the cliff off near the Chapultepec castle rather than surrender to American forces. (Reese, 2012, p. 287)

In comparison to the expressive and creative oral language use in class, written language and critical thinking skill development is not as emphasized as oral Spanish. Students' academic writing is limited to copying and dictation and the teacher and parents' focus more on spelling and grammar accuracy not rather than on developing content and creative and critical thinking skills (Smith, Jimenez, & Martinex-Leon, 2003).

Brown (2016) studied the literacy practice of a Mexican extended family residing in a mobile home park in southwest U.S. Through half a year of informal conversations and observations Brown found that the extended families had rich literacy resources of knowledge. They had unique practices like story nights where generations of the family came together to share and teach family stories to each other. They created a learning environment outside the school setting. Brown argued for the U.S. teachers' need to expand their views toward literacy education to include communal events where language minority families' preferred literacy forms and practices were valued in teaching children from those backgrounds.

How Do Mexican Students Learn Subject Matter Knowledge? In Mexican secondary schools, Spanish and mathematics receive the most attention and are taught an hour every day during the week (Herrera, 1996). Beginning in the lower-secondary school, students are taught physics, chemistry, biology, the history of Mexico, general geography, civics, and world history as different subjects in contrast to general science and social studies in elementary schools. It is also at this level, students begin to learn a foreign language, and the most popular foreign languages are English and French (James, 2002; Rosado, Hellawell, & Zamora, 2011).

Unlike high schools in the U.S., Mexican upper-secondary schools or preparetoria are affiliated and run by colleges and universities. Students pick one of the two specialized schools which focuses on either academic/general education or college bound or vocational/technical education. Also, in upper-secondary schools for the college bound students, they select one of the two tracks: humanities and social sciences or science and mathematics (Lopez-Bonilla, 2015). Using extensive interviews, Herrera (2015) investigated Mexican secondary school students' experiences and views toward learning the history of Mexico using English as a medium of instruction. Despite many Mexican students' initial skeptical or even negative views toward using English to learn Mexican history, they recognized the merit and embraced both the language and subject matter challenges as one of the students reflected "(W) used it to interpret the Independence of Mexico and I feel good because we did something about our traditions and country in English" (p. 113). Her research is testimonial evidence that it is crucial for the U.S. subject matter teachers to pay close attention to ELLs' previous schooling in their native countries in order to effectively teach the subject matter knowledge in English. Lisa reflected on the strength of her education in Mexico like this:

> Mexican students are more advanced in mathematics because the emphasis by the school and teacher on learning mathematics. I've learned many concepts earlier than USA students in my class. I learned how to solve equations in 6th grade, and my sister, who is in Mexico at the moment, is taking calculus and she is now in 10th grade. Also, our mathematics learning focuses on mental math, totally different from the US mathematics learning. After being here for over a year and learning math using the U.S. way, I find myself forgetting about my strength in mental math. I wish the U.S. teacher allows us to learn mathematics in both ways.
>
> — *By Lisa, 10th grade ELL*

Naslund-Hadley, Varela, & Hepworth (2014) studied the 6th grade mathematics and science classroom video-taped discourses in three Latin American countries: Paraguay, Dominican Republic, and Nuevo Leon of Mexico. They found that although the classroom discourse in the Mexican school showed a predominant focus on procedural knowledge, drilling, and memorization, there were occasions where the mathematics and science teachers engaged students actively by connecting the concept to their own lives and developing their analytical thinking skills. Mexican mathematics and science teachers even tried to implement inquiry-based instruction and experiential learning though not as frequently as the American teachers do. Those teachers questioned the textbook quality and accuracy as well as curricular constraints. They argued for the need for American teachers to increase an awareness of what secondary ELLs bring to the classroom in order to connect and build upon what they have learned back in their native country and work with them effectively.

What Does All of This Mean to Teach ELLs from Mexico? As shown in above discussion on Mexican education, Mexican Spanish speaking ELLs are not from a homogenous group. Rather, they come from varied geographic locations and with varied educational, socioeconomic and cultural backgrounds, and native language and literacy levels and needs. Therefore, teachers must make a conscious effort not to lump all Spanish speaking ELLs into one category viewing them just as native Spanish speakers. Reviews of the educational system, traditions, and practices inform teachers that they should view those students not just as English language learners, but as literacy learners, cultural learners, and subject matter learners (Turner, 2017). According to Cummins (1979a), students who enter the classroom with developed higher order literacy skills in their first language often fare better and catch up quickly both in subject matter knowledge and English because of the shared and interdependent nature of academic language and cognitive foundation.

Tap into Mexican ELLs' Previous Language and Literacy Backgrounds. Subject matter teaching and learning is also cultural bound besides language bound. It is imperative for the subject matter teacher to learn about where their ELLs come from and how they are taught in their home country, including their familiar ways of learning and genres of reading and writing.

As shown by both research and students' revelations, the folklore can be a wonderful resource for illuminating the cultural values and passing on cultural and literacy traditions when working with Mexican ELLs. Teachers can discern common and distinctive features in the folklores across cultures when teaching literary elements and patterns. By encouraging students to share, express, and perform the literary genre that they are familiar with, the teacher enables them to develop their own voices and become active learners. Blending the genre and participation form that is known to those students with the new genre and form will build connections between the old knowledge and the new knowledge.

Capitalize on Mexican Students' Literary Strengths. Knowing that there is a strong family tradition of literacy learning, subject matter teachers should tap into that background and family resources. Survey Mexican students for their collective cultural traditions and expressions, such as proverbs and oral expressions can be a welcoming first step to involve those students in the learning process. Even for social studies, mathematics, and science teachers they can always find something unique to connect to what those students know in their home cultures and families. Using culturally familiar examples will instill interest, engagement, and participation in class discussions and stimulate learning how to read, write, and think in English.

DOMINICAN PUBLIC EDUCATIONAL SYSTEM

As a fast-growing immigrant population, students from the Dominican Republic have become the largest foreign born ELL population (17%) in New York City public schools in recent years (New York City Department of Education, 2016). Although the Dominican ELLs' native language is Spanish, they have many unique and different characteristics, beliefs, traditions, and expectations from Spanish speaking ELLs from South America and Caribbean America. Despite the relatively close proximity in the geographic location to the U.S., the Dominican students often reported a cultural shock when they first came to the U.S. as shown in James' words:

> I came to America two years ago from the Dominican Republic with my parents. My dad got relocated by his company and our family moved to New York City and lived here ever since. My home language is Spanish, but I took English when I was back in the Dominican Republic. I had quite a few cultural shocks when I first came to the US. For one, most Americans seem to be rushing to get somewhere and there is a schedule that everyone has to meet. In the Dominican Republic, people are very relaxed. You don't have to show up on time all the time, including go to school on time.
>
> — *By James, 11th grade ELL*

Difficulties with English language learning have been noted by many Dominican students. Yefry, a 7th grader from the Dominican Republic, has been in the U.S. for two years. When asked, he told his English language arts teacher the following:

> I did not learn English when I was in school in the Dominican Republic. So, it was *very* difficult for me to learn English when I first arrived here. I know I need to do better in schoolwork in English, but I don't know how to study for English. I go to a Spanish speaking church on Sundays. The sermon is all in Spanish. I watch Spanish TV daily and listen to Spanish music, but I enjoy watching American shows, such as comedies.
>
> — *By Yefry, a 7th grade ELL*

How is the Educational System in the Dominican Republic Different from the U.S. System? The Dominican Republic is a tropical country located in the Caribbean Sea between Haiti and Puerto Rico. The official language of the Dominican Republic is Spanish. The Dominicans are racially and ethnically diverse with 16% of the population from Spanish European backgrounds, 11% from Haitian background, and 8% from Taino Indian background. The majority of the Dominicans (73%) comes from the mixed racial and ethnic backgrounds (Bedggood & Benady, 2010; Dominican Republic, n.d.).

According to Wikipedia, an overall literacy rate of the Dominican Republic was 91.8% in 2015 (List of countries by literacy rate, 2017). Public schools in the Dominican Republic consist of eight years of elementary school and four years of secondary school (i.e., grades 9–12). The compulsory education the Dominican Republic is eight years from grades 1 through 8. The classroom in the Dominican Republic schools is a lot bigger with up to 55 students in one class on average (Education in the Dominican Republic, n.d.).

The curriculum of basic and public education in the Dominican Republic is controlled by three government organizations: the State Secretariat for Education, the Ministry of Education, and the National Institute of Professional and Technical Training the Secretariat of Public Education. Curriculum and learning standards, including the reading materials and teaching guides are regulated by the government mandating the teacher to stick to the prescribed guides. There is a national exam at the end of each grade at the secondary level for students to pass in order move onto the next grade; however, students in the lower grades do not have national exams to be promoted to the next grade (Education System in the Dominican Republic, n.d.).

The school year in the Dominican Republic starts in early September and ends in late June, consisting of 180 days of classes, similar to the schools in the U.S. Recently, in an effort to promote literacy education, the government extended the school day from five hours to seven hours. A typical school day begins at 8:20 a.m. and ends around 2:30 p.m. with a 30-minute lunch break at noon. Elementary students spend about four hours a day, five days a week in school; while secondary students spend at least seven hours a day, five days a week in school. In the morning before class, students raise the national flag and sing the national anthem. The differences between the U.S. schools and the Dominican Republic schools are K–12 grade students stay in the same school in one building rather than going to different schools and buildings. Also, in the Dominican Republic schools, students stay in the Dominican in the same classroom throughout the day, semester, and year, while the teacher travels from class to class (Manning, 2014).

Although the percentage of enrollment in the Dominican elementary schools is similar to the U.S. schools, the drop-out rate is different. About 90% of the Dominican children enroll in elementary school in 2012, however, the dropout rate was high about 25.2%. In comparison, the U.S. students' enrollment in elementary school was 92% and the drop-out rate from the elementary school was

6.9%. For students who graduated from the elementary school in the Dominican Republic, only about 40% go on to secondary schools (Manning, 2014).

Why Do the Dominican Schools Operate Differently? The history of education in Dominican Republic has gone through many ups and downs. Basic and public education was put into the Constitution after its independence from the Haitian rule in 1844. However, it was not until after overthrowing the dictatorship of Rafael Trujillo in 1961, that public education was improved tremendously (Jimenez & Lockheed, 1995; Smith, 2014).

The Dominican Republic society is divided into two separate societies: the Haves and the Have-Nots. Often people living in the city or urban area tend to have more social connections and economic means. As a result, there is a huge difference in the educational opportunities and experiences between urban and rural teenagers. People in the urban areas have convenient public transportation and more opportunities for education and many own their homes and cars, thus the urban family has become more and more westernized and education is placed as a top priority.

In rural areas, however, having children often means to have extra helping hands to support the family and take care of parents when they get old. Thus, education is not as a top priority in comparison to fulfilling filial responsibilities and meeting daily survival needs. Rural schools often lack school resources, such as textbooks and technology, and even teachers. Often running water and plumbing facilities as well as electricity are luxuries rather than necessities. Thus, rural education is characterized by a low enrollment, and a high dropout rate. Many rural schools only have one or two classrooms to hold multi-grade students and provide education up to only 4th or 6th grades (Foucault & Schneider, 2009; Heath & Sobol, 2013).

Those who continue their education to secondary schools or even college are mostly from middle- and upper-class families. Even though basic education is free, textbooks are not free. As a result, many parents cannot afford the textbook for their children in the rural schools. So, education becomes a privilege that only those who have economic means can afford. For children and teenagers living in poor and rural communities, daily survival, supporting the family, and fulfilling filial obligations become a top priority than learning to read and write (Heath & Sobol, 2013).

Similar to many collective cultures, such as China and Mexico, the Dominican Republic culture is a collective culture well known for its strong family values, loyalty, respect for the elderly, optimism toward life, and work ethic. The Dominican people value kinship, family, and have a tradition of taking care of the elderly. The country is rich in its folklore and oral literature. The Dominicans are fascinated by mystic creatures and supernatural beings and beliefs. Many Dominican students often have a fond memory of their schooling back in the Dominican Republic like what Andrea remembers:

My time in school in the D.R. (the Dominican Republic) was a happy time because I know all my teachers from primary school to middle school, and they were nice to me. In D.R. the students stay in one class from grade one, and the teachers will follow you throughout grades and teachers. So, we all feel like a big family.

— By Andrea, a 10ʰ grade ELL

The Dominican Republic has a long history of migration, and the U.S. has been the most popular destination for many Dominicans. It is very common for a person born and raised in the Dominican Republic to have a close family member living in the United States (Amuedo-Dorantes & Pozo, 2010). These families with members migrating to the US are considered fortunate since many here in the U.S. will help the families still living in their native country by sending money home, and some of their financial support contributed to supporting children to go to school (Amuedo-Dorantes & Pozo, 2010).

How Do Dominican Students Learn the Spanish Language, Reading, and Writing Skills? The curriculum for urban primary school students in the Dominican Republic consists of Spanish, mathematics, social studies, science, physical education, music, and art. A high school student's day in urban schools consists of Spanish, mathematics, social studies, literature, recreational activities, physical education, science, and computer science. The language arts curriculum in the lower grades is teacher-driven. Students have a book in hand while the teacher reads and the students recite each word later. As they progress through the grades, students start reading full-length books and write book reports. Some of the similar classroom practices that are shared with the U.S. classroom are the teacher assigning the book reading, assigning students to look for words in the dictionary for definitions, and modeling the use of the new vocabulary and literary devices. However, a priority is given to the author's point of view rather than the reader's personal views and creative and critical reading (Watkins-Goffman & Cummings, 1997).

Writing an essay in the Dominican Republic is also similar in structure to writing an essay in the U.S. Some of the similarities include having an introduction, body, and a conclusion. One major difference is that students living in the Dominican Republic are asked to collaborate in their essay writing, such as composing a group essay. Another difference is a more emphasis on analyzing the textual structure, summarization, and language use. The language arts teachers often equate good writing to error free writing (Hache de Yunen & Montenegro, 1993; Watkins-Goffman & Cummings, 1997).

Herrero (2006) studied two New York City junior high school ELA teachers' using their Dominican ELLs' oral literature, such as cuentos de herencia or historias de calumnia in Spanish to engage and promote their students' learning of English as well as to build their literacy skills in Spanish. Students collected those oral literature narratives and presented them to the class while critiquing and revising the narrative through discussions and writing. Herrero's research findings suggested that those ELLs were capable of doing critical literary analysis when doing a group project for which they had deep knowledge and were passionate about. In doing so, Herrero found that "students used their own linguistic and cognitive resources to present, critique, and write narratives rooted in the oral traditions of their cultural community" (p. 19).

How Do Dominican Students Learn Subject Matter Knowledge? The history of the Dominican Republic echoes the history of the U.S., as it relates to European settlers, colonization, the slave trade, and independence. Michelle, a 10th grader from the Dominican Republic, got excited when her social studies teacher invited her to share the characteristics of the Dominican political system before learning the three branches of the U.S. government. Her social studies teacher's willingness to listen to what she learned back home made her see the relevance in the topics and volunteered to compare the U.S. and Dominican political systems. Garcia, another 10th grader, fondly remembers his experience in the social studies class back home:

> I remember my school days in D.R. like yesterday. I love social studies. I studied really hard on the day for my social studies presentation. I was nervous, but I was able to understand all the material and presented well. My social studies teacher told me I did a good job. I felt proud of myself. This is something I missed in the U.S. and I don't feel like a highly achieving student anymore. The social studies topics are so difficult and new. I constantly feel bad about not being able to do things that I used to in schools back home in the DR.
>
> *— By Garcia, a 10th grade ELL*

In contrast to the U.S. science and mathematics instruction, the science and mathematics lessons in the Dominican Republic secondary schools focus more on memorization of the concepts (Naslund-Hadley et al., 2014). According to their cross-national studies of mathematics and science classroom instruction in secondary schools in Paraguay, the Dominican Republic, and Mexico, they found that students in those countries had very limited opportunities to do science. They did not have access to science labs nor opportunities to work through the concepts using the scientific method. Often the teacher does the demonstration and asks the students to memorize the procedures and the results due to a lack of resources. However, the science teacher did use real-life examples to connect the topic to students' lives to make the lesson relevant and meaningful.

In mathematics, a high priority is placed on the memorization of mathematical procedures and formulas rather than on developing skills in critical thinking and problem solving. Majority of the mathematics class time is spent on practicing the low-level mathematical problems using the formulas and correct procedures (Naslund-Hadley et al., 2014). Students are not expected to think critically and solve problems using novel ideas or procedures. Caroline remembers her favorite school event like this:

> My favorite memory is participating in the math competition in middle school back in the Dominican. I used to be a part of the math team in my school competing with

the math teams from other schools. We would have a tournament where we had to answer tough question about math. I forgot about those questions, but I remember my school winning the tournament and was one of the best in our school district. I was assigned to speak in front of all students, parents, and teachers at the trophy ceremony.

— By Caroline, an 11ᵗʰ grade ELL

Although secondary ELLs from the Dominican Republic may have had science learning experience back in their home country, however, that experience can be varied depending on the school and location of their previous schooling. Many rural schools in the Dominican Republic do not have the facilities and equipment. Carlos moved to the United States from the Dominican Republic three years ago at the age of 14. Although he has been progressing nicely with English, he is having more difficulty with academic English in such classes as biology. Carlos told his biology teacher that he had never had a lab in his biology class back home, so he did not even know how a lab works and names of the lab equipment even though he had learned many biological topics and terms back in the Dominican Republic.

What Does All of This Mean to teach Dominican ELLs? Reviewing issues related to educating Dominican students' native language, culture, and literacy experiences, the subject matter teacher can find a way to reach out to those students by modifying the curriculum incorporating what students know into the lesson. Many of the above literacy experiences discussed and articulated by the students here can serve as a springboard for their learning in the American classroom.

Listen to the Dominican Republican ELLs' Previous Learning Stories. Garcia's and Caroline's fond memories of their previous social studies and mathematics learning are very telling. Engaging those students in sharing the knowledge about the topic of the lesson, literacy skill, or educational and cultural background offers the teacher a way not only to connect the lesson to the students' old knowledge, but also to diagnose their baseline in order to differentiate and provide support. Even students' talking and writing about their previous learning in their native language is important. With the help from the Spanish native speaking colleagues, the teacher can identify the students' literacy skills and academic knowledge in their native language, which can be used as an effective anchor to build on the new knowledge in English.

Build on Similarities in Subject Matter Instruction. To prevent the Dominican students from being onlookers in the classroom discussions, teachers need to know more about the shared similarities in their culture, political, and educational systems to find ways of engaging those students. As shown by research and students' own words, many topics in the Dominican schools in social studies, science, and mathematics are also topics taught in the U.S. schools. Uncovering both similarities and differences in teaching and learning between the two cultures cannot only be a powerful validation for those students but also a meaningful opportunity for engagement in critical thinking through those comparisons and contrasts.

CHAPTER 5

PLANNING SUBJECT MATTER LESSONS FOR ELLS

A lesson plan is an objective driven, curriculum-based, and student-oriented writing genre used by the teacher to guide instruction. A typical secondary lesson lasts for about 45 minutes, though some are longer for 90 minutes (a block schedule consisting of two related subjects and covering two periods), while others are shorter, depending on the grade level, school, and subject matter. A typical lesson plan at the secondary level normally consists of the following ten identifiable components:

1. Students (including their gender, grade level, language and literacy levels, and learning needs);
2. Context of the lesson (what comes from and after this lesson and how the lesson is situated in the unit);
3. Learning standards, including standards for professional, state, and national organizations;
4. Curricular objectives (the learning goals to be achieved after the lesson is completed);
5. Aim (the central question that drives the whole lesson for students to be able to answer by the end of the lesson);

Teaching English Language Learners in Secondary Subject Matter Classes, pages 87–112.
Copyright © 2019 by Information Age Publishing
87

6. Do now (the motivational techniques or warm-ups that grab the students' attention and get them ready for the new knowledge);
7. Procedures (the development of the lesson and meaty part of the lesson, including teacher questions, teaching strategies and techniques used, learning activities, structure, sequence of the lesson, etc. In teaching ELLs, procedures also include ways that the teacher accommodates those students and differentiates instruction according to students' levels and needs);
8. Assessment (specific ways and tools for the teacher to check for students' understanding and performance at the beginning, during, and the end of the lesson);
9. Follow-up (homework and project derived from the lesson); and
10. Materials (handouts, reading materials, technology, lab equipment, etc.).

HOW TO PLAN A SUBJECT MATTER LESSON WITH ELLS IN MIND?

In comparison to a lesson plan for English proficient students, an ESL oriented subject matter lesson plan has additional three components used to tailor to ELLs' English language proficiency levels and address their previous cultural and educational backgrounds. Those components are language objectives, ESL anticipated language difficulties, and cultural notes.

Now after learning the ESL teaching principles (see Chapter 1), individual ELLs' portraits of their second language learning and acculturation experiences (see Chapter 2), and their native cultural and educational backgrounds this is a good time for the subject matter teacher to draw on all that knowledge to design a subject matter lesson with those students in mind. In the following, those three components of the ESL oriented subject matter lesson plan will be discussed and illustrated with discipline-specific examples shown by the end of the chapter.

Planning for Language Objectives. As language is the medium of instruction, an ESL oriented subject matter lesson plan begins with language objectives that bridge this gap between the language and literacy skills required for the lesson and ELLs' actual English proficiency levels. While the curricular objectives are often derived from the subject matter specific learning standards, language objectives should be based on ELLs' English language proficiency levels Clancy & Hruska, 2005; Dong, 2004b; Fairbairn & Jones-Vo, 2010; Haynes & Zacarian, 2010; Regalla, 2012). In New York State, ELLs' English proficiency levels are outlined as follows:

Entering (Formerly Beginning)
A student at the Entering level has great dependence on supports and structures to advance his or her academic language skills. As measured by the NYSESLAT, a student at this level has yet to meet the linguistic demands necessary to demonstrate proficiency in a variety of academic contexts within this grade level.

Emerging (Formerly Low Intermediate)

A student at the Emerging level has some dependence on supports and structures to advance his or her academic language skills. As measured by the NYSESLAT, a student at this level has yet to meet the linguistic demands necessary to demonstrate proficiency in a variety of academic contexts within this grade level.

Transitioning (Formerly Intermediate)

A student at the Transitioning level shows some independence in advancing his or her academic language skills. As measured by the NYSESLAT, a student at this level has yet to meet the linguistic demands necessary to demonstrate proficiency in a variety of academic contexts within this grade level.

Expanding (Formerly Advanced)

A student at the Expanding level shows great independence in advancing his or her academic language skills. As measured by the NYSESLAT, a student at this level is approaching the linguistic demands necessary to demonstrate proficiency in a variety of academic contexts within this grade level.

Commanding (Formerly Proficient)

A student at the Commanding level is now designated as a Former ELL, and entitled to receive two years of continued ELL services. As measured by the NYSESLAT, a student at this level has met the linguistic demands necessary to demonstrate proficiency in a variety of academic contexts within this grade level. (Commissioner's Regulation Part 154, 2015, pp. 7–8)

Language objectives include ELLs' learning the CALP, such as vocabulary, sentence structures, and discourse patterns used in the lesson. Also, selected BICS level vocabulary may need to be taught in order to explain the CALP level words. For example, in order to learn the concept of "probability" in mathematics students need to have some knowledge about "chance," "event" and "outcome." If ELLs do not understand those basic words, then the subject matter teacher needs to teach those words before tackling the meaning of probability.

Language objectives should also address reading and writing skills required for the lesson, such as how to read a word problem or a scientific paper, write an argumentative essay or a lab report, etc. Finally, language objectives include discipline-specific language patterns, sentence structures, and discourse functions. For example, if a mathematics teacher designs a lesson on inequalities, then s/he needs to teach key English comparative phrases and sentence structures like "more than" "less than," "no greater than" in order to teach how to read word problems about inequalities.

Planning for ESL Anticipated Language Difficulties. Once ELLs' language proficiency levels are identified and the curricular and language objectives are written, subject matter teachers need to focus on the key ESL language difficulties and design strategies to overcome those difficulties in the lesson. ESL anticipated difficulties often include: CALP level vocabulary such as disciplinary words and general academic words and even BICS level words used to learn the CALP, reading and writing challenges, difficulties with disciplinary language structures, etc. Teachers need to identify specific ESL language difficulties and design effective ways of addressing those difficulties. Based on what we have learned in Chapter 1, subject matter teachers can develop strategies to address those difficulties. Below are a sample of those strategies (see Chapters 8, 9, and 10 for more on this topic):

Using ELLs' Native Language to Overcome ESL Language Difficulties. Research has shown that many CALP vocabulary words share similarities in meaning and function across languages (see Chapter 1). There is a positive correlation in ELLs' academic language and literacy skills and subject matter knowledge learning between their native language and English (Cummins 1979a,b; Dong, 2013, 2016, 2017; Esquinca 2011). Cummins argued that language and concept can transfer across languages based on the shared foundation in cognition and language at the CALP level (1979b). Therefore, providing ELLs with native language support can even the playing field for them and set a positive tone of inclusion and appreciation of what those students bring to the learning task.

For example, in planning a lesson on "exponent" in mathematics, a mathematics teacher should first pause and question whether the English word "exponent" might be foreign to ELLs who are very limited in English proficiency. However, at the same time, mathematics teachers need also to consider these students' native language literacy learning history to find out whether they have already learned this concept in their native language in schools back home. If so, the student's native language should be used to facilitate the learning in English. When the ELL recognizes the vocabulary in their native language, their schema is activated. They may only need to learn another pronunciation and spelling of the word they already knew in their native language, thus reducing time for the teacher to explain the concept in English and opening up the possibility of learning and performing at a higher level.

Languages from the Romance language family share many cognates with English in disciplinary vocabulary, including exposant in French, ekspozan in Haitian Creole, exponente in Spanish, expoente in Portuguese, and esponente in Italian. Cognates are the words that have similar sounds and spelling with the same meanings across languages. Using translation, the teacher enables ELLs to learn concepts faster.

Subject matter teachers do not have to be multilingual in order to do the word-level translations. They can use websites, such as the Google translation (see http://translate.google.com/) or ask the ESL or bilingual or foreign language teacher who is fluent in that language in their school to assist. They can even ask their advanced bilingual students or ELLs to help with the translation. In a subject matter class with both English proficient students and ELLs, the subject matter teacher can prepare a multilingual glossary handout and give it to their low-level ELLs before class. By doing this, ELLs won't be lost during the lesson but will have something familiar to help with their comprehension and participation (see Table 1.1 in Chapter 1).

Using Visuals and Graphic Organizers. Visual aids, graphic organizers, and multimedia/technology have been commonly used in all classrooms. When used effectively with adjustment and careful selection, they can be a powerful tool to achieve ELLs' comprehension and understanding. With the availability of multimedia and technology resources in many schools and classrooms, subject matter teachers should include them in their lessons. When selecting those resources, subject matter teachers should keep in mind three important rules of thumb:

1. Select those teaching resources/materials that ELLs can relate to and have some familiarity. Some of the political cartoons and pop cultural visuals, though visually rich, require a cultural insider's knowledge in order to comprehend. Therefore, pre-teaching of that cultural knowledge may be needed.
2. Subject matter teachers should be mindful about the caption, legend, directions given along with the visual materials. As ELLs' language is limited, language support is needed by simplifying or using ELLs' native language to do the caption, directions, legends. Even a word web or a chart may not be simple enough for ELLs.
3. Finally, just because it is a multimedia and technological resource, it may not mean it is readily accessible to ELLs. ELLs are often confused and overwhelmed by the PowerPoint slides used by the teacher with no language modification or cultural support. Board work, handout, assignment, tests, etc. all pose possible difficulties for ELLs, thus needing language and cultural support.

Using Non-Verbal Means. There has been a long history of using the Total Physical Response (TPR) technique in second language teaching. Developed by Kunihira and Asher (1965), the TPR was designed to reduce the Affective Filter in language learning and follow the children's first language development principle to enhance comprehension. Initially the TPR was used only for BICS level in second language learning. Later on, it was expanded to learning the CALP (see Dong's 2011 book for a sample of TPR illustrations of CALP level vocabulary learning). The effective TPR technique requires the teacher to 1) select challenging academic words, that are difficult to define and comprehend, 2) break down the abstract concept into manageable chunks for physical commands and illustration, 3) model and direct students to do a sequence of movements and show facial expressions to convey meaning, 4) have students translate the verbal instructions and commands into physical actions and expressions, and 5) engage students in reflection on what the word means and how the meaning is communicated through the TPR.

For example, the concept of "star-crossed lovers" in Shakespeare's *Romeo and Juliet* can be illustrated using the TPR. The teacher asks two students to stand facing each other with two groups of the students standing behind each student to act as their families to hold them back. Then the teacher asks the class questions, such as what happened here and what "star-crossed" means. Afterwards, the teacher shows an excerpt of the movie to illustrate further the concept of "star-crossed" and has students describe their understanding of the concept in either English or in their native language. Following the TPR procedure, the teacher can then give a multilingual glossary, activate ELLs' prior knowledge, and do a read-aloud of a modified version of the play to discuss the concept further.

Another example of the TPR can be used to teach the human's immune system. The biological term in focus here is macrophage, the immune system cells that fight invading germs. The teacher groups the class into two groups with one group standing outside the classroom door trying to get in and the other group standing inside the classroom preventing the other group from getting in. Afterwards the teacher asks the class to describe what they saw and heard and what functions the human immune system has performed. Based on the TPR demonstration, the teacher can then use the multimedia, hands-on, vocabulary, reading and writing instruction to explore the concept in more depth.

Modifying Teaching Materials. Subject matter readings, notes on the board, PowerPoint slides, directions given in class at secondary level can be difficult. Anticipating these difficulties, subject matter teachers need to simplify and modify their questions, board work, directions, and reading materials. The key is to make the both language and subject matter knowledge accessible and comprehensible to ELLs (see Chapter 8 for more examples on this topic). Even the wording of the "Aim (the central question for the lesson)" and "Do Now (warm-up exercise to tap into students' prior knowledge)," a typical New York Stare school required classroom routine, might need to be rephrased, based on ELLs' English proficiency levels (see examples of such modifications and differentiation by the end of this chapter).

Planning for Cultural Notes. In Chapter 1, we learned that the acculturation process takes time and learners' motivation to expose and adapt to the 2nd culture. It also requires the teacher to welcome, encourage, inform, and support the learner through the acculturation process (Acton & Felix, 1986; Edwards, 2015; Harklau, 1994; Meyer, 2000; Rubinstein-Avilla, 2006; Schumann, 1978; Watkins-Hoffman & Cummins, 1997). In the previous chapters (see Chapters 3 and 4) we also learned that different cultures have different school systems, cultural values, and classroom practices. Subject matter teachers do not teach in a vacuum, rather, they teach in an environment that mainstream American culture is valued (Gay, 2010; Lee, 2010; Moll et al., 1992). Some of the classroom routines and learning tasks that the subject matter teacher asks the student to read, write, and discuss may not only be foreign to ELLs but also may be against their cultural beliefs, traditions, and expectations. Therefore, subject matter teachers do have a responsibility to not only be aware of but also use ELLs' home cultures and previous education when they plan their lessons (Dong, 2004, 2009, 2013–2014, 2017; Freeman & Freeman, 2009).

Cultural notes refer to planning for differences, un-familiarities, or even clashes in teachers' expectations, classroom routines, teaching examples and materials between the U.S. mainstream culture and ELLs' native cultures. Subject matter teachers should consciously seek ELLs' previous learning history and experiences to design more tailored instruction (Choi, 2013; Irizarry, 2011; Ladson-Billings, 1995; Moll et al., 1992; Ramirez & Jaffee, 2016; Tang & Dunkelblau, 1998; Woude, 1998). Below I discuss some sample teaching strategies used to plan for the Cultural Notes:

Survey ELLs for Their Native Literacy Learning Experiences. In New York City secondary schools, the majority (74.3%) of ELLs had grade level equivalent education in their home countries when they came to the U.S. (New York City Department of Education, 2017). All this prior learning experiences, if used effectively, provide access and stimulate interests in learning. Even for SIFE students (the students with interrupted formal education), their life experiences, oral language, and cultural experiences gained in their home country can be utilized and bridged to learn the new language and subject matter knowledge, ELLs often respond enthusiastically when the teacher demonstrates a sincere interest in these students' previous learning. One way of doing this is by inviting these students to talk and write about their previous literacy experiences. Below is a sample survey about ELLs' native language and literacy backgrounds:

- What is your native language?
- When and how did you learn to write in your native language?
- What writing assignments do you remember that your teachers back home in your native country assigned to you?
- How did your teachers back home go about teaching you how to write in your native language?
- What are the differences between writing in English and writing in your native language?
- Do you write in your native language now? If so, what do you write about and to whom?

Below are some responses from ELLs when asked about their fond memories of learning to read and write in their native language back in their home countries.

As a kid I liked to read the Chinese funny book. The first book I ever read is a Chinese book called Funny Master. It's about an old man who is very funny and he tells jokes in the book. I like his jokes. I love to write stories about myself in those funny books. Now I am in the 7th grade and I don't read those funny books any more.
— *By John, an 8th grade ELL*

When I was in China, I loved reading books. I always started reading as soon as I got home, and usually forgot to do my school homework. Because of this, my dad yelled at me a million times, even had beaten me for reading. He felt that math was more important than literature… I still read and write in my native language. I read a Chinese newspaper called *World Journal* every day for usually about half an hour to an hour. I also write my daily journal in Chinese, not so often though, maybe I should call it a weekly journal, and sometimes even a monthly journal.

— By Maria, a 10ᵗʰ grade ELL

The most influential book I read was a book about a Korean emperor. I got it for Christmas. In Korea, teachers check your journal entries every day. I wrote about my trip to a mountain and I received a certificate for it. That was the first piece of writing that I received a certificate for and I was proud of it. In the 3ʳᵈ grade, my teacher congratulated me on my writing because I copied down the whole book. That made me more confident as a writer.

— By Kim, a 9ᵗʰ grade ELL

Here in America the school is different from my country. In Colombia we stay in one room all day and we have the same teacher for all classes or sometimes we have a different teacher but we stay in the same room. But here we have different rooms and different teachers. Another difference is that the teacher in my country speaks Spanish and teaches in Spanish. But here many teachers can speak Spanish but they don't teach in Spanish. The textbooks we use here for social studies talk about America and Colombia, not like the books we had back in Colombia, it was all about Colombia. But in math they teach the same as it is here.

— By Sam, an 11ᵗʰ grade ELL

Back in the Philippines, I took Tagalog, my native language. But English was my subject language. I have learned English since Kindergarten. But I am still placed in ESL classes. I don't know why. What is more is that we are treated like we don't have any intelligence. What we learned in ESL is like what we learned in kindergarten. Teachers here don't know that what we had learned back home was far more and far advanced in science and math than American students in the same grade. I was very insulted by all this.

— By Peter, a 9ᵗʰ grade ELL

It was hard to make friends here because each class has different people in it. In my school back in Poland, all the students have all their classes together for all four years of high school. It's easier to make friends that way. Also, we don't need to run around to find our classrooms between breaks because we have the same classroom all day and the teacher comes to us to teach. So the between the break chaos really threw me off the first few weeks when I came here.

— By Maria, an 8ᵗʰ grade ELL

These students' writings offer a window into their previous education. By listening to ELLs' previous literacy experiences, subject matter teachers will gain a deeper understanding of where those students come from and find their strengths and interests to capitalize. In addition, subject matter teachers can survey ELLs about the subject matter they teach. Those surveys can be both administered at the beginning of the year or semester and at the beginning of a new unit or even a new lesson (Tables 5.1–5.4).

TABLE 5.1. Surveying ELLs for Their Previous Writing History

Your Name:

Your Native Language:

Language that you can write:

When did you learn to write in English?

Where did you learn to write in English?

Under each statement, check the blank that you think fits you best.

a.   I am good at reading in English.   Agree__   Disagree__

b.   I am good at writing in English.   Agree__   Disagree__

c.   What kinds of writing did you do in your school back home?

    ___stories   ___journals   ___research papers

    ___essays   ___poems   ___letters

    ___no writing at all   ___other (please specify)

d. How did your teacher teach you how to write back home?

    __brainstorming ideas   ___class discussing on the topic

    __writing an outline   ___asking for more drafts

    __providing a model of good writing   ___revising my papers

    __correcting and commenting on my writing   ___using peer responses

    __reading famous writers' works as models   ___lecturing on how to organize

    __memorizing good phrases and words   ___teaching grammar and words

    Other (Please specify)_

e.   How frequently did you write for school back home? (write down the number of times you wrote for school work)

    __1~2 times a week   ___3 more times a week

    __1~2 times a month   ___3 more times a month

    __Other (Please specify)

Mark the following expectations that apply to you.

f.   I expect my writing to be corrected word by word by my English teacher.

    ___Yes   ___No

g.   To me, copying words from the text without saying where they are from is acceptable

    ___Yes   ___No

h.   I like to have my friends or my classmates read what I have written in English.

    ___Yes   ___No

i.   I use the following sources when I write in English:

    ___a native language dictionary   ___a grammar book

    ___a writing manual   ___an English dictionary

    ___a bilingual dictionary   ___a thesaurus

    ___other (Please specify)

TABLE 5.2. Surveying ELLs for Their Previous Mathematics Learning History

Your home country:

Your native language:

I have learned mathematics for _____ years.

	Agree	Disagree
I am good at mathematics.	_____	_____
I did well in mathematics in my native country.	_____	_____
Mathematics is my favorite subject back home.	_____	_____
I believe mathematics will be useful in my future.	_____	_____
My parents push me to learn mathematics.	_____	_____
Mathematics is difficult to learn.	_____	_____
Learning mathematics in English is difficult for me.	_____	_____

In my native country, I learned math through (check all the relevant answers)

_____memorizing mathematical rules and formulas

_____practicing problems over and over again

_____asking for help from someone who is good at math

_____taking notes from the teacher

_____reading the mathematics textbook

_____going over a mathematics workbook

_____working with my peers or classmates on mathematical problems

_____Other (please explain)

My mathematics teacher back home taught us math by (check all the relevant answers)

_____explaining the rules and formulas

_____demonstrating how to solve a problem

_____assigning us to do many exercises every day

_____asking us to memorize the rules and formulas

_____teaching us how to think

_____grouping us into study groups to work on mathematical problems

_____other (please explain)

Is there any difference in the writing of mathematical expressions or in ways of solving problems in mathematics you learned back home compared with math you learn here in the U.S.?

How different is the way of teaching by your math teacher back home compared with your mathematics teacher here?

What is the most important factor influencing how well you do in mathematics here in the U.S.?

What is your biggest problem in learning mathematics now?

TABLE 5.3.   Surveying ELLs for Their Previous Social Studies Learning HIstory

Your home country:

Your native language:

What topics did you learn in social studies? (Mark the ones you learned)

_____Your country's history

_____Your country's geography

_____Your country's government

_____Global/world history

_____US history

_____Other (please list any topics that are not on this list)

How did your social studies teacher teach history in class?

_____From the teacher's lectures

_____By reading the textbook

_____By reading historical figures' biographies

_____By memorizing historical facts and famous people's sayings

_____By watching historical films

_____By writing research papers and essays

_____Other (please explain)

What are some of the U.S. history events and people you have learned?

What social studies topics did you enjoy most? Why?

How did your social studies teacher teach history in class in your home country?

Who influenced your social studies learning most in your home country?

What are some of the historical events and/or people you would like me to know about your home country?

What are some of your difficulties in learning social studies in English?

What are the major differences in social studies learning in your home country and here in the U.S.?

TABLE 5.4   Surveying ELLs for Their Previous Science Learning History

Your home country:

Your native language:

1. A good science reader is a learner who

    a. Reads fast

    b. Memorizes what s/he reads

    c. Understands all the words

    d. Always makes guesses

    e. Does other things (Please explain.)

2. Do you like reading about science in your native language? Why?

3. Do you like learning science in your school back home? Why?

4. What did you learn in science before coming to America?

    a. Plants

    b. Animals

    c. Chemistry

    d. Physical science

    e. Other (Please explain.)

5. How did you learn science back home?

    a. Reading and memorizing the textbook

    b. Listening and memorizing the teacher's lecture

    c. Taking the test

    d. Writing science papers

    e. Doing science projects

    f. Other (Please explain.)

6. How do you read the science textbook in English?

    a. translate the reading into my native language

    b. look up in a dictionary for every new word (my native language dictionary)

    c. read more slowly and memorize each word

    d. read aloud to practice my pronunciation

    e. ask my friend from my country for help with reading

    f. do other things (Please explain.)

7. How is it different in class between your learning back home and learning here in the U.S.?

8. What is most difficult for you to learn biology in English?

Use ELLs' Culturally Familiar Examples. Lacking exposures to American mainstream culture and education system, ELLs are often limited if not at a total loss with the prototypical examples and analogies used by the subject matter teacher in class. Furthermore, subject matter textbooks and readings are often written with an assumption that the readers grew up in the U.S. with similar experiences and background knowledge (Dong, 2009, 2011, 2013, 2013–2014, 2016, 2017; Freeman & Freeman, 2009, 2015). Therefore, when teaching ELLs, subject matter teachers should plan culturally familiar examples for ELLs.

For example, in revising his word problem used to teach the concept of probability, Sean changed the setting of his word problem to what his ELLs are familiar with, their home countries. Learning that those students travel back and forth between the U.S. and their home countries at least a couple of times a year, he revised his word problem as follows:

> You won a free trip to one of the following countries of your choice: Puerto Rico, El Salvador, or the Dominican Republic. You can also choose to fly in the first class or economy. What is the probability of you choosing to fly first class and going to Puerto Rico?
> *— By Sean, a pre-service mathematics teacher*

In teaching the concept of an animal cell, Robert, a high school biology teacher learned that his ELLs may not understand the prototypical analogy: a city, factory, etc. that he would normally use with his English proficient students. From the ESL Robert learned that many of his ELLs with a rich agricultural and rural background could be a resource for learning. Robert adjusted his cell analogies by asking his ELLs to generate their own culturally familiar analogs, such as farm, village, etc. to gain a meaningful understanding of the concept. By exploiting what his ELLs know, Robert helped them fully understand the complex structures and functions of an animal cell (Dong, 2011).

In addition, subject matter teachers should systematically engage students in using their prior knowledge to learn. It also sends a message that ELLs' prior knowledge though set in a different educational context still is a valuable and relevant resource. Below are the examples of how this can be done in social studies (Dong, 2017):

Teaching Topic 1: Three Branches of the Government

Writing prompt to tap into prior knowledge: Who has the most power in your native country and why?

Teaching topic 2: Civil Rights Movement

Writing prompt to tap into prior knowledge: Were you treated differently when you first came to the U.S.? How and why?

Teaching topic 3: Revolutionary War

Writing prompt to tap into prior knowledge: When is your country's Independence Day? What did you learn about your country's independence from foreign occupation? (p. 4)

Lee, an earth science pre-service teacher, learned that her ELL students were confused with the textbook reading that contained predominantly U.S. examples, such as Mt. St. Helens using to explain key concepts about volcanoes. In planning her tutorial lesson on this topic, Lee gathered examples of volcanoes from each of her ELLs' countries. Her students had sparks in their eyes when they saw something they already knew on Lee's PowerPoint slides. Armed with what they already know, they were eager to learn the new concepts.

Although there are many commonalities in numerical systems and symbolic language shared between languages and cultures, how mathematics is taught and learned is language and culture specific. The mathematical procedures used to demonstrate solutions, steps of doing proofs, teaching examples and analogies, classroom discussions and activities are all shaped by culture and prior learning. Debra, a 10th grade mathematics teacher of a bilingual Chinese mathematics class, selected her teaching examples from her ELLs' familiar setting: Chinese architectures, such as the Temple of Heaven and the Bird's Nest when teaching the concept of "reflection" and "rotation."

Lisa, a middle school mathematics teacher encouraged her Korean ELLs to use the mnemonic device that her students learned back in South Korea to learn the concept and steps of distribution. Her Korean students used the city initials of their home country like: Pohang-East Sea-Mokpo-Daegu-Ansan-Seoul to remember PEMDAS (Parentheses, exponents, multiplication, division, addition, and subtraction) (Dong, 2016).

Conduct Cross-Cultural Literacy Learning Comparisons. Once the ELLs' previous cultural and educational backgrounds are uncovered, subject matter teachers can plan for some purposeful comparisons and contrasts to engage ELLs in critical thinking and learning (Dong, 1998, 1999a,b, 2004a,b). For example, what is considered to be good writing in different cultures around the world can explore ELLs' views and practices of writing in their native language. The reflections can be very enlightening and informative for both the teacher and students to understand each other. The new understanding will enable students to see why their American teacher asks them to write or learn differently. Below are some ELLs' responses to the differences between writing in English and writing in their native language:

Academic Writing in Bangladesh

One difference is that here in English when we write a paragraph, we have a main idea. And for that main idea, we have to give details to support the main idea. The details have to be so clear that everybody can understand [them]. But in my country [Bangladesh], my culture, sometimes, we were not encouraged to give details, we just gave some hints. And nobody had any problem understanding these hints.

— By a Bangladeshi ELL

Academic Writing in China

In China there is no I. There is "we." The word "I" is used as a bad word like "individual." This is disrespectful to the government in China. To be selfish is very bad in China.

— By a Chinese ELL

My Chinese teachers helped me know how they wrote by explaining the words they chose and ideas they wrote about. We can copy their words and this is a way of learning flow to write.

— By a Chinese ELL

I must memorize beautiful phrases and sentences included in dictionaries hoping that I may use them in future writing assignments. I must quote others writing and turn to other essays for help and reference and turn to handouts containing famous quotes for reference in writing.

— By a Chinese ELL

I consider it important to memorize sentences to write better. If the English teacher required me to write a long English essay, I would turn to famous sayings and sentences derived from famous writers and essays on the same topic. I would imitate what other people say and use their sentences in my essays. I would use famous sayings, proverbs, and quotable phrases quite often, just as I use them very often in writing Chinese essays, for I consider they are essential in writing Chinese and English essays.

— By a Chinese ELL

Academic Writing in Japan

In Japan we are modest and polite. What we call old fashion way. We are trained to appreciate our feelings and the writer's intention of writing not directly. We try to use what we call "guessing skill." Write as not directly as we can and read as not directly as we can.

— By a Japanese ELL

All the teachers here wanted was example, example, example, concrete, concrete, and concrete. I can't understand why the reader must be told everything. Why must we be so obvious in English writing?

— By a Japanese ELL

Academic Writing in South Korea

I began to write in my native language, Korean, when I was nine-year-old. I had to write my diary as homework almost every day. I am still writing diaries. I write about the most important thing that happened to me, my feelings about the school and my friends, and my dreams. It helps me learn to write in English too.

— By a Korean ELL

Academic Writing in Pakistan

Back in Pakistan, my teacher would assign us to copy directly from the textbook using loose-leaf paper. This helped me with writing. I am still using this method when I have trouble understanding the reading or have difficulty in getting started with a writing task in English.

— By a Pakistani ELL

My teachers always read good essays from my classmates in front of the class I also like to read my classmates' work because it can help me to find the differences between theirs and mine. I can absorb their merit in order to improve my own writing. My teachers were used to teaching us writing this way.

— By a Pakistani ELL

Academic Writing in Poland

There are a lot of things different between the two languages, English and Polish. Sometimes when I write, I like to write it in a general way not specific... In Polish, when we wrote papers, we didn't have to give statistics or write sentences specific, such as what happened first, and then the next, and giving examples. We were supposed to just give clues rather than being specific.

— By a Polish ELL

When I was in the 7th and 8th grades in Poland, my teacher gave us I lot of books to read; and based on the reading, she was preparing topics for the assignments. ...She gave us a lot of freedom in our writing. Our assignment could have different forms of our choice: it could be a letter, a monologue, a dialogue, defending one's position. We had to write what the author's point was, who the main characters were, how can we compare them with our lives and our experiences, and what our personal opinion was about the book.

— By a Polish ELL

Academic Writing in Russia

In Russian, we usually have a very big introduction and a big conclusion. For example, if we are supposed to write about computer use in modern life, we are supposed to start like this "Mathematics was greatly appreciated by our great leaders, now it is used more in the technology such as computers." We can give a personal example, but not much because the teacher does not value that much of it. We are supposed to give a political and historical background. In the conclusion, we kind of finalize the result. I should prove the advantages of the use of the computer by saying yes, by the examples that I give in this composition, I have proven the idea that I said in the beginning.

— By a Russian ELL

When I came to the United States, I learned a new word "brainstorm." In Russia, I have never thought before writing and never made a list of things to write about. I just sat down, took a pen and paper and started to write. It was never me who wrote, it was my pen. In Russia, students do write a lot. In my middle school years, we used to write compositions for 10–15 pages. I had one great teacher. She did not give us any unusual techniques, but she explained to each and every student any mistakes he or she made, and told us how to write better. She gave us such nice topics that everyone wanted to write. The teacher told us: "You think you are students? No! You are writers!"

— *By a Russian ELL*

Academic Writing in Peru and Mexico

The most satisfying school assignment that I can remember was when I had to do a research project in my high school back in Peru. The project was about some of the pre-Inca cultures in my country. In the field research I had to go to some ruins in the mountains with my fellow students. The trip was fun and the ruins were a nice place to visit with a lot of tourists around. In my group I had to be the leader because I was

TABLE 5.5. Shared Themes and Concepts Between Cultures in History*

Historical Events	Possible Connections	Shared Concepts
Immigration	• Personal immigration stories	• Assimilation • acculturation
Civil War	• Chilean Civil War (1891) • El Salvador Civil War (1980–1992) • Chinese Civil War (1945–1952) • Korean Civil War (1950–1953) • Dominican Civil War (April 1965–Sept. 1965)	• Conflict • Economic • Inequality • Emancipation • Reconstruction
WWII	• Battle of the Caribbean (1941–1945) • Battle of the River Plate (Dec. 13, 1939) • Rafael Trujillo: Dominican Dictator (1930–1938) • Sino–Japanese War (1937–1945) • Battle of the Atlantic (1939–1945)	• Dictatorship • Propaganda • Fascism • Communism • Isolationism
Industrial Revolution	• Railroads were built in Argentina, Mexico, Peru, and Brazil 1870–1913 • Export–import development and expansion in South America 1900–1930 • Chinese Industrial Revolution 1960s–1990s	• Colonialism • Imperialism • Expansion • Modernization • Trade
American Revolution	• Haitian Revolution (1791–1804) • Brazilian Revolution (1820–1822) • Colombia Revolution (1808–1824) • Mexico Revolution (1910–1920)	• Tyranny • Independence • Monarchy • Liberty
Great Depression	• Chilean crisis of 1982 • Chinese stock market crash (2015) • Indian economic crisis (1991) • Asian financial crisis (1997) • Russian financial crisis (1998)	• Recession • Welfare • Reform • Economy • Debt

*(Dong, 2017, p. 148)

the one with more background knowledge about the subject. At the end our research paper was about 40 pages long, full of graphs and pictures.

— By a Peruvian ELL

When I was more proficient in Spanish in Mexico, we started to read the famous authors like Miguel de Cervantes and other famous Spanish novelists. They influenced me a lot in my style of writing. I fell in love with the way how they used the written word in their novels. Since then, I started to use complex sentence structures in Spanish with a great many fancy words. Thanks to them, I gained a vast knowledge of the Spanish vocabulary.

— By a Mexican ELL

By systematically incorporating ELLs' prior knowledge into the lesson plan and using the cultural notes, the subject matter teacher creates a rich and inviting learning context to motivate and engage them, thus making the subject matter learning in English meaningful and effective. Below is an example of such connections made between the U.S. history events and history events happened in ELLs' home countries (Table 5.5)

SAMPLE PLANNING ON ESL COMPONENTS OF SUBJECT MATTER LESSONS

Taking all the above three ESL lesson plan elements together, I offer examples to illustrate those three components for an ESL oriented subject matter lesson plan below:

Sixth Grade ESL Oriented Art Lesson on Shading

Curricular Objectives:
The students will be able to identify and describe the sequence of shading
The students will be able to shade a sphere with side or low lighting.

Language Objectives:
Students will be able to give an example of interesting shadows in their daily lives.
The students will be able to comprehend and use key shading vocabulary to describe the shading process in pairs.

ESL Anticipated Difficulties and Strategies:
ELLs may lack vocabulary power to describe shadows and the shading process and sequence. I will provide those ELLs with a multilingual glossary of basic terms before class. I will also demonstrate using those words to illustrate their meanings. During the shading seat work I will walk around the room to monitor the student's progress and ask them to use the new words to describe the shading sequence.

Cultural Notes:
Although shadows are common concepts used all over the world, their use and connotation may not be shared among cultures. Certain cultures may view shadows as

something dark and bad. Also, the way that shading is taught in an art lesson may vary from culture to culture. Therefore, I will first survey ELLs about superstitions practiced in their native cultures, myths related to the shadow in their culture and ask them to bring some pictures to illustrate shadows in their daily lives and/or culture. In doing so, students will activate their prior knowledge before learning the new concept and art technique.

Aim (Central Question):
What is shading?

Motivation/Do Now:
Take a look at those pictures (shadowy pictures) and describe what you see.

Tenth Grade ESL Oriented English Language Arts Lesson on "Harlem"
Curricular Objectives:
Students will be able to understand Hughes' metaphorical use of language to express the American Dream in his poem "Harlem."
Students will be able to write about their American Dreams, mimicking Hughes' poem.

Language Objectives:
The students will be able to differentiate the literal dream from figurative dream such as the American Dream.
The students will be able to understand and use Hughes' hypothetical questioning technique, its use and functions.

ESL Anticipated Difficulties and Strategies:
In this poem, quite a few words express metaphorical meaning that may be unfamiliar to the ELL students, such as dream deferred, fester, crust, sags. These words are used by Hughes so vividly, creating powerful imagery. So, a multilingual glossary on metaphorical meanings of those words is necessary. In order to really see what Hughes means, a group drawing exercise will be used to facilitate ELLs' understanding of the poem.

Cultural Notes:
This lesson is geared toward the multicultural classroom of today and is especially fitting after the recent tragic events. The ELLs may not be familiar with the term "American Dream" though that dream might be what has brought them here; therefore, this term will be defined in class. To activate students' prior knowledge, I will ask them about their journey to America. Using their own personal experiences, the new vocabulary and mimicking Hughes' poem, ELLs will do a group poem writing to express their American Dreams.

Aim (Central Question):
How did Langston Hughes depict (show) American dream in his poem "Harlem"?

Motivation/Do Now:
What were your, your parents', or your grandparents' dreams?
What brought you over to the U.S.?
What is your dream? Have you realized your dream yet? How so?

Eighth Grade ESL Oriented Family and Consumer Science Lesson on Healthy Foods

Curricular Objectives:

Students will be able to identify and explain how current dietary guidelines are used to help meet human nutrition and wellness needs.

Students will be able to use the guidelines to construct their MyPlate and discuss their rationales for it.

Language Objectives:

Students will be able to identify parts of the MyPlate and key components of the dietary guidelines.

Students will be able to read a modified newspaper article about the American dietary guidelines and discuss their findings in groups based on the reading comprehension questions.

Anticipated ESL Language Difficulties and Strategies:

As the lesson focuses on the American dietary guidelines using American food, ELLs may be at a loss for words. I will provide them with a visual multilingual glossary. I will also download visuals from online to illustrate those typical American foods. In addition, I will use foods in the school cafeteria as one set of examples as students may be familiar with those foods.

Cultural Notes:

Although there are many commonalities shared across cultures, food is culture specific. Also, what foods are considered to be healthy or even grain or vegetable can vary from culture to culture and family to family. This lesson can be a great way to incorporate student's cultures and use their identification with food groups in their own cultures was an entry into the lesson. When ELLs' prior knowledge is out in the open, they can engage and find the lesson meaningful and interesting. Besides ELLs' cultural knowledge, I will also introduce American food groups to draw parallels.

Aim (Central Question):

What is the recipe for good health?

Motivation/Do Now:

Write down what you eat at home for breakfast, lunch, and dinner. Try to describe it, even if it is written in your native language.

Ninth Grade ESL Oriented Mathematics Lesson on Probability

Curricular Objectives:

Students will be able to understand the basic principle of probability.

Students will be able to solve a probability problem using data collection and analysis.

Language Objectives:

Students will be able to define key vocabulary related to probability.
Students will be able to interact with each other using English while solving the probability problem.

Anticipated ESL Language Difficulties and Strategies:

There are quite a few words which can pose difficulty for ELLs to really understand the concept of probability, such as experiment, outcome, die, possible, chance, etc. Some of these words' meaning is different from the meaning used in basic communication, such as die, chance. Therefore, I will provide ELLs with a multilingual glossary. Also, some verbs used in the activity, such as flip and toss can be demonstrated using physical movements.

Cultural Notes:

Although ELLs may have prior knowledge about the concept of probability in their schooling back home, still transferring that knowledge into English may not be automatic. Also, the concept related to probability, such as fair game, equal chance may not be familiar cultural concepts for some ELLs depending on their cultural and religious beliefs. In addition, some of the examples used in the lesson can be culturally specific, such as lottery, gambling, insurance, etc. So, I will use what students know as a starting point to go into the lesson, for example, the number of times that they are given a homework assignment.

Aim (Central Question):

What is probability?

Motivation/Do Now:

What is the chance that my teacher will give me homework today?

Seventh Grade ESL Oriented Physical Education Lesson on Muscles

Curricular Objectives:

Students will be able to understand and name the major muscles of the body.
Students will be able to interact with their peers to demonstrate the functions of those muscles.

Language Objectives:

Students will be able to learn key vocabulary related to muscles.
Students will be able to use the TPR and peer interaction to demonstrate their understanding using English.

Anticipated ESL Difficulties and Strategies:

Terms used to describe human anatomy can be hard to pronounce and learn by regular English speakers, let alone ELLs. The muscle terms included in this lesson can be new for ELLs. Thus, I will use a multilingual visual glossary to illustrate those words. Students whose native language is from the Romance language family may have an advantage as some of those words are cognates between their languages and English. As not every ELL's native language is derived from the Romance language family, I plan to teach using the TPR and to ask students to touch, feel, listen, and say one word at a time in pairs.

Cultural Notes:

Even though human anatomy terms are used across cultures, the examples and ways used to teach them are culturally specific. For example, for my non-ELLs I will use weight lifting and football as a prime example to discuss how different muscle groups work and get trained. However, working with ELLs, I plan to survey students for their favorite sports back in their home countries and use those sports as prime examples for illustration and discussion. Finally, I plan to do an online search to gather cultural familiar examples and expand my knowledge in this area as well.

Aim (Central Question):

What are the main muscles of the body?

Motivation/Do Now:

Tell us a sport that you often play back in your home country (either in English or your native language). What is it called and how is played?

Ninth Grade ESL Oriented Biology Lesson on Cell Theory

Curricular Objectives:

Students will be able to define the concept of an animal cell, its structure and function.

Language Objectives:

Students will be able to understand the key vocabulary related to the animal cell. Students will be able to demonstrate their understanding of the cell theory through physical movements, visuals, and peer interactions.

ESL anticipated difficulties and strategies:

There are quite a few key vocabulary/concepts to be taught in this lesson. Besides using visuals and glossaries, I will use analogies that are familiar to ELLs to explain the complex and abstract vocabulary. Also, a multilingual glossary will be used to facilitate understanding. Finally, TPR will be used to engage students in using movements to learn key vocabulary words.

Cultural Notes:

Taken into consideration that ELLs may have taken science curriculum with different sequences, the concept of cell, though many native English-speaking students have been introduced to in their middle schools, may not be so for the non-native English speaking students. Therefore, students' prior knowledge should be assessed. In the case where students have not learned this concept, I need to teach both prior knowledge and new cell concepts. In giving examples, I need to be mindful about ELLs' comprehension of culturally specific references by including ELLs' familiar examples.

Aim (Central Question):

What is an animal cell?

Motivation/Do Now:

Draw a map of our school and label different parts, such as cafeteria, principal's office, etc.

Eleventh Grade ESL Oriented Social Studies Lesson on the Causes of the Civil War

Curricular Objectives:

Students will be able to identify the economic, social, cultural and geographical differences between the North and the South before the Civil War.

Students will be able to compare the Northern and Southern Regions of the United States.

Language Objectives:

Students will be able to learn vocabulary and concept of those differences.

Students will be able to use this new information in their reading and writing.

Students will be able to work in groups to interact with each other in English and talk about those differences using newly learned vocabulary.

ESL Anticipated Difficulties and Strategies:

There are quite a few key vocabulary/concepts to be taught in this lesson. Besides using visuals and glossaries, I will use a multilingual glossary to enable ELLs to transfer concepts from their native languages to English, i.e., Civil War, economy, cause, climate, etc. Finally, a TPR (Total Physical Response) exercise will be used to engage students in using movements to learn key vocabulary words.

Cultural Notes:

Teaching U.S. history can be challenging due to the specific geographical, economic, and historical details of the subject matter are often culturally specific. However, the overall theme of Civil War could allow for the use of ELLs' prior knowledge because most countries around the world have experienced the Civil War, and at the very least a civil unrest. Also, most countries consist of different regions with different types of land, culture, religious beliefs, economies, etc. I will tap into ELLs' prior knowledge about their own counties to help with the students' understanding.

Aim (Central Question):

What are the causes of the American Civil War?

Motivation/Do Now:

Did you learn about the Civil War in your country? If so, when did it happen and how did it start?

PLANNING FOR COLLABORATION WITH ESL TEACHERS

To respond to increasing ELLs in our schools, a collaboration between the ESL and subject matter teachers has become a necessity if not a requirement in many New York City schools. Collaboration comes in different forms, ranging from spontaneous and informal communication between the two teachers about the shared students to a formalized and long-term collaboration where two teachers join forces to plan the lesson, teach it, and assess it for the benefit of ELLs. In recent years we have seen several models of teacher collaboration in New York City schools (Graziano & Navarrete, 2012; Honigsfeld & Dove, 2008) as shown in Table 5.6.

Different from the traditional ESL instruction, nowadays more and more teachers from different fields come together to teach/assist ELLs' learning in the same classroom. Research has identified several benefits for teacher collaboration like this (Davison, 2006; Graziano & Navarrete, 2012; Tasdemir & Yidirim, 2017). First, collaboration especially in the push-in, ENL, using an inclusive model makes it possible for the ELLs to learn from and interact with both ESL and subject matter teachers in the same classroom at the same time during the lesson. ELLs can ask for help when there is a confusion and difficulty and do not have to wait until after class to go to their ESL class to ask for help.

Also, ELLs feel more included rather than isolated from the subject matter teacher and their English proficient peers. In a collaborative teaching environment, ELLs are exposed to the same material sometimes twice from the two teachers who have different expertise and teaching styles, thus increasing their comprehension and understanding. Teachers in the same classroom can also discuss and find solutions to the problem on site and adjust their teaching immediately.

Finally, collaboration like this is beneficial to both teachers. For ESL teachers, being exposed to the subject matter curriculum and assessment provides them

TABLE 5.6. Teacher Collaboration Models and Characteristics

Model	Key characteristics
One teaches and one assists	The subject matter teacher teaches up front to all students, while an ESL/ENL teacher working with ELLs on the side either individually or in a group.
Parallel teaching	The class is divided into two groups. One group is taught by the subject matter teacher while the other by the ESL/ENL teacher in the same classroom and at the same time.
Alternate teaching	Subject matter and ESL teachers rotate, taking turns to teach at different points during the lesson or on different days of the week.
Team or co-teaching	Both teachers teach side by side at the same time during the lesson. The subject matter teacher uses the ESL methods to teach the subject matter while the ESL teacher uses language to highlight the subject matter and address ESL difficulties and cultural points.

with insights and authentic opportunities for teaching language through the subject matter. In turn, their language support and assistance become more tailored and meaningful to ELLs. For subject matter teachers, collaboration offers opportunities to learn about ESL teaching methodology and differentiate their instruction according to ELLs' language levels and cultural needs. This leads to more student awareness and improvement on their own instruction.

Over the years research has shown that effective teacher-teacher collaboration has the following key ingredients (Graziano & Navarrete, 2012; Pawan & Craig, 2011; Slater & Mohan, 2010; Tasdemir & Yidirim, 2017):

- There is complete administrative support from the district, school, and departments. Both ESL and subject matter teachers are given time, resources, incentives, and support to work as a team in planning and delivering of the lesson, designing curricular materials, and adjusting instructional and assessment strategies.
- The district, school, and departments provide a clear purpose, guidance, and training on how to collaborate with each other and have established explicit expectations and accountability measures.
- Collaborating teacher pairs share mutual understanding and responsibility. Both teachers are respectful toward each other's disciplines and credentials and willing to learn from each other to better serve their students. In addition, both teachers are open and flexible about the differences in each other's personality, teaching style, and communication preference for the benefits of the students.

There are the following four specific ways for the subject matter teacher to collaborate with the ESL teacher in lesson planning:

Communicate with the ESL Teacher Early on to Learn About ELLs in Subject Matter Classroom. Collaborative lesson planning should start as early as the school assigns a subject matter teacher to a collaborative team with an ESL teacher. If that is not the case, once the subject matter teachers have learned that they have ELLs in their classes and their ESL teacher(s), the subject matter teacher should reach out to the ESL department and/or ESL teacher(s) to gather information about their ELLs' English proficiency levels and learning needs, length of time in the U.S., cultural and previous educational backgrounds, and family situation. Often the ESL teacher who shares the same ELLs is a good contact person to get that information.

Share Your Curriculum and Assessment Content with the ESL Teacher. It's often a good idea to inform the ESL teacher of the subject matter unit wide key concepts with general curricular objectives or a week-long instructional plan and the teaching context. This way the ESL teacher can have a curricular and assessment context and offer more insights and a systematic plan for differentiation for ELLs. For an ESL oriented lesson plan, I have discussed a few key elements of tailoring the subject matter lesson to ELLs' levels and needs in this chapter.

Those can be the starting points for the subject matter teachers to focus on when discussing the ways of differentiation with the ESL teacher.

Keep in mind, the ESL teacher has training and expertise in teaching ELLs. They may offer local ESL resources, ranging from multi-media support to modified readings to providing native language support. Be willing to show the ESL teacher your design for the three key areas for differentiation, such as language objectives, ESL anticipated difficulties, and cultural notes. Be open, flexible, and professional about their suggestions for using more culturally relevant questions and teaching examples, such as the wording of the subject matter teacher's directions, test questions, and homework and/or project guidelines.

Explore Possible Cross-Cultural Differences. As we have talked about in this chapter and chapters before, secondary ELLs are not blank slates when they come to the subject matter teacher's classroom. Rather, most of them have already acquired their native culture and have gone through grade level equivalent education in the subject matter. All that prior knowledge should be tapped into and utilized effectively in the subject matter teacher's instruction. If the subject matter teachers are unfamiliar with their ELLs' prior knowledge, the ESL teacher is the one to consult with besides surveying the subject matter teacher's students about their native language, culture, and schooling.

Establish a Routine of Communication with the ESL Teacher. Effective collaboration requires both teachers to have regular discussions and updates on the shared ELLs' progresses and problems. This way the subject matter teachers do not have to wait until the day before a big test or when the student has failed class. Be courteous and consistent and take initiatives in communication with the ESL teacher. With regular communication, the subject matter teacher and the ESL teacher can be on the same page, identifying problematic areas to address as well as monitoring progresses made which will inform the subject matter teacher's instructional decisions in order to be sure that the subject matter teacher's ELLs' needs are met, and they are supported in the subject matter teacher's classroom.

CHAPTER 6

ASSESSING ELLS IN SUBJECT MATTER CLASSES

Assessment is a collection of ongoing and systematic information about students' learning for the purpose of improving students' learning and informing instruction. Assessment gives the teacher an opportunity to gauge students' progress or a lack of progress in order to tailor instruction toward their needs. A good assessment should go hand in hand with instruction and integrated at various points in the lesson, including before the lesson, during the lesson, and after the lesson.

For ELLs, especially entering and emerging ELLs, the traditional verbal based assessment, such as oral participation and written work, may not be feasible and useful because students are going through the Silent Period and/or have limited speaking and writing abilities to demonstrate their intelligence in English. Therefore, it requires the subject matter teacher to use authentic or alternative assessment to track the ongoing progress of ELLs. Below is a sample veteran ESL language teacher's advice for subject matter teachers to do in class and meaningful assessments:

Assessing ELLs, particularly those who are still in their Silent Periods, not yet ready to verbalize their thoughts in English, eliciting non-verbal responses is a great way to assess. For those who are at the stage of one word or phrase responses, such as emerging and developing ELLs, we provide them with sentence starters for them to complete the sentences themselves. Fill-in-the-blanks are great, especially if we're

Teaching English Language Learners in Secondary Subject Matter Classes, pages 113–124.

looking for key words. Listening to ELL group work allows me to observe the ELL's engagement with their peers. For intermediate to advanced level ELLs (from developing to transitioning), I like to engage them in peer and self-assessment. For those assessments, I model first and then give specific guidelines such as appropriate words and sentences and the rubrics for students to document each other or their own progresses and areas for improvements. This is a great way to promote their self-awareness and social and communication skills as long as the teacher has established a positive learning environment. —By an ESL teacher

In this chapter, I provide a few vignettes to illustrate common dilemmas and effective ESL strategies used to assess ELLs in subject matter classes.

ASSESSMENTS FOR ENTERING AND EMERGING ELLS IN SUBJECT MATTER CLASSES

Ashgan, a Newcomer in Her Silent Period. When Ashgan first came to Ms. G's 9th grade global studies class, she did not speak much English. She sat straightly in her seat every day with her notebook open and seemingly paid attention to what went on in class. However, from what she was told by the school, Ms. G learned that Ashgan just arrived in the U.S. a month ago from Egypt and spoke Arabic and French. But the teacher was not given any information about Ashgan's language status in her global studies or her educational history back in her home country. Knowing that Ashgan had almost zero English language skills, Ms. G wondered what the starting point should be for Ashgan's global studies learning. "How can I tell that she is learning?" "How can I make sure that she understands what I am teaching?" "To be fair to all students, do I grade her equally as others in class?"

Talking to Ashgan's ESL teacher turned out to be the best thing. Ms. G. decided to do the following. First, she arranged Ashgan to sit close to her desk in order to have frequent observations of her behavior, to give her help when needed, and to make sure that Ashgan followed what went on in class. Seated closely to the teacher, Ashgan communicates with Ms. G. through signs and facial expressions.

Second, soon after Ms. G. paired Ashgan with Sue, a peer who spoke French at home and who was also a second language student herself. Ms. G. believed that Sue's native language and her experience with second language learning could encourage more personal involvement and assistance. Ms. G would check on the pair during her lesson and gained more insights about Ashgan from Sue's feedback. Sue would interrupt her lesson by asking her to clarify something for Ashgan. Ms. G. knew it was time to re-arrange seat for Ashgan when she saw Ashgan become more at ease and interact more frequently with Sue in French. This time she placed Ashgan in the middle of the students who did not speak her native language. Ms. G. wanted to create an environment where Ashgan would be encouraged to learn English.

Third, based on her daily observations, Ms. G. adjusted the grading system to accommodate Ashgan's needs. In the first two months, she did not assign Ashgan a letter grade. From Ashgan's ESL teacher Ms. G learned that it was premature to evaluate Ashgan's progress using the same criteria that she used for the rest of her class. With the help from the ESL teacher, she designed a profile chart to document Ashgan's progress. Ashgan received only a "credit/noncredit" grade for the first two marking periods. It was not until November when Ms. G. noted a breakthrough in Ashgan's oral English. Her language improved exponentially during group work. Her notes were complete in English, and her test performance showed a remarkable improvement (Table 6.1).

Some mainstream subject matter teachers may have concerns over the fairness in assessing a newcomer ELL differently from the rest of the class. While I respect these teachers' efforts to treat all students equally, I believe that blind equality runs the risk of not recognizing that a student's individual needs and backgrounds. Ignoring these backgrounds and needs and forcing everyone to be treated equally will be a disservice to these ELLs and will leave them feeling alienated, inferior, and disengaged. Like siblings in Fu's book (1995) many new immigrants who came to America need to adjust both academically and socially besides learning new language skills. Instead of giving these students a pass or fail grade, it is more productive to give them time to become familiar with the learning environment and provide opportunities for them to demonstrate their abilities.

TABLE 6.1. Classroom Assessment Matrix for Beginning (Entering and Emerging) ELLs

Non-verbal learning behavior	• Student is alert/ interested or • confused/ disoriented/bored	• Open the book and the notepad. • Show signs of readiness for learning.	• Nod or smile or pay attention to the lesson and class talks. • Use signs to communicate to peers and to the teacher.	• Follow the directions Copy notes.
Verbal behavior	• Write numbers, dates and own name when asked. • Notes are taken, either complete or marked in L1.	• Talk to peers in L1 or in English. • Ask questions from peers. • Ask for help after class or in class when the teacher walks by.	• When asked, gives a word answer or Yes/no responses. • Tackle the test or homework in some way either in L1 or in English.	• Frequent use of dictionary or glossaries to follow the reading or the discussion.
Group work behavior	• Sit close to the group and face the group members.	• Pay attention to what goes on in group talks.	• Get the book or the handout ready for the task.	• Communicates with the group members for clarification and help.
Social behavior	• Walk into the class alone or with friends, on time or late.	• Sit and talk with friends in L1.	• Smile to the peers and be friendly to others and the teacher.	• Have eye contact with the teacher and be able to say simple greetings.

Good assessment should be a means rather than an end to motivate students' learning and inform teachers' instruction (Boyd-Batstone, 2013; Wiggins, 1992). With a more enrollment of ELLs in subject matter classes, subject matter teachers need to adjust their assessment strategies to those ELLs' needs and levels. Research has argued that continuous assessment is an integral part of improving instruction for ELLs (Abadiano & Turner, 2003; Ortega & Minchala, 2017).

Assessing Yi's Biology Learning. Yi Lin has only been in the U.S. for five weeks. She is 15 years old and placed in the 9th grade biology class taught by Tom. She is from Taiwan and appears to be in her Silence Period. She answers to almost every question with a nod or headshake. Even when Tom asked if she was Yi, she shook her head but said "yes." The ESL teacher told Tom that Yi had some English back home in Taiwan, and even though she did not speak, she understood more than she appeared. Despite the ESL teacher's reassurance, Tom still had concerns about her. His question is how can I assess Yi's performance if she does not speak or perform on the test? She performed poorly on the first two tests. On her first test, she wrote nothing but a few Chinese words. On her second test, Yi did not respond to the question of "Why photosynthesis is useful?" at all. Instead, she wrote the complete formula of the photosynthesis from memory. "Is Yi really learning? How can I in good conscience give her a passing grade with this kind of work?"

Tom's questions are typical subject matter teachers' questions in working with newcomer ELLs. Fortunately, Tom reached out to the ESL teacher in the school to ask for advice. Tom showed Yi's work to her ESL teacher. To his surprise, the ESL teacher saw something that Tom did not see. She saw the improvement between Yi's first test and her second test. She told Tom that even though Yi did not respond to the question on both tests, her writing down the whole formula of the photosynthesis on the second test revealed that one, she understood that the question was about photosynthesis, two, she tried to respond by using her knowledge, and three, she had paid attention in class and kept good notes. To the ESL teacher, all this showed a big leap in Yi's second language learning. Judging by the improvement and effort, Yi should be given a passing grade.

The ESL teacher also advised Tom to use continuous daily assessment of Yi's performance. One assessment strategy is in class observations. Following the ESL teacher's advice, Tom designed a profile sheet of Yi, detailing her second language development over the semester. He would go around the room to observe the students' discussions during peer work and group work and look for any signs of communication issues from Yi. Tom found out that Yi was actually very active in peer and group work through her active interaction with her Chinese peers. Although Yi did not show much verbal communication in English, however, observations made Tom see that Yi did involve herself and was on task through careful listening and following what her peers did.

Very soon Tom's profile was filled with details about Yi. He could see exactly where Yi was in her development in both English and biology and how he could adjust his instruction to push Yi forward. Based on his observations, Tom told Yi to show her notes to him in class by marking the parts of the lesson where she struggled to understand. By reviewing Yi's notes regularly Tom gained a better understanding of Yi's biology and language learning and also got a sense of his own instruction. One day in class Tom casually mentioned something about guinea pigs. The next day, he walked over to Yi and found a big question mark about that part of the lesson. She did not understand it. This alerted Tom to be more cognizant about some of the cultural references that he makes in class.

In teaching of mitosis, Tom learned from Yi that although she had copied everything into her note pad, she still did not understand the concept and her electronic translator did not help either. This led to Tom's follow-up lesson through a use of construction paper to demonstrate the cell division and the process of mitosis. Students were divided into groups of five to verbalize the process using the manipulative. Tom sat in Yi's group and showed Yi step by step the mitosis process. By the end of the lesson, Yi was able to show the correct process involved in mitosis using the manipulative.

Assessment should not stop here. Constant and ongoing assessment should help subject matter teachers adjust their expectations and raise their standards accordingly. Too often those teachers hold low expectations for ELL students (Fu, 1995; McKeon, 1994). Language learning like subject matter knowledge learning is not linear, rather it is recursive and has cognitive and language leaps. So, although an ELL student may not do much on the first test, a month later, s/he may attempt to answer a lot. Therefore, using classroom observations and daily assessment, a subject matter teacher can gauge ELL students' progress, set up a new goal and expectations for them, and push them to catch up with their English proficient peers. Below are some general guidelines for assessing beginning ELLs in subject matter classes:

- Conduct ongoing classroom observations to document ELLs' learning behaviors and academic performance in class. Arrange ELLs to sit close to your desk or sit with students who speak their native language so that you have an easy access to see their facial expressions and have their native speaking peers help translate key points of the lesson.
- Allow ELLs to use their preferred language to demonstrate their understanding. For ELLs who have received literacy education in your subject matter in their home country and are literate in their native language, giving them an opportunity to use their native language to describe the key concepts can be both motivational and beneficial. Even if the subject matter teacher is not proficient in that language, using technology, such Google translation and peer help can get those beginning ELLs engaged in the lesson.
- Establish an assessment chart of ELL students (see Table 6.1), especially those who are at a beginning stage of second language learning. Monitoring and documenting each ELLs' progress, strengths, and weaknesses

helps the subject matter teacher revise their expectations of ELLs and adjust their instruction and assessment accordingly.

- Use multiple assessment strategies rather than relying on the test results or writing in English alone to get a holistic view of ELL students' performance. In order not to penalize those ELLs for their lack of English language skills, teachers must use creative and diverse assessments, including using physical responses, visuals, drawings, labeling, and hands-on assessments to measure comprehension and understanding of the subject matter knowledge when ELLs cannot adequately demonstrate it verbally in English.

- Be mindful of your beginning ELLs' language levels and modify your assessment methods, tools, and grading systems to provide ELL students with a chance to respond and a shot at learning. Consider adjusting your grading system according to those students' English levels. Rather than using one rubric for all students or giving out failures to those ELLs, it is more productive and meaningful to grade those students by their progress, especially in the early stages of their second language learning.

ASSESSMENTS FOR INTERMEDIATE AND ADVANCED ELLS IN SUBJECT MATTER CLASSES

Assessing ELLs During Class Discussions. Recognizing that some of his students were not used to class participation and comfortable with deferring to the teacher as an authority in their previous schooling, Mike, another biology teacher, used varied strategies to constantly train his students to talk about science in class. Mike's lecture was loud and clear. He used wait time when he asked a question. He did not only call on those who raised their hands, but also those who kept silent once he sensed they were ready to participate. For example, knowing that Win had been in his biology class for almost a year, but still did not speak a word in class, he tried to nudge her to join in the class discussion (Dong, 2002).

Teacher:	So, another reflex is blinking. Everybody blinks, you blink your eye. It is not voluntary. Reflexes are involuntary. How does blinking protect you? Do you know what *protect* means?
Student 1:	To keep you from harm.
Teacher:	OK, so how does that protect you? How are you doing this with your eye, opening and closing? How is that protection? Win Xiang?
Win Xiang:	(didn't answer)
Teacher:	Want to help her out? (pointed to her neighbor)
Student 3:	Keeping it from [becoming] dry.
Teacher:	Did you hear what she said? (asked Win Xiang again)
Win Xiang:	(nodded her head but still didn't answer verbally).
Teacher:	Did you hear what she said just now? Can you repeat what you said? (asked the whole class)

Student 4:	Keeping it from [becoming] dry.
Teacher:	Can you repeat what he just said? (walked to Win Xiang and asked her for the third time)
Win Xiang:	Keeping it from dry weather [sic].
Teacher:	Good. Can somebody repeat what Win Xiang said loud so that everyone can hear it?
Student 5:	When your eyes are dry you blink to moisten it [sic].
Teacher:	Guys, did you hear that now? It keeps the eyes from getting dry and keeps dirt from getting into the eye, so it protects it.

Here we see an example of Mike's use of several turns to get Win to participate in the class discussion. Two interesting elements in teaching and assessment come out. First, instead of leaving a quiet student alone, Mike held a high expectation of her. That expectation is based on Mike's daily assessment and observations. Sensing that Win has acquired the language power by now, he nudged Win to articulate her understanding orally. Second, Mike demonstrates that good assessment is an integral part of teaching. By using elicited responses from other students first to set up a non-threatening environment, Mike prompted Win to speak up in the end. This incident turned out to be a turning point for Win. After that incident she participated regularly in class.

Using Miscue Analysis to Assess ELLs' Reading Comprehension. For intermediate or advanced ELLs, there is also an increased need to assess their literacy and thinking skills alongside with their language skills. Very often these students have already developed BICS and may appear to be fluent in oral English. However, that oral fluency may disguise problems with the written English and mislead the teacher into believing that these students should be equally fluent and proficient with reading and writing skills.

In comparison to other literacy skills, reading skills, specifically, are often hidden and difficult to evaluate. Students with reading difficulties can go unnoticed for quite a long time. Therefore, there is a need for the subject matter teacher to learn some basic assessment techniques used to evaluate ELLs' reading comprehension and behavior in order to identify their reading needs and abilities. One informative and easy to use tool is the miscue analysis, (Ebe, 2010; Goodman et al., 1987).

The miscue analysis requires the teacher to first assign a student to read aloud a reading passage that is appropriate to her level. During the read-aloud, the teacher take notes on the text to mark the student's miscues, including the mispronunciation, misread, miscomprehension, etc. After the read-aloud, the teacher asks the student to retell the story or summarize what s/he has read. Then the teacher analyzes her notes of the read-aloud and groups the miscues into several categories. Three commonly used categories include semantic acceptability (whether the miscues fit with the meaning), syntactic appropriateness (whether the miscues interrupt the sentence flow), and graphical resemblance (whether the miscues match the actual words or phrases in some way). The analysis offers the teacher an in-

TABLE 6.2. Miscue Analysis of ELLs' Reading Comprehension I

There were only hills and valleys of water around me now. When I was in a valley I **could** see nothing
         #   coo

and when the canoe **rose out** of it, only the ocean stretching away of away.
               rollz ou   #

Night **fell** and I drank from the basket. The water cooled my **throat**.
   fall   dero

The sea was black and there was no **difference** between it **and** the sky. The waves made no **sound**
Da   different   (omit)   soun

among **themselves**, only **faint noises** as they went under the canoe or struck against it. Sometimes the
     themself   faded noise   #

noises seemed angry and at **other** times like people laughing. I was not hungry because of my fear.
noise   seem   another

The first star made me feel less afraid. It came out low in the sky and it was in front of me, **toward** the
                                                           estoward

east. **Other stars** began to appear all around, but it was this one I kept my gaze open. It was in the
     another star

figure that we **call a serpent**, a star **which** shone green and **which** I knew. Now and then it was hidden
               called spart   whi
  whi

by **mist**, yet it always came out brightly again. Without this star I would have been lost, for the waves
  mis

never **changed**. They came always from the same direction and in a manner that **kept** pushing me away
   change   (omit)   kep

from the place I wanted to reach. For this reason the canoe made a path in the black water like a snake.
    #   #

But somehow I **kept** moving **toward** the star **which** shone in the east. Excerpt from <u>Island of the Blue</u>
     kep   estoward   whi

depth understanding of the student's reading behavior and patterns of miscues. That gives the teacher an idea of the student's language and reading abilities. The following are two examples of such an analysis done by two English teachers with their native Spanish speaking ELLs (Tables 6.2 and 6.3).

Assessing and Scaffolding ELLs Academic Skills. Chamot and O'Malley (1994) emphasized the importance of cultivating effective learning skills and outlined major learning skills across academic disciplines for ELLs. Among these, note-taking skills, though appear simple and straightforward, can be overwhelming for an ELL. The learner has to juggle multiple tasks, such as listening, reading, and writing all at once while making notes in class. In addition, effective note-taking involves students not only copying what is on the board but also drawing a meaningful roadmap that identifies key points and summarizing crucial information. Organization and consistency of the notes are two indicators of effective

TABLE 6.2.   Continued

Analysis

There are altogether 26 miscues in a short reading of about 250 words. Maria, a 8th grader, made an average of one miscue every ten words. A closer examination of these miscues shows that the majority of these miscues are second language pronunciation problems. Maria's native language is Spanish and I can see some native language influences here such as her difficulty in pronouncing the /th/ sound, and omissions of certain sounds in words ending with "t" "s" and "d". However, Maria's retelling shows that she has achieved basic understanding of the text. Her miscues at the semantic level such as "faded noise" "called spart" "rollz out of" do not seem to distract her from getting an overall meaning. At first I thought she might not understand the word "serpent" but she told me that she got the idea at the end because of the phrase "the black water like a snake."

When I look at Maria's writing, she has trouble with certain word endings, such as verb –ed ending and the third person singular. All this reveals a need for her to practice on these forms of language both orally and in writing. Also, Maria's use of the context clues to understand the word "serpent" excites me, and maybe I can structure something for her and the whole class to learn how to use contextual clues in reading.

note-taking. Subject matter teachers should check students' notes and model effective note-taking strategies rather than assume that ELLs can take notes.

Brian, a middle school social studies teacher uses a systematic approach to teach note-taking skills to his ELLs. In the beginning of the semester, after finding out that his ELL students had very limited and incomplete notes, Brian provided a handout each day before class that outlined key information while including a few blanks for his ELL students to fill in the missing information. By the end of the lesson, he would quickly go over the notes as a whole class to check for understanding. As the semester went on, blanks in Brian's handouts became bigger and longer and finally his ELL students would no longer need Brian's handout to take notes. Table 6.4 is a sample handout that Brian used with his ELL students.

Besides the above effective assessments, subject matter teachers can use writing assignments to assess ELLs. In New York City public schools, teachers routinely design and use multiple writing assignments before, during, and after the lesson. Those assignments can be a short "Do Now," a warm-up writing exercise for students to activate their prior knowledge or skills about the lesson or an "Exit Slip," a quick response from the student about what s/he has learned and what s/he is still confused about or has questions before the lesson ends. Sometimes, a modified version of the writing exercise and teacher modeling is needed for the low-level ELLs. Students can write it using personal writing or even their native language or using drawing, captions, graphic organizers, etc. to express their understanding and knowledge about the topic. At those levels, word or phrase level English expressions should be allowed. For the intermediate level ELLs, students can write using scaffolds, such as sentence frames, such as I learned in class today that _____, I like to _____, and fill-ins. After modeling and giving examples, they can also write in paragraphs.

TABLE 6.3. Miscue Analysis of ELLs' Reading Comprehension II

It is a miracle that New **York** works at all. The whole thing is **implausible**. Every time the residents
        Yerk   impossible

brush their teeth, millions of gallons of water must be drawn from the Catskills and the hills of

Westchester. When a young man in Manhattan writes a letter to his girl in **Brooklyn**, the love message
Wetchester   Brookleen

gets blown to her **through** a **pneumatic** tube-pfft-just like that. The **subterranean** system of telephone
            thoughts # poomatic   subferranean

cables, power lines, steam pipes, gas mains and sewer pipes is reason enough to **abandon** the island to
                                                     abondon

the gods and the weevils. Every time an incision is made in the pavement, the noisy **surgeons** expose
        #   surginias

ganglia that are tangled beyond belief. By rights New York should have destroyed itself long ago, from
gang

panic or fire or **rioting** or failure of some **vital** supply line in its circulatory system or from some deep
            reeoting   veetal

labyrinthine short **circuit**. Long ago the city should have **experienced** an **insoluble** traffic snarl at some
laboratory   cirweet   experience   insollable

impossible bottleneck. It should have **perished** of hunger when food lines failed for a few days. It
                               perish

should have been wiped out by a **plague starting** in its slums of **carried in** by ships' rats. It should have
                    plagoo staring   carrying it

been **overwhelmed** by the sea that licks at it **on** every side. The workers in its myriad cells should have
      overwhelm   in

succumbed to **nerve**, from the fearful pall of smoke-fog that drifts over every few days from Jersey,
           nervez

blotting out all light at noon and leaving the high **offices** suspended, men **groping** and **depressed**, and the
blooting   office   grouping   depreesed

sense of the world's end. It should have been **touched** in the **head** by the August heat and gone off its
                                 touch   hear

rocker. Excerpt from <u>New York</u> by E. B. White

Subject matter teachers should keep in mind that although developing and transitioning ELLs have shown a tremendous jump in their second language learning and class performance, still disciplinary literacy skills often take a long time (see Chapter 1 on the length of time for ELLs to catch up with their native English speaking peers in CALP). Therefore, teachers still need to modify and adjust their instruction and assessment to provide comprehensible input while teaching challenging disciplinary vocabulary and subject matter specific discourse patterns to prepare those students for the standardized tests.

TABLE 6.3. Continued

Analysis

There are 30 miscues in this read-aloud by Richard, a 11th grader whose native language is Spanish. After reviewing the transcript and Richard's retelling, I realized that he did not understand the reading. There are some native language influences such as pronouncing the words with an – ed ending. But most of the miscues he made were semantic miscues, such as "grouping" for "groping", "reeoting" for "rioting", "insollable" for "insoluble", and "impossible" for "implausible." These miscues prevent him from understanding the story. Richard's retelling was very sketchy, an indication of a failure to comprehend the story. Before this exercise, I thought Richard could handle a reading material like this one, since he had been in the U.S. for more than five years and was mainstreamed in his middle school. However, the finding of the miscue analysis has made me think again. Richard revealed that he had trouble with big words and with what he called "woofy" language or figurative language use. I wonder whether the problem here is due to the use of big words or figurative language use or both.

This miscue analysis is a wake-up call for me to see where my students are at in their reading abilities. I am re-examining the reading materials that I use with this class in general and Richard in particular. Richard's reflection on his own reading process made me wonder whether this is a prevalent problem for other students. I plan to give Richard another miscue analysis using a reading material that is descriptive. I also plan to investigate my other ELL learners on this.

TABLE 6.4. The Cause of the American Revolution

The Cause of the American Revolution
I. French and Indian War:
• Fought between the _____ and the _____ in North America and ended in 1763. The _____ won the war and took complete control of North America.
• _____
• In order to pay off their massive debts, the British began to place heavy _____ on the _____.
II. Sugar Act:
• Placed heavy _____ on _____ which was being sold in the colonies.
• _____

DIFFERENTIATED ASSESSMENTS ACCORDING TO ELLS' LEVELS

Language support and challenge should go hand in hand in instruction and assessment. Differentiated writing assignments with increased expectations and language support have proven effective for the ELLs (Adamson & Coulson, 2015; Cooks & Sunseri, 2013–2014; Fairbairn & Jones-Vo, 2010). For example, when planning a lesson, the subject matter teacher can design a writing assignment that takes into account his or her ELLs' varied English proficiency levels. Below is sample reading and writing assessments differentiated by ELLs' levels (Fairbairn & Vo-Jones, 2010)

For Beginning ELLs (Entering and Emerging ELLs)
Language-Based Expectations: Using non-verbal and/or BICS level self-introduction or even native language to describe the learning topic orally

Reading Expectations: Demonstrating their comprehension and understanding using translated and modified texts and/or assignments/tests

Writing Expectations: Giving word level responses and/or native language responses in writing

For intermediate/advanced ELLs (Developing/transitioning ELLs)
Language-Based Expectations: Delivering a short presentation on the learning topic orally

CALP Level Vocabulary: Using appropriate CALP level vocabulary in class talks and presentations

Reading Expectations: Showing comprehension of a short reading passage and/or with reading modifications; correctly reading the diagrams and charts to show their understanding

Writing Expectations: Using CALP appropriate sentences in the disciplines to write and demonstrate skills in composing a word web, outline, Venn diagram, T-Chart, writing captions (p. 282)

CHAPTER 7

READING AND VOCABULARY INSTRUCTION FOR ELLS IN SUBJECT MATTER CLASSES

Secondary students face challenging academic reading requirements in subject matter classes and on the standardized tests. Reading in subject matter classrooms at the secondary level focuses more on students' reading to learn, learning vocabulary, and reading to write to demonstrate the newly learned subject matter knowledge. Typical kinds of secondary subject matter readings are:

English Language Arts: poems, short stories, plays, non-fictions, graphics, newspaper articles, biographies, literal critiques, speeches, online resources, etc.

Mathematics: word problems, test directions, equations, tables, data, proofs and procedures, graphics, online resources, etc.

Science: textbooks, popular science articles, lab manuals, test directions, tables, data, graphics, online resources, etc.

Social Studies: internet readings, textbooks, primary sources (speeches, court and political documents, letters), newspapers and magazines, graphics, political cartoons, captions, artifacts, diaries, tables, data, biographies, maps, online resources, etc.

Teaching English Language Learners in Secondary Subject Matter Classes, pages 125–157.

SUBJECT MATTER READING AND
VOCABULARY CHALLENGES FOR ELLS

For ELLs who are limited in English proficiency both at BICS and CALP levels and come from diverse linguistic, cultural and educational backgrounds, they encounter additional three challenges besides common challenges as English proficient students face with secondary academic reading. These areas are: language challenges/vocabulary challenges, educational challenges, and challenges with cultural and prior knowledge

Language and Vocabulary Challenges. Unlike English proficient students who have already acquired the BICS level English proficiency characterized by grammar fluency, oral language fluency, and daily communication skills, many secondary ELLs must learn both BICS and CALP simultaneously due to a late start of learning English and an urgent need to pass the standardized tests and meet high school graduation demands in a timely fashion.

Reading in English for ELLs differs greatly from reading in their native languages. ELLs must first visually adjust themselves to the text orientation from vertical to horizontal as in Chinese, Korean, and Japanese literature reading or from right to left to left to right as in Urdu and Arabic reading. Next, they have to learn the basic sound-letter correspondence in order to use that knowledge to help with reading in English (Figueredo, 2006; Harrison & Krol, 2007; Sipra, 2013). If their native language does not have similar or lacks sound-letter correspondence like Chinese and Urdu, they have to learn those reading skills in English from the very beginning.

English proficient students have already acquired the BICS level oral language and vocabulary by the time when they go to elementary school. By the time they enter high school they have acquired about 25,000 words in English (Nation, 2006). However, ELLs' vocabulary often starts from a handful of English words if any. Because of their very limited vocabulary size and knowledge, ELLs often find the reading materials assigned by the subject matter teacher well above their language proficiency levels (Irbahim, Sarudin, & Muhamad, 2016; Nagy & Townsend, 2012; Nation, 2006, 2015). As soon as the reading starts, they encounter a large number of unknown words that overwhelm them during the reading.

Educational Challenges. Research has shown that ELLs' approaches to the reading materials, expectations, and reading skills gained in their schooling back in their home countries may not be consistent or overlap with the approaches and skills taught in the American schools (Chapters 3 and 4). For example, in certain cultures reading instruction is teacher-centered and geared toward memorizing sacred or religious or well-known literacy texts and complex vocabulary. In those cultures, teachers are an authority and reading comprehension is all about word for word close analysis given by the teacher to parse and transmit information to the student rather than reading for self-expression and multiple perspectives using the reader-oriented, inquiry, and cooperative learning approaches as in U.S. schools.

Furthermore, American academic texts have their preferred ways of organizing information, presenting disciplinary language patterns, ideas, and thoughts using evidence based and argument-driven using deductive thinking (see Chapter 1). Finally, ELLs may not have had enough exposure to various genres and kinds of texts and ways of written communication used in different subject matter classes. All this is compounded by their lack of grammatical knowledge, American cultural knowledge, and limited vocabulary, all adding to their difficulties in reading in English (Beeman & Urow, 2013; Dong, 1998, 1999a,b, 2011; Matalene, 1985; Shen, 1989; Yum, 1988).

Cultural Challenges. Besides their lack of American mainstream cultural knowledge in general, many ELLs feel foreign if not conflicted about the topics and background knowledge discussed in the reading in American schools. Coming from different cultural backgrounds, ELLs' views toward literacy, written language, belief systems, and self and group and family relationships may be totally different if not contradictory with the American teacher's views. While American educational values individualistic thinking and stress on the developmental growth and building critical and creative thinking skills through reading, other cultures, such as the Asian and Latino cultures value conformity and view the text as a presentation of the absolute truth, not up for debate. The teacher holds that truth and pass it onto the student (see Chapters 1, 3, and 4).

Despite those ESL related reading challenges, secondary ELLs do have some advantages on their side. Research has shown that ELLs with strong native language and literacy skills often learn quicker and perform better than ELLs with weak native language and literacy skills, particularly in academic reading (August et al., 2005; Cummins, 1979a,b; Dong, 2009, 2013–2014; Freeman & Freeman, 2009; Marino, 2011). This is due to their familiarity with the school literacy practices and having had basic understanding of how schools operate and subject matter knowledge base they have built in their schooling back in their home country. Armed with language and literacy skills gained in their native languages and subject matter knowledge, these students automatically compare and contrast languages and literacy practices for similarities and differences. That prior knowledge can be used to their advantages, often called transfers at the different stages of language and literacy learning in English (see Chapter 1). An example of this linguistic and literacy knowledge and skill transfer is the use of cognates between English and their native languages.

As we learned in Chapter 1, second language proficiency for academic purposes takes longer time (i.e., 5–7 years) to acquire, especially for discipline-specific vocabulary and literacy skill development. We also have learned that if an ELL has developed the CALP in his or her native language, those literacy and cognitive skills can be transferred to English as long as the subject matter teacher encourages such a transfer. With increasing demands on disciplinary reading skills on the standardized tests across all subject matter areas, all subject matter teachers must be knowledgeable about language and literacy requirements in their disciplines. They must also familiarize themselves with ELLs' previous educational backgrounds and native language and literacy skills (see Chapters 3 and 4). In this chapter I discuss two major areas of ESL reading instruction for subject matter teachers to facilitate and help with ELLs' reading about subject matter in English. They are:

1. Modify the discipline-specific reading materials according to ELLs' language levels and needs; and
2. Teach reading skills and vocabulary before, during, and after reading.

MODIFY THE DISCIPLINE-SPECIFIC READING MATERIALS FOR ELLS

Given that ELLs come to U.S. schools at different times with varying levels of proficiencies in English, subject matter teachers should provide modification and simplification of the reading materials, notes, and directions used on the tests and in daily lessons. Research has suggested that reading modifications through simplification and language support tailored to ELLs' language levels provides those students with access to challenging reading and increase comprehensible input (Ellis, 1993; Krashen, 1981; Nation & Deweerdt, 2001, Noguchi, 1998; Porter, 2009; Schmitt & Carter, 2000). According to Nation (2001), if the reader has to consult a dictionary for a new word in every sentence, then the reading passage is too difficult for the reader, thus needing modification. "Good pedagogy involves helping learners reach their goals through suitable staged steps. In the beginning and intermediate stages of language learning, controlled texts are among the most suitable means of bringing the important strands of learning from meaning-focused input and fluency development" (p. 63). Jameson proposed five guidelines for modifying and simplifying reading texts for ELLs across subject matter classes (Table 7.1).

Subject matter teachers need to go through the assigned reading and re-organize, and even rewrite it for their ELLs first. Those modifications and simplifications can be done by subject matter teachers, or selected from various existing reading materials, or using online sources. Below are some examples:

Parallel Reading. Parallel reading is to provide ELLs with more than one version of a text under study by tailoring each version to a specific level of English proficiency (Samuel, 1995). Those versions can be adapted from juvenile literature, popular newspapers and magazines, trade books for low level students (as long as they are not infantilizing and have quality and accurate subject matter information) or can be re-written by the teacher. They can be a life-saver for differentiated instruction.

Many juvenile literature works and popular newspaper articles are good candidates for such a selection. Using this kind of extensive reading drawn from such a rich reservoir of language use and expressions over time, students will develop their vocabulary and language skills as well as their conceptual knowledge. Dif-

TABLE 7.1. Guidelines for Text Simplification

Guideline	Original Text	Simplified Version
1. Make a long sentence into several short sentences.	The various possible results of the experiment are outcomes, and the collection of all possible outcomes of an experiment is the sample space (S).	A probability experiment has many results. These results are called outcomes. The sample space is a collection of all the outcomes.
2. Change passive voice into active voice.	The number of outcomes in event E is denoted by n (E), and the number of outcomes in the sample space S is -*	We name the number of outcomes in event E, n (E). We name the number of outcomes in the sample space S, n (S)
3. Underline key points or words and define these points or words if necessary.	To calculate the probability of an event, you count the number of outcomes in the event and in the sample space.	To calculate the probability of an event, you count the number of *outcomes* (results) in the *event* (a specific result) and in the sample space (a collection of all the results).
4. Turn narratives into lists.	To calculate the probability of an event, you count the number of outcomes in the event and in the *sample space*. The number of outcomes in event E is denoted by n (E), and the number of outcomes in the sample space S is denoted by n (S).	To calculate the probability of an event: 1. Count the number of all the outcomes in the sample space. 2. Count the number of the specific events that you are interested in. 3. Divide the number of the specific events from the number of all the outcomes in the sample space.
5. Use charts and diagrams to illustrate relationships among key concepts and words.	The various possible results of the experiment are outcomes, and the collection of all possible outcomes of an experiment is the sample space (S). Finally, any sub-collection of a sample space is an event (E).	

ferent groups or individuals in class can be given different parallel texts to read and they can come as a group to establish as many parallels. New vocabulary terms will be explained in the passage and given a pronunciation aid. After reading one version of the text, students can be challenged to read a high-level text but of the same content, and be asked for comparisons between the texts to reinforce the understanding.

Subject matter teachers should keep in mind that the modification and simplification are not the end goals but rather the scaffolds to support the ELLs to work toward the end goal: being able to read the original text. Also, most ELLs have language handicaps in their initial stage of second language learning, but not cognitive handicaps by any means. Those scaffolds should be gradually removed as the students become more proficient in English. So, teachers should not stop at the modification and simplification, but rather develop a process with the aim of enabling ELLs to read the original text in the end. Beene (2017) discussed scaffolding guidelines for ELLs' social studies reading according to their English proficiency levels (Beene, 2017, p. 27):

> **Entering/Emerging ELLs:** Read the complex and detailed reading about the topic in their native languages first, then read a short and simplified version about the topic in English. Allow students to discuss with a partner in their native language and English.
>
> **Transitioning/Expending ELLs:** Read the modified reading about the topic in English, maintaining the key concepts and details of the original reading with vocabulary support. Require students to discuss the reading with a partner in a group using English.

Below are parallel reading examples in various disciplines:

Parallel Reading Examples in Biology

The Original Text

In all but a few small ecosystems, the autotrophs are plants and other photosynthetic organisms. They trap energy from sunlight and use it for the synthesis of sugars and starch. These substances can be changed to other organic compounds that are needed by the plant, or they can be broken down for energy. Heterotrophs can only use the chemical energy stored in organic compounds for their life processes. These organic nutrients must be obtained from the bodies of other organisms—either plants or animals. Because autotrophs are the only organisms in an ecosystem that can produce organic compounds (food) from inorganic compounds, they are called producers. Since heterotrophs must obtain nutrients from other organisms, they are called consumers.

Within an ecosystem, there is a pathway of energy flow that always begins with the producers. Energy stored in organic nutrients synthesized by the producers is transferred to consumers when the plants are eaten. Herbivores are the primary consumers, or first order consumers. The carnivores that feed on the plant-eating animals are secondary consumers, or second-order consumers. For example, mice feed on plants and are first-level consumers. The snake that eats the mice is a second-level consumer, while the hawk that eats the snake is a third-level consumer. Since many consumers have a varied diet, they may be second-, third-, or higher-level consumers, depending on their prey. Each of these feeding relationships forms a food chain, a series of organisms through which food energy is passed. Feeding relationships in an ecosystem are never just simple food chains. There are many types of organisms at each feeding level, and there are always many food chains in an ecosystem. These food chains are connected at different points, forming a food web.

— *From Schraer & Stoltze (1995, p. 828)*

Simplified Version

Living things depend on each other for energy. Most of the energy in an ecosystem comes from the sun. The energy moves from the sun to organisms within an ecosystem. There are two main groups of organisms in ecosystems: producers and consumers. Producers take in energy from the environment. The tree is a producer. Most producers take in energy from the sun. All of the other organisms in an ecosystem are consumers. Consumers, like the bird get energy from other organisms. Some consumers get energy by breaking down dead organisms and wastes. This type of consumers is called decomposers. For example, when the tree loses its leaves, they are broken down by decomposers, such as bacteria in the soil.

Energy flows from producers to consumers in an ecosystem. The path of energy between producers and consumers in an ecosystem is called a food chain. What might happen if a change in the environment killed the tree? An important food source would be lost. The flow of energy in that ecosystem would change. Many organisms would die without other sources of food.

There are many food chains in an ecosystem. These food chains are all connected to one another. In fact, the organisms in an ecosystem may be a part of more than one food chain. All food chains in an ecosystem taken together are called a food web. A food web is called a web because the many different paths of energy in an ecosystem are like a web of many food chains. The loss of the tree in the food chain will affect not only the organisms in that food chain but also the organisms in other food chains in the ecosystem. The loss of the tree will affect the whole food web. (from Pignatiello et al., 1998, p. 171.)

Modified Version Using Storytelling

There was an old lady who lived near a pond. She was scientist and enjoyed using a microscope. With her microscope she could see tiny things. One day she went to the pond and filled a jar with the water from the pond. She brought it back home and put a sample of it under the microscope. This is what she saw: algae converts sunlight to energy.

The next day she went back to the pond and found a fish. The fish ate the algae. She catches the fish and brings it home. Accidentally, she leaves a lid to the bucket off and her dog eats the fish. The dog choked on the fish and died in the yard. Flies and birds picked on his remains. The rest of the dog's body decomposed and became fertilizer for the plants in the back yard. The old lady was sad, but as a scientist, she understood all of this was part of the food chain. (Teacher-made reading)

Modified Version Using Poetry

In a wild forest a baby plant once said
"Mommy plant, when will be my turn to die?"
"When it's your time to die, there's no place to go
but this cycle of life you should know.

Of the beasts that eat meat,
You should not have fear, but beware

Of the plant-eating herbivores,
Such as cows, mice, horses, and deer.
We as autotrophs, can form our own good,
But to eat other animals we believe is quite wide.
These are the carnivores, eagles, and lions,
They sit on the top of this food chain
Without ever trying.

Even these animals have fear too
Because they die, return to the earth and
Become food for me and you. (Teacher-made poem)

Parallel Reading Examples in English Language Arts

Prologue of Shakespeare's *Romeo and Juliet*
Original Text:

Enter CHORUS.
Chor. Two households, both alike in dignity,
In fair Verona, where we lay our scene,
From ancient grudge break to new mutiny,
Where civil blood makes civil hands unclean.
From forth the fatal loins of these two foes
A pair of star-cross'd lovers take their life;
Whole misadventured piteous overthrows
Do with their death bury their parents' strife.
The fearful passage of their death-mark'd love,
And the continuance of their parents' rage,
Which, but their children's end, naught could remove,
Is now the two hours' traffic of our stage;
The which if you with patient ears attend,
What here shall miss, our toil shall strive to mend.

— From Durband (1985, p. 1)

Modified Version Using Storytelling

Once upon a time there lived in Verona two great families named Montagu and Capulet. They were both rich, but they were enemies. A Montagu wouldn't speak to a Capulet if s/he met one another in the street-nor a Capulet to a Montagu. If they did speak, they would say rude and bad things to each other. That often ended in a physical fight. Because of the bad blood between the two families, even the servants were often fighting with each other.

— From Nesbit (1997, pp. 105–106)

Modified Version Using Questions

What would happen if you fell in love with someone you knew your parents and friends would not approve? What would you do if the two people you trusted and counted most failed you in a crisis?

— Morris (1993, p. 76)

Modified Version Using Poetry

I have a story from another age,
A tale of resentment and bitter rage.
In fair Verona, where I set my scene,
Violent fights had become routine.
Two noble families were locked in this fight,
Hatred burned in their souls; they could never unite.
One was Capulet, the other Montage,
And neither household would change its view.
The bad blood runs deep in generations,
Even the servants were mean and fight in the street.

— From Burdett (1998 p. 5–6)

Guidelines for Designing Parallel Readings in Social Studies. Modified readings in social studies include textbooks, newspapers, and even primary source documents. Primary source documents give a real human touch and diverse views of the writer who records the history, thus those texts enliven the subject matter discussion and deepen students' learning and thinking about history (Avalos et al., 2007; Monte-Sano, 2011; Morgan & Rasinski, 2012; Price, 1998). Though primary source documents are commonly used in the social studies classroom, they are seldom examined for ELLs' reading difficulties. A primary source reading is especially challenging for ELLs because of the reader's unfamiliarity with the cultural and historic context of the text, the writer's background and intention, the use of complex and difficult vocabulary, and varied sentence structures. In addition, a variety of genres used as a primary source, such as letters, memoirs, legal documents, newspapers and magazines, political speeches, essays, cartoons, etc. challenge the reader to extend expository reading skills used for textbook reading to narrative reading and even argumentative reading. Therefore, social studies teachers must carefully select the primary source documents and modify them to provide comprehensible input for ELLs (Gewertz, 2012; Price, 1998). There are five criteria to use in primary source document selection for ELLs:

1. **Length:** Consider cutting down the length of the primary source document in order for the lower level ELLs to have sufficient time to do close reading. Often an excerpt of the original document is preferred.
2. **Vocabulary:** Simplify outdated or complex vocabulary in the text and provide a glossary on the site or embed those words in the text to facilitate ELLs' reading comprehension.
3. **Context:** Provide ELLs with relevant background knowledge and contextual clues about the reading first in order for the ELLs to have a general idea and

purpose going into the reading. Even the clothing, furniture, and landscape where the artifacts or political cartoons need to be introduced.

4. **Quality:** Examine the quality of the source and document. It can be the content quality and the source quality, referring to whether the text/handwriting is legible to read, the painting or cartoon is visually clear to view, or the audio is loud enough to hear. Preferably, if there is a written text along with an audio version of that source, then both should be accessed and used to enhance reading comprehension.

5. **Bias:** Consider the intended audience, purpose, and possible bias, including the bias from the author and the teacher in primary source document selections. ELLs often are unaware of the background information about the primary source documents, let alone possible bias issues. In addition, as many ELLs come from a country where the opinion given by the government or religious leaders or mass media is the only opinion and "right" opinion, social studies teachers should prepare students to read for biases in language structures, accents, and vocabulary choices used by the authors/artists from different sources besides the subject matter knowledge.

Parallel Reading About the Dropping of the Atomic Bombs
Original text:

In May 1942, only seven months after the Fermi experiment succeeded, President Roosevelt had set up the super-secret Manhattan Project to prepare to build a bomb. But it took another three years and a cost of $2 billion for the Manhattan Project to do the job...By the time the bomb was perfected, the Germans and Italians had already surrendered. Of the enemies now only Japan remained. On July 26, the Allied leaders gave the Japanese a solemn warning that "the alternative to surrender is prompt and utter destruction." Still they did not surrender.

Should the United States use the atomic bomb? No one knew how long Japan would hold out. Despite the terrifying fire raid of March 10, 1945, when more than 100,000 people died and much of Tokyo was destroyed, the Japanese militaries appeared determined to resist. If the war dragged on and Americans had to invade Japan, it might cost a million lives. The atomic bomb, President Truman knew, might kill many thousands of innocent Japanese. But life for life, the odds were that it would cost less.

— From Boorstin and Kelley (1989, pp. 589–590)

Modification Based on the News Report

Washington, Aug. 6—The White House and War Department announced today that an atomic bomb, possessing more power than 20,000 tons of TNT, a destructive force equal to the load of 2,000 B–29's and more than 2,000 times the blast power of what previously was the world's most devastating bomb, had been dropped on Japan.

— From (Shalett, 1945)

Modification Based on Truman's Radio Report

Having found the bomb, we have used it. We have used it against those who attacked us without warning at Pearl Harbor. We have used it in order to shorten the suffering of young Americans. We shall continue to use it until we completely destroy Japan's power to make war. Only a Japanese surrender will stop us.

— From Truman's radio report to the American people (1945)

Modification Based on John Hersey's *Hiroshima*

After the atomic bomb was dropped, Dr. Sasaki helped those who were nearest him first. He noticed soon that the corridor was crowded. Most people in the hospital had suffered dreadful burns. He realized then that casualties were pouring in from outdoors. There were so many that he began to pass up the lightly wounded to attend to the seriously wounded. All he hoped to do was to stop people from bleeding to death.

— From Hersey (1946, p. 106)

Other text modifications can be having the reading text translated into the ELLs' native language for the beginner ELL. Give multimedia adapted texts, such as the audio and movie versions of the text. Ask for help from the ESL and bilingual teachers in the schools. Often, those teachers have a rich collection of ESL appropriate and translated subject matter readings and modified readings done by themselves ready to use with ELLs. In addition, there are online resources for reading modifications. Below are a few online sources that provide level-specific and modified readings:

Online Sources for Modified Readings

Newsela provides several "levels" of the same newspaper articles, along with accompanying online quizzes, that students can read and take. For a small fee, teachers can create a virtual classroom, assign articles and monitor student progress. However, students can read the articles for free without having to pay anything.

News in Levels offers similar resources, but without the ability to track student progress online. The site is free.

For the Teachers has similar leveled articles available for download. It, too, is free.

Breaking News English

Text Compactor lets you paste text into it and then automatically shares different versions with fewer words. It seemed to work pretty well when I tried it.

Rewordify is like a super-sophisticated Text Compactor on steroids. You can read my previous post about it: "Rewordify" Is One Of The Most Unique Sites Out There For English Language Learners & Others.

Reader Laurie suggests *Embedded Reading*. which has these kinds of similar "leveled" texts in English, as well as in other languages.

I learned about *CommonLit* from the amazing educator Suzie Boss at her recent *Edutopia* post. It's a neat site that doesn't actually provide the "same" text written for different "levels." What it does do, however, is provide leveled readings—with prompts—on the same theme. It's pretty neat. (They've just added many new features—see "CommonLit" Now Lets Teachers Create Free Virtual Classrooms.)

Books That Grow has a library of texts that have each been edited to be made accessible to different reading levels. And it has some other unique features—teachers can create virtual classrooms to assign and/or monitor what students are reading and students can click on words that are new to them to see definitions and hear how they are pronounced. They are also planning on adding comprehension questions. The texts can be read on any device.

Kids Discover has several levels for social studies instruction—for a price that does not seem to be unreasonable.

Simplish. Automatically simplifies and/or summarizes text

ReadWorks. Now provides "same" texts at different level

Resources for Teachers has a number of the same articles written for different reading levels.

Scholastic has a small number of audio-supported same text at different levels (they also have a few more here). In addition, their *Storyworks* program has many more, though it costs about $8 per student to use.

Using Audio Books Along with the Reading Text. Research in second language learning has supported instruction that involves ELLs' multi-modalities and engages their listening, viewing, and reading skills all at once. Audio recorded books can expose the second language learner to the language modeled by native speakers, enhance their ability to make the sound and meaning connection in the new language, and immerse the student in a pure enjoyment through the audio impact which silent reading cannot achieve. Slow paced audio books adjusted to ESL students' language proficiency levels is an effective learning tool for ELLs. These books can also be used for whole class reading or listening activities. See below for a list of selected titles of audio books was compiled by Recorded Books.

The Adventure of Huckleberry Finn by Mark Twain (8 cassettes/11.75 hours)
The Adventure of Tom Sawyer by Mark Twain (5 cassettes/7 hours)
Animal Farm by George Orwell (3 cassettes/3.25 hours)
Anne Frank: The Diary of a Young Girl (6 cassettes/9 hours)
The Call of the Wild by Jack London (3 cassettes/4.5 hours)
The Chocolate War by Robert Comier (5 cassettes/6.5 hours)
The Contender by Robert Lipsyte (4 cassettes/5.25 hours)
Fahrenheit 451 by Ray Bradbury (4 cassettes/5.5 hours)
A Light in the Forest by Conrad Richter (3 cassettes/4 hours)
My Antonia by Willa Cather (6 cassettes/8.5 hours)

Number the Stars by Lois Lowry (3 cassettes/3.5 hours)
The Outsiders by S. E. Hinton (4 cassettes/5.5 hours)
The Pearl by John Steinbeck (2 cassettes/2.75 hours)
The Red Badge of Courage by Stephen Crane (3 cassettes/4.5 hours)
Shabanu: Daughter of the Wind by Suzanne Fisher Staples (5 cassettes/6.75 hours)
Summer of My German Soldier by Bette Greene (6 cassettes/7.75 hours)
Things Fall Apart by Chinua Achebe (5 cassettes/6.5 hours)
To Kill A Mockingbird by Harper Lee (9 cassettes/13.5 hours)
Where the Red Fern Grow by Wilson Rawls (6 cassettes/7.75 hours)

Recorded Books
2700 Skipjack Rd.
Prince Frederick, MD 20678
1-800-638-1304
(www.recordedbks.com)

Dual Language Reading. Dual language reading (texts written in both ELLs' native languages and English) is another effective way especially for beginning ELLs to make a transition from their native language to English and become engaged in the reading. Research has suggested that dual language reading materials (i.e., picture books, novels, trade books, poetry, nonfiction) were more effective for ELLs (Ballenger, 2008; Beeman & Urow, 2013; Freeman & Freeman, 2006; Garcia, Johnson, & Seltzer, 2017; Walker, Edwards, & Blacksell, 1996; Welie et al., 2017). They not only ease ELLs' difficulty in reading in English but also build a valuable bridge between home language and school language as well as enhancing metacognitive knowledge. It can be used creatively to help students compare two languages and two versions of the same content, leading to ELLs as a knowledgeable peer to offer insights about the text in their native language and what and how it is similar or different from the English version. The following is a sample of such reading materials:

Spanish/English

Bofill, F. (1998). *Jack and the beanstalk—Juan y los frijoles magicos*. San Francisco: Chronicle Books

Johnston, T. (1996). *My Mexico—Mexico mio*. New York, G. P. Putnam's Sons.

Lachtman, O. (1998). *Big enough—Bastante grande*. Houston, TC: Pinata Books.

Reisner, L. (1993). *Margaret and Margarita—Margarita y Margaret*. New York: Greenwillow Books.

Reisner, L. (1998). *Tortillas and lullabies—Tortillas y cancioncitas*. New York: Greenwillow Books.

Vietnamese/English

Trugen, T. (1987). *The little weaver of Thai-yen village—Co be tho-det lang thai-yen*. San Francisco: CA: Children's Book Press.

Chinese/English

Ching, E., et al., (1991). *Two bushels of grain: forget the turnips!* Cerritos, CA: Wonder Kids Publications.

Ching, E., et al., (1991). *The Blind man & the cripple Cerritos.* CA: Wonder Kids Publications.

Ching, E., et al., (1991). *Sun Valley: A stone carver's dream.* Cerritos, CA: Wonder Kids Publications.

Shepard, A. (2001). *Lady White snake: A tale from Chinese opera.* Pan Asian Publications (U.S. A.), Incorporated.

Zhao, Q. (1998). *Liang Shanbo and Zhu Ying Tai,* Beijing, China: New World Press.

Bengali/English

Attard, E. (2011). *Ali Baba and the Forty Thieves.* UK: Madeleine Lindley Ltd.

Curtis, C. (2008). I Took the Moon for a Walk. UK: Madeleine Lindley Ltd.

Maclaren, T. (2008). *Yum! Let's Eat!* UK: Madeleine Lindley Ltd.

PRE-READING VOCABULARY INSTRUCTION

According to second language learning research, vocabulary learning and reading comprehension go hand in hand. Often strong readers have a large size of academic vocabulary and developed a deep understanding of academic words besides a good understanding of subject matter knowledge. According to Nation (2006), on average, the reader needs to understand 98% of words in a text in order to achieve comprehension without help from the dictionary. In order to enable ELLs to catch up quickly with their English proficient peers in reading comprehension, subject matter teachers must include vocabulary instruction in their subject matter reading instruction, even with modified reading. Vocabulary instruction for reading comprehension is all about developing ELLs' understanding of word meanings and learning how the word is used and related to other words in the text. Armed with key vocabulary knowledge before going into the reading, ELLs are less distracted from and frustrated by constantly stopping at the sight of a new vocabulary and can focus on the main ideas in the reading.

What and How Many Words to Select to Teach? In secondary subject matter classes, there are three tiers of vocabulary for all students to learn (Laufer & Aviad-Levitzky, 2017; Moss, Lapp, & O'Shea., 2011; Nagy & Townsend, 2012; Snow, 2008):

Tier one vocabulary: the BICS level vocabulary (often English proficient students have mastered BICS by elementary or middle school. In reading personal and narrative texts, those words appear with a high frequency.

Tier two vocabulary: academic words used in the classroom discussions across disciplines and on the test, for example, compare, contrast, analyze, complex, specific, significance, principle, response, research, etc. Those words are used with a high frequency in the classroom and academic readings and they are different from Tier one vocabulary in that they are the hallmark of a becoming mature, intelligent, and literate person.

Tier three vocabulary: discipline-specific vocabulary appearing in a low frequency and limited to a specific discipline, such as Industrial Revolution in social studies, photosynthesis in science, kneading in family and consumer science, circumference in mathematics, dynamic warm-up in physical education, irony in English language arts, etc. Words in this tier are often abstract and complex, requiring intensive and focused learning.

Research has also shown the benefit of the teacher selecting fewer words (5–8 words in one reading) and doing an in-depth instruction of Tier two and Tier three vocabulary (Nagy & Townsend, 2012; Snow, 2008). Vocabulary selections can be both teacher-based and student involved. A pre-reading vocabulary questionnaire is effective to poll the class for their word knowledge on the incoming reading. It is useful for the teacher to give a list of words and ask each student to respond to:

- Words that I know
- Words that I don't know at all
- Words that I saw before, and I guess the meaning of this word is…

While selecting words to teach before reading, subject matter teachers should know that there are ESL, bilingual, and literacy teachers in the schools for them to ask for advice and gather resources. The rule of thumb in vocabulary instruction especially for ELLs is less is more. On the one hand, subject matter teachers do not want to overwhelm ELLs by requiring them to learn 20 words at one time; on the other hand, they should focus more on in-depth understanding and using the new vocabulary in order to gain a global understanding about the text that they read.

Multilingual Visual Glossary. Secondary ELLs' native languages will always have a strong influence on their learning English and subject matter knowledge (August et al., 2005; Cummins, 1979b; Dong, 2009, 2013–2014). Especially at the beginning and intermediate stages of second language learning, their native language is something that they can draw on to make sense of challenging academic reading. While reading in English, there is a natural tendency for ELLs to translate the unknown words into their native language in their heads, especially for beginning ELLs. Understanding and tapping into this prior knowledge will help subject matter teachers teach abstract and complex academic vocabulary and accelerate on ELLs' language learning in English. One strategy is to provide a multilingual visual glossary of the new words to give it to ELLs before the reading. As Cummins' Language Interdependence Theory argued (1979b), there is a shared foundation in academic language across languages (see Chapter 1). For Romance languages as Spanish, Portuguese, French, Italian, and Haitian Creole there are many cognates in academic vocabulary shared among those languages. Even for students who come from non-Romance language backgrounds, vocabulary gained in their previous education in their native languages can still be used when the connection is made and encouraged by the teacher (see Table 1 for samples of multilingual glossary in Chapter 5).

Infusing Vocabulary Support Into the Reading Materials and Instruction. In addition to the glossary, subject matter teachers can infuse native language translation and vocabulary modification into the reading material to provide language support. This way ELLs do not have to consult a dictionary so frequently to find the definition of the new words, thus reducing reading interruptions, saving time, and facilitating a global understanding of the text. Below is an example of biology reading on hibernation with language support (Dong, 2011):

Hibernation (Hibernacion)

In the fall, mammals (mamíferos), such as mice and squirrels, gather and store food. Woodchucks and skunks develop thick layers of fat. These adaptations (adaptacion), and others (otros), help many animals (animales) survive the cold winter months when food is scarce. Some birds and insects (insectos) migrate (emigran) from the forest to warmer climates (climas) where food is abundant (abundante). Small animals, such as snakes and chipmunks, spend the winter in burrows in a sleeplike state called hibernation (hibernación). During hibernation an animal's body temperature (temperatura) is lower and its heartbeat and breathing rates decrease. Hibernation allows an animal (animal) to survive the winter on very little energy (energía). In the spring the animal "wakes up."

— From Brockway, Gardener, & Howe (1985. p. 128)
and the parentheses were inserted by a science teacher

In a subject matter class with both English proficient students and ELLs, the teacher can prepare a glossary handout or infused reading passage like above and give it to the ELLs who need language support.

Providing ESL Friendly Word Definitions. ESL researchers have demonstrated that often the dictionary definitions for English proficient readers are not always helpful or even may do disservice if the subject matter teacher relies on giving out the dictionary definition as the only way to teach vocabulary (McKeown, 1993; Miller & Gilda, 1985). They are written for native English speakers, not for ELLs. As a result, ELLs find those definitions using new words to explain the new words. Also, many dictionary definitions include multiple meanings of the word using complex sentence structures creating a maze for ELLs to go through in order to find the most appropriate meaning. Therefore, using the "look it up in a dictionary" strategy does not work here in preparing ELLs for the reading. New language learners may only need a basic definition of the new word to get the relevant meaning across. Subject matter teachers can use ESL dictionaries, learner dictionaries, or teacher-made definitions to ensure comprehensible input (Manyak, 2007). Below is a list of varied definitions about photosynthesis comparing regular English and ESL dictionaries:

American Heritage Dictionary **Definition of Photosynthesis**
The process in green plants and certain other organisms by which carbohydrates are synthesized from carbon dioxide and a source of hydrogen (usually water), using light as an energy source. Most forms of photosynthesis release oxygen as a byproduct.

Oxford American English Dictionary **Definition of Photosynthesis**
The process by which green plants and some other organisms use sunlight to synthesize nutrients from carbon dioxide and water. Photosynthesis in plants generally involves the green pigment chlorophyll and generates oxygen as a by-product.

Merriam-Webster Learner Dictionary **Definition of Photosynthesis**
The process by which a green plant turns water and carbon dioxide into food when the plant is exposed to light.

Cambridge ESL Dictionary **Definition of Photosynthesis**
The process by which a plant uses the energy from the light of the sun to make its own food.

— Underlined sections were marked by a science teacher

Subject matter teachers can also make a definition game like the fill-in-the-blank, asking ELLs to participate in generating definitions following the teacher's guidance. In so doing, those students will be engaged in actively thinking about the words not just passively memorizing the word definition. Below is an example of such a student-generated definition with the teacher's language support before reading about photosynthesis. The italicized parts are for ELLs to fill with the words based on their understanding of the concept and reading:

Photosynthesis has two parts: Photo means *light*, synthesis means putting together. Plants make their own food *to eat* from *the sunlight and water*. This whole process is called *photosynthesis*.

— Modified definition produced by a biology teacher

Activating Prior Knowledge. Second language learners are not empty vessels when they come to the subject matter classroom; rather, they bring a collection of prior knowledge, including their native languages, subject matter knowledge, and literacy skills acquired in their native language back in their native countries (Dong, 1999a, 1999b, 2013–2014, 2017; Fisher, Frey, & Lapp, 2012; Marino, 2011; Salinas, Franquiz, & Reidel, 2008). Even for students with limited or interrupted schooling subject matter teachers can still tap into their life and cultural experiences and oral fluency to teach subject matter knowledge. Allow ELLs to use their native language with peers for a quick brainstorm to discover what they know about a topic before assigning the reading text. If the subject that cultural knowledge is a critical factor in learning, such as in social studies and English language arts, look for ways to activate ELLs' prior knowledge, including everyday experiences, and prepare them for academic reading (see Table 7.2).

TABLE 7.2. Logical Connector Use in Everyday English and Mathematics

Example	Function of Connectors	Equivalent Forms	Mathematical Meaning
If it stops raining, then I will go for a walk.	predicting a future action	If p, then q ($p \rightarrow q$)	p is true except when hypothesis p leads to a false conclusion q.
You can pass the test only if you study.	stating a fact	p if and only if q ($p \leftarrow > p$)	p and q are true only when p and q are both true *or* both false.
Sue likes golf and Lee likes swimming.	paralleling two statements giving cohesion	p and q ($p \wedge q$)	p and q are true only when both are true.
The school bus is late or my watch is fast.	giving choices and alternatives	p or q ($p \vee q$)	p or q is true when any one of the statement is true.

Pre-Reading Multimedia Tour or Picture Walk. Each time before handing out a new text for ELLs to read, subject matter teachers need to give a multimedia tour or a picture walk about key concepts and ideas discussed in the reading. This technique not only helps students connect to the reading using multiple senses but also stimulate interests in the reading (Beeman & Urow, 2010; Campbell & Cuba, 2015; Falk & Linder, 2009; Porter, 2009). Highlight the cover of the book, pictures and graphics, bold print, headings, glossaries, etc. Show students how to use those elements to preview the text and predict what the reading is about. Pre-reading an informational or expository text for ELLs requires subject matter teachers to direct students' attention to available tools presented in the text, including titles, headings, bold/italicized print, maps, graphs, visuals, captions, bullet lists, etc. as ELLs may not have exposure to and know how to use those elements to achieve reading comprehension. Students can also view media sources and the internet about the topic that they will be reading and discuss what they know and what they think will be covered individually or in pairs and groups.

Predicting and Questioning. Asking prediction questions before reading encourages active and purposeful reading (Caldron, 2007; Grant & Fisher, 2010). Keep in mind that ELLs may not bring the same kinds of background knowledge to a text as English proficient students, thus their predictions may sometimes be different or even contradictory to what the teacher has expected. Remember the goal of making pre-reading predictions is to develop active and purposeful reading skills and habits. ELLs' predictions should be encouraged and bridged into the lesson rather than being dismissed. Model and give ELLs' sentence starters to assist their predictions, such as, I predict... My guess is ... I think ...

The following predicting questions are about fiction reading:

- Sample reading prediction questions are:
  - Look at the title/picture/graphs/headings. Can you predict what this reading is all about?
  - What do you know about this topic?
  - What do you want to know about this topic?
  - What questions would you like to ask the author about this topic?
  - What do you think will happen in the reading?
  - Why do we read this text?

Pre-reading predictions and questions can also focus on the five Ws (what, who, when, where, and why) and one H (how). Remind students to draw on what they learned from the multimedia tour/picture walk in generating their questions and predictions. Also invite students to draw on their prior knowledge about the topic under study. The following are sample predicting questions about informational and expository texts:

- Based on the multimedia tour/picture walk, what do you predict about the main idea of the reading?
- Based on the multimedia tour/picture walk, how do you think the author will present this topic?
- Who do you think are involved in this research?
- When and where do you think the research took place?
- Are you familiar with this topic? If so, what do you know about it? If not, what do you want to know about this topic?
- Why is this topic important?

VOCABULARY AND READING
INSTRUCTION DURING THE READING

Academic reading at the secondary level often requires students to close read complex texts for the purpose of comprehending difficult concepts and demonstrate their understanding afterwards (August, McCardle, & Shanahan, 2014; Boyle, 2012–2013; Fisher & Frey, 2014; Freeman, 2015; Lapp et. al., 2013). There are five effective close reading strategies to be used during reading:

1. Making text notes;
2. Asking questions;
3. Using student questions to drive reading comprehension;
4. Predicting the word meaning from the context; and
5. Read-aloud combined with think-aloud.

Making Text Notes During Reading. Note-taking with ELLs begins with ELLs' circling or underlining the key words or new words in the text as they read along. Reading notes can be written on the margin of the text or put on post-it notes. For low level students in English proficiency, teachers can model, train

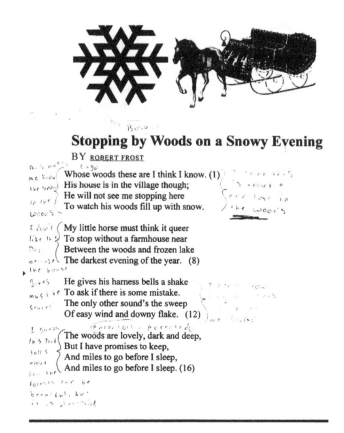

FIGURE 7.1. ELL-Note Taking on Reading Frost's Poem

students how to take notes. In order to take good notes, ELLs need to be trained and supported by sentence starters for language support, such as, "I don't understand..." or "I'm confused about ..." or "I agree with ...." Give sample notes so that students see what and how they should interact effectively with the text and articulate their thoughts during the reading (Blackwell & McLaughlin, 2005; Grant & Fisher, 2010; Tovani, 2000).

Unlike secondary English proficient students who have done note taking during reading in their early grades, ELLs need models and explicit teaching on how to take notes by connecting the text to personal experiences, other texts, or prior knowledge as well as noticing the confusions and unknowns during the reading. In doing so, it helps students become active and reflective readers. Phrases like, "This reminds me of..." "I can relate because..." are useful sentence starters for helping students to make connections. Figures 7.1 and 7.2 are two sample notes taken by ELLs:

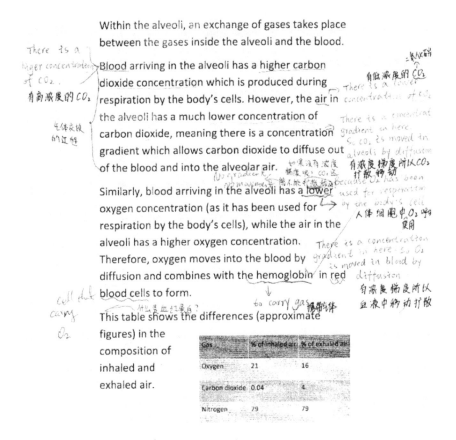

FIGURE 7.2. ELL Note-Taking on Gas Exchange

In above notes, two ELLs use what they learned and followed the teachers' modeling to take notes on gas exchanges and reading Frost's poem. In the gas exchange note, the student uses both Chinese and English to highlight the key concepts make connections, and asks questions, such as "What happens when there is no concentration? What is red blood protein?" This language switching is an important step for the beginning ELLs to take in order to think and write critically (Woodall, 2002). In the other notes, the ELL connects the poem to his life and uses those connections to make meaning about the poem.

Asking Questions During Reading. As mentioned in the beginning section of this chapter, good readers make predictions, ask questions, and use them to drive their reading, figure out the unknown, and develop their critical thinking and independent reading skills (Calderon, 2007; Dong, 2009; Grant & Fisher, 2010; Lems, Miller, & Soro, 2010; McKeown, Beck, & Worthy, 1993). Subject matter teachers need to show how to come up with questions first and then provide sample questions to model and train ELLs in questioning about the reading.

Christine, an English language arts teacher focuses on modeling and training her ELLs three types of questions during reading: questions about the text and the author, questions about connecting the text with the reader, and questions about connecting the text with the world around us. Here is a sample of the questions her class asked during their reading of "Sally" a chapter in Sandra Cisneros' *The House on Mango Street* (1991).

Questions about the text:
What does Sally look like?
What does the author mean when she describes Sally as having "eyes like Egypt"?
What relationship does Sally have with her parents?
What are the feelings that Sally has about staying in Mango Street?
How does the author feel about Sally?
How are the author and Sally similar or different?

Questions about the reader:
Do you think Sally is misunderstood by others? Why?
Do you know somebody who looks like Sally? Explain.
Would you be friends with Sally if she were in our class? Why or why not?
What advice would you give to Sally?
Do you often worry about what other people say about you? Why or why not?

Questions about the world around us:
Why did Sally's father say that her beauty is trouble?
Why does Sally's father keep her away from the outside world?
If Sally were a boy, do you think her father would treat her differently? Why or why not?
What does it mean to be a beautiful girl in your culture?
What does it mean to be a beautiful girl in American culture? (Dong, 2009, pp. 24–25)

Developing reading skills for ELLs takes time and involves training and language support. Subject matter teachers need to model the ways to show how they wrestle with the unknowns, confusions and ask questions during the reading. Following the teacher's modeling the students can then proceed to do the same with the reading. Below is a sample of close reading questions in biology based on the modified text made by the teacher:

Ecological Succession
Although ecosystems appear **stable** (calm), they do **undergo** (experience) change. Change **occurs** (takes place) because the living organisms *present* in the ecosystem **alter** (change) the environment. Some of the changes tend to make the environment more suitable for new types of organisms and less suitable for the existing organisms. Thus, the original organisms in an ecosystem are *slowly replaced* by other types. A new community **replaces** (does the job of) the original community

in the ecosystem. Over time, this community gradually replaced by still another community. The process by which an existing community is slowly replaced by another community is called ecological succession. In land environments, ecological succession usually **depends on** (decides) the types of plants that are present at any given time. Plants **determine** (decide) the type of community that develops because plants are producers. The types of animals that can **survive** (continue to live) in the community depend, directly or indirectly, on the types of plants.

> — *From Schraer & Stoltze (1995, p. 835)*
> *The parentheses and the boldface words were marked by a biology teacher.*

Student questions generated during the reading:

Why does a change occur in an ecosystem?

Is the change always good or bad?

Why do plants determine the types of community that develops?

What does "slowly/gradually replace" mean?

How can we replace "present" for another word?

Using Student Questions to Drive Reading Comprehension. Research has indicated that there is a positive relationship between the class talking about the text and students' reading comprehension (Dong, 2013–2014; Michener, Proctor, & Silverman, 2018; Wolfe, 2004). John, a science teacher, has established a question-seeking routine in his 6th grade general science class composed of all ELL students. John firmly believes that science learning begins with questions, and second language learners are capable of thinking about science as any other students. To John, despite that ELLs often lack the language power to express their intelligence they do not lack the thinking power, so they should not be treated like small children. Instead, they should be challenged as their English proficient peers are in science classrooms. According to John, there are no stupid or low-level questions, even a basic comprehension question can be used as a departure for inquiry to arrive at deeper reading comprehension. The process of generating questions and discussing them, according to John, is a valuable part of learning how to think about science. Here is an excerpt taken from the discussion on the relationship between the environment and human beings (Dong, 2006, p. 25).

Anna:	What are gnus? They talk about gnus on this page, but I don't know what they are.
Teacher:	Let me read the paragraph. (A few minutes were devoted to the reading.) You're right, Anna, it talks about the lions eating the gnus, but what are gnus? Me being the teacher, I have no clue! Well, does anyone know what a gnu is?
Maria:	Maybe it's a small animal.
Teacher:	How small?

Maria:	(showed about 5 inches in length)
David:	Maybe it's a lizard.
Anna:	Maybe it's in the picture on this page?
Teacher:	Maybe you are right, I don't know.
Cynthia:	Well, I think it's a big animal.
Teacher:	Why?
Cynthia:	Well, we read the passage, and it says that if these gnus were no longer living, then the lions would go hungry. Well, I know that lions are big animals and so I think they must eat big animals. I think the lions would starve if they didn't eat big animals because they provide more food.
Teacher:	I think you have a point. Did everyone understand?

As shown in the above example, using the meaning construction of gnus as the center for the discussion, John invites students to hypothesize and ponder their own answers and thoughts. In John's class, students are not only encouraged to ask questions but also to give rationales for their answers, thus developing a habit of active learning and thinking. Rather than giving a quick dictionary definition of the word "gnus," John is willing to entertain the ambiguity and uses it as a teaching moment to stimulate students' active thinking about the science and concepts behind the word. John's feedback is interesting, "Me being the teacher, I have no clue!" "Maybe you are right, I don't know." His responses issue an invitation for an open discussion and placing the teacher as one of the learners. In addition, acknowledging the student's question and echoing students' responses without an explicit evaluation placed the students' voice at the center of the discussion, thus sustaining the discussion. Furthermore, John gives time for the class to pose hypotheses and to think about their responses, read aloud the excerpt, and look at the pictures in the text, which all leads to high-level thinking responses.

Predicting the Word Meaning from the Context. Predicting the meaning of new words from the contextual clues in the text trains all student readers to develop reading fluency and vocabulary knowledge and gain deeper understanding and independent reading skills (Grant & Fisher, 2010; Nation, 2001). Fluent and efficient readers can let go of the dictionary but use contextual clues to read for meaning and global understanding. However, ELLs, especially at the beginning stage of second language learning tend to be too reliant on a dictionary alone. When students are heavily dependent on the dictionary, their reading fluency and comprehension can be disrupted and slowed. That results in not only a very slow reading pace but also losing concentration and sight of the main ideas of the text. That increases their affective filters and discourages their reading motivation if the text is long and filled with new words.

Researchers have offered helpful tips for second language learners to gain skills in predicting the word meaning from the context (Folse, 2004; Nation, 2008; Thornbury, 2002). A word of caution though, a successful prediction requires the text that has at least 90% of the words that students know already, about one new word every other line. If there are too many new words, then it's not feasible for guessing anymore. So, text selection and modification are critical first steps for the teacher to teach this reading skill. Also, the teacher needs to provide a context-rich reading text with a high frequency of occurrence of the new word and ample contextual clues for the reader to apply reading comprehension skills (Zahar, Cobb, & Spada, 2001).

Reading research in such expository texts as textbooks, research articles, newspaper articles, speeches, etc. has suggested that there are clear contextual clues to be taught systematically and regularly for the reader to use them to achieve meaning and promote vocabulary learning. To integrate Nation's (2008) suggestions and field-tested strategies, I summarize the following six key contextual clues. They are:

1. Example clues: the example within the sentence or between the sentences has already illustrated the word meaning in the text
2. Relationship clues, the clues can be inferred from the linking words, such as *but, however, and, so*, which give a clue to the relationship of the word to its context.
3. Restatement clues: The writer of the text includes a definition or synonym around the new word explaining the meaning of that word immediately, especially in textbooks.
4. Background knowledge clues: the reader is called on to draw his or her background knowledge, or real-life knowledge to associate with the new word.
5. Discourse level clues: the reader can deduce the meaning of the word from information that has been discussed thus far from the previous paragraphs.
6. Grammatical clues: using such grammatical knowledge as parts of speech, word formation, the location of the word, or punctuation

Read-Aloud Combined with Think-Aloud. Read-aloud is a reading technique often used in lower grades, which English proficient students follow the teacher's oral reading as a model to sound out words, paying attention to pronunciation, and gain good understanding of the reading. For ELLs who didn't grow up in this culture, they will benefit greatly from this technique. In addition, the read-aloud combined with think-aloud, as the teacher verbally expresses her thoughts during the read-aloud to make meaning of the text, offers ELLs additional insights into how the teacher works through the text to make meaning (Calderon, 2007; Grant & Fisher, 2010; Haynes & Zacarian, 2010; Lems et al., 2010).

In choosing the text for the read-aloud, care should be given to the text that is challenging enough but not too overwhelming for ELLs. It should not be too long. Pause at different points of the read-aloud to illustrate how to decipher the word meaning from the context, make connections between the reading and personal experiences and culture. During the read-aloud, students can have the text to follow along silently. Teachers can also assess students' understanding at different points of the read-aloud by asking for the student's understanding and perspectives on the topic at the same time. Afterwards, the teacher can ask the students to jot down effective reading strategies they just used and revisit those strategies taught for reading comprehension. Below illustrates such a discussion based on reading a mathematics word problem (Dong, 2016, p. 539):

Six people can be seated at a single dinner table. For the Thanksgiving dinner, Yi Fan's Mom places two tables end to end, so 10 people can be seated. How many tables must be placed end to end to seat 22 people?

Below is the conversation on how to read a word problem by Sue, an 8th grade mathematics teacher with her ELLs:

Sue read aloud the problem to the class (The problem is posted on the wall).

Amber:	End to end, what does it mean, Ms. A.?
Teacher:	Good question. Let me draw a picture for you (draws the picture on the board). This is an important point in the problem. "End to end" means the tables all line up in a row with each table touching another table (moves two desks to put them together). Do you understand how the tables are placed?
Amber:	Oh, I see.
Wanfang:	Ms. when you combine two tables, you are losing some seats.
Teacher:	Can you come and show to us? (Wanfang points at the picture to show how a connected table loses seats when both sides touch other tables.) Great point! So, tables 2, 3, 4, etc. can only seat how many people?
Amber:	Four people not six anymore.
Teacher:	Yes. But what about those end tables like this table and that one (points to those two end tables). How many people can sit at each of those end tables?
Oscar:	5 because only one side of that table is touching another table.
Teacher:	Excellent. Now on your notepad write down those important words/ phrases following the UNITE, the steps we just did. Make sure to follow this reading technique and write down your process clearly. I'm walking around to help you if needed. (After 15 minutes of writing) Ok, let's go over what we have come up. We now know what the question is and information needed to solve this problem. Can we set up our equation now?
Wanfang:	Mine is $4x+2=22$
Teacher:	Why is that?
Wanfang:	One side of my equation is 22 because that's the total number of people to be seated. And we know the middle tables can only seat 4 people. So, the total number of the tables should be $4x$. But two end tables can seat one more person each, so that is two more.
Teacher:	Excellent.

Following is the mathematics teacher's board work to illustrate the word problem reading technique, UNITE:

FIGURE 7.3.   UNITE: Word Problem Reading Instruction

READING AND VOCABULARY INSTRUCTION AFTER READING

Reading instruction does not stop at the closure of the reading. After ELLs have completed the reading and reading comprehension activities, subject matter teachers still need to build on what they have achieved through a series of post reading activities. Below are the three after reading instructional strategies:

1. Using graphic organizers
2. Teaching discipline discourse patterns
3. Teaching writing about the reading

Using Graphic Organizers. Graphic organizers, such as Venn Diagrams, word webs, character attribute charts, and concept maps, etc. are helpful in reducing the language demands, visually illustrating connections among abstract vocabulary concepts embedded in the reading (Calderon, 2010; Grant & Fisher, 2010; Lems et al., 2010; Oliver, 2009). A pictorial presentation of the relationships between concepts and information can deepen students' understanding of the reading material. Types of commonly used graphic organizers are:

Venn-Diagram. A Venn diagram has two adjacent circles intertwined with each other with an intersection in the middle. It presents similarities in the middle intersection and differences on the sides. It illustrates the comparisons and contrasts of the two concepts depicted in the reading. While students are reading, they can jot down the comparisons and contrasts in the circles. Alex, a social studies preservice teacher, tutors Rebecca, an 11th grade ELL who came from the Dominican Republic three years ago. Talking with Rebecca in both English and Spanish on several occasions, Alex found out that Rebecca was seriously behind in her social studies learning not only because of her limited English proficiency, but also her lack of knowledge of Western and American history and culture. Rebecca's school work was negatively impacted as her parents repeatedly pulled her out of the school to return to their home country for extensive periods throughout the school year. Because of all this, her social studies teacher mistook her for one of the newly arrived ELLs. The class was learning WWII, Rebecca knew very little about the Nazi Germany and was overwhelmed by the new material and vocabulary. However, she knew a lot about Rafael Trujillo, the Dominican dictator in WWII, from her previous schooling. Alex went online and studied Rafael Trujillo and decided to use Rafael Trujillo as both a way in and as an example to teach Rebecca about Hitler (Figure 7.4).

Armed with his Spanish skills and Google translation website, Alex translated key vocabulary and an excerpt of Hitler's autobiography into Spanish. In a series

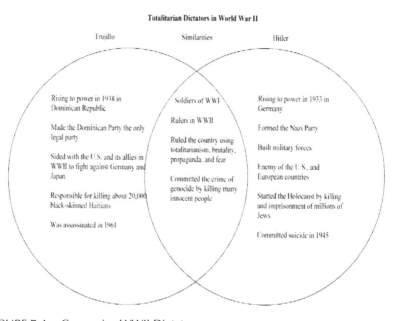

FIGURE 7.4. Comparing WWII Dictators

of tutorial lessons, Alex engaged Rebecca in discussing and reading about Rafael Trujillo, then Hitler, and finally comparing and contrasting the two dictators using newly learned social studies concepts in a Venn diagram (Dong, 2009, p. 32):

Concept Map. Concept map is a map to illustrate the relationships among the concepts (Bruna, Vann, & Escurdero, 2007; Dong, 2013; Novak & Gorwin, 1984; Oliver, 2009). It centers on one key concept and branches out to show the sub-concepts and inter-connected links between the concepts. Concept maps are effective in helping students organize and express abstract and complex ideas in the reading and develop their thinking skills. Jean, a biology preservice teacher, was tutoring three middle school ELLs from Ecuador. The lesson was on applying the concept of biomes to New York State. After consulting with the ESL teacher, Jean realized that her students may not be familiar with the geographic surroundings of New York State due to their new arrival status, however, they probably know about the biomes in Ecuador. Jean adjusted her lesson by asking her students to talk about the weather, temperature, plants, and animals in Ecuador first and then

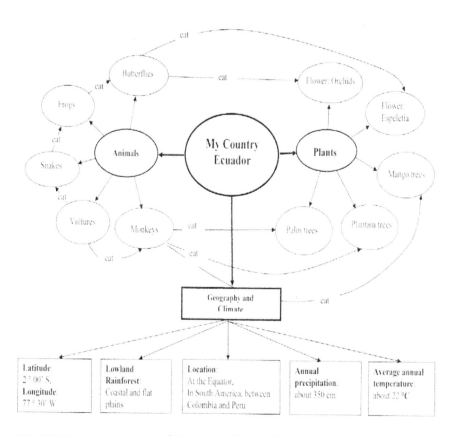

FIGURE 7.5.   Concept Map of Ecuadoran Biomes (Dong, 2013–2014)

compare all that with New York State. This guided inquiry during and after the reading is significant because Jean got her students to apply their prior knowledge to a new learning environment, and in doing so, students were able to achieve a new understanding (Dong, 2014, p. 56).

Disciplinary Discourse Patterns. Research on language use has revealed various discourse patterns in discipline-specific reading (Gee, 2008; Grant & Fisher, 2010). The general distinctive discourse pattern in academic reading is characterized by an organization of principle/concept definition→explanation→application. In addition, there is a unique discourse pattern in each discipline:

Discourse Patterns Used in Mathematical Texts. Even though some ELLs may be very proficient in mathematics and fluent with algorithm skills, they may not understand the concepts or the reasoning behind their calculations. At the secondary level reading, the mathematics text is interwoven between written English and symbolic mathematical language. If unfamiliar with this kind of mathematical reading, ELLs may not progress to the higher-level mathematics courses.

Barwell (2009) and Gerofsky (1996) discussed the three discourse components of a typical mathematical word problem: a set-up component, an information component, and a question component. Although sometimes these three components may collapse into one or two lengthy sentences, they are still observable. In component one, there is often a story line offering a simple plot and characters, aiming at activating the reader's appropriate background knowledge about the problem (Martineillo, 2008; Noguchi, 1998). Logical connectors, such as "if...then," "if and only if," or, "and," "either...or," used in mathematical texts are critical in understanding the reading for problem solving (Dong, 2013–2014, 2016; Esty, 1994; Hoffert, 2009). One way to use logical connectors during the reading is to use these learners' English grammatical knowledge to compare and contrast the use of these connectors between daily English and academic language (Table 7.3):

Discourse Patterns Used in Social Studies Texts. A typical social studies textbook reading has several language patterns to represent ideas using logical links. They are: illustration, sequence, comparison and contrast, cause and effect, and problem and solution (Dong, 2009, 2017). In order to follow the writer's train of thought and make meaning of the reading, a reader must be aware of these links and how the writer uses those links to organize the writing. Schleppegrell,

TABLE 7.3. Organizational Links Used in Academic Reading

Function	Organizational Links
Sequence	first, second, third, at the same time,
Cause/effect	because, consequently, therefore, thus, as a result, hence, resulting
Compare/contrast	than, by contrast, in comparison, however
Emphasis	in particular, specifically, in addition, moreover, furthermore,
Conditional	if...then, although, suppose

Achugar, and Oteiza (2004), and Schleppergrell and Oliviera (2006) took a linguistic view to examine the social studies textbook reading. They highlighted the social studies texts by the events (the writer's use of action verbs), participants (the writer's use of nouns), the relationship between the events and participants (the writer's use of tenses, voices, connotations, etc.), and points of views (the writer's use of adjectives, phrases, and modifiers). Social studies teacher should first survey the text for those language and discourse patterns and logical links before teaching it.

Discourse Patterns in Science Texts. Like other academic reading at the secondary level, secondary reading in science has taken a distinctive shift from personal and narrative reading to expository and even argumentative and research reading. Look at the following texts used in science learning (Gee, 2008, pp. 59–60):

> **Text 1.** Heliconius butterflies lay their eggs on Passiflora vines. In defense the vines seem to have evolved fake eggs that make it look to the butterflies as if eggs have already been laid on them (from a popular science magazine article).

> **Text 2.** Experiments show that Heliconius butterflies are less likely to oviposit on host plants that possess eggs or egglike structures. These egg mimic are an unambiguous example of a plant trait evolved in response to a host-restricted group of insect herbivores (from a scientific article).

> **Text 3.** The destruction of a land surface by the combined effects of abrasion and removal of weathered material by transporting agents is called erosion... The production of rock waste by mechanical processes and chemical changes is called weathering (from a science textbook).

According to Gee (2008), these three texts reflect unique scientific writing styles used for different purposes and audiences: scientists, nonscientists and general public, and students of science. The popular science magazine article (shown in Text 1) is easiest for student readers because of its reader friendly and familiar text structure similar to what students read in early grades, such as using a person or animal as a subject to engage the reader to think about the survival journey that butterflies go through.

In Text 2, the writer takes on a scientist's view by building evidence and making claims through the use of objective and impersonal structure, argumentative and research writing in discourse patterns. The subject of the sentence begins with "experiments" and throughout the short excerpt where the writer argues and proves logically with evidence to support the claim: "Heliconius butterflies are less likely to oviposit on host plants..." The writer uses those scientific words to argue the his or her point of view to convince fellow scientists and advance scientific knowledge.

Text 3 is distinctive in its use of the nominal sentence structure, and the sentence begins with a complex concept, "the destruction of a land surface..." The writer does not start his or her sentence with a person or a natural event, rather using an abstract noun and a complex sentence that is filled with the passive sentence structure and a series of Tier 2 and Tier 3 vocabulary. This style of writing is often used in the textbook writing, where the writer used the definition→ 📖 explanation→application discourse pattern to communicate with the reader in a dictionary-like writing style with one definition after another connected by the organizational links. See Table 7.3 for frequently used links in academic readings.

Writing About the Reading. For ELLs, after going through the pre-reading and during reading exercises, writing about reading is a natural progression for them to use the reading and language and subject matter knowledge learned in a purposeful way. Summarizing is frequently used in the subject matter classroom. It requires students to understand and consolidate what they just read and put the text into a short version to demonstrate their understanding (Calderon, 2007; Chauncey, 2011; Grant & Fisher, 2010; Haynes & Zacarian, 2010). In summary writing, students are asked to compose using their own words to highlight and organize the key ideas of the reading and important details. Writing a summary about the reading offers students another way of gaining a deeper understanding and mastering information discussed in the reading. A summary should always be shorter than the original text.

Below are the steps for subject matter teachers to teach how to write a summary:

- Read the text one more time to select main ideas.
- Write all the main ideas in sentences using students' own words.
- Group those sentences in a logical manner using appropriate organizational links students just learned.
- Read what is written this far and add sentences or words to make those main ideas clear and meaningful to the reader.
- Compare what they wrote with the text they just read. If they copied sentences from the original text, be sure to change them into students' own words.
- Check for spelling and grammar.

Also, as some ELLs come from a culture where copying or borrowing words even sentences without acknowledging the source is an acceptable learning behavior in their previous schooling, learning to write a summary using their own words is challenging. They may unknowingly commit plagiarism (Dong, 1999; Kostka & Maliborska, 2016; Lems et al., 2010). Therefore, subject matter teachers must teach the importance of American academic integrity and consequences of committing plagiarism while teaching how to summarize and how to paraphrase (Doolan & Fitzsimmons-Doolan, 2016; Shi, 2004). Below are the steps for subject matter teachers to teach how to paraphrase based on the reading:

- Read the text one more time to select main ideas and key details that support those main ideas.
- Change the main ideas and key details gathered from the text into their own words and sentences.
- Use a dictionary or a thesaurus to help with word selections, such as synonyms.
- Break down the long and complex sentence from the original text into two or three short sentences.
- Read the sentences over to make sure that they changed words and sentences but do not change the meaning of the original text.
- Organize their sentences into a logical manner using appropriate organizational links learned.
- Combine all the sentences into paragraphs and check for spelling and grammar.

CHAPTER 8

WRITING AND VOCABULARY INSTRUCTION FOR ELLS IN SUBJECT MATTER CLASSES

In comparison to other language skills writing is the most challenging skill for English proficient students to acquire, let alone ELLs. In secondary schools, learning to write requires students to go beyond writing for personal communications and expressions to demonstrate their critical thinking skills, understanding of subject matter knowledge and academic language. English proficient students who were born in the U.S. have marked stages in their development of writing skills through schooling from letter writing, to making letter and sound associations, to inventive spelling, to writing in phrases and sentences, to personal narratives, and to writing expository and argumentative essays.

STAGES IN ELLS' WRITING DEVELOPMENT IN ENGLISH

Different from English proficient students' writing development, ELLs who have obtained their native language and literacy skills often show a different English writing developmental process than their native English-speaking peers. Second language researchers have identified the stages that school-aged ELLs go through in their learning to write in English. Early researchers focused on the developmental stages of acquiring English grammatical structures (Brown, 1973; Krash-

Teaching English Language Learners in Secondary Subject Matter Classes, pages 159–186.
Copyright © 2019 by Information Age Publishing
159

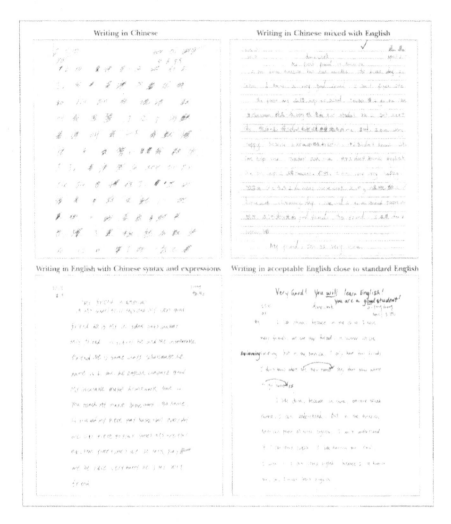

FIGURE 8.1. Developmental Stages of ELLs' Writing in English

en, 1982) and characteristics and sequence in ELLs' oral language acquisition in English. Recent studies have examined second language learners' acquisition sequence of writing skills using ELLs' writing samples. Figure 8.1 is an illustration of secondary ELLs' writing development in English (Freeman & Freeman, 2006; Fu, 1998, p. 8).

The writing sample in the upper left-hand box (Figure 8.1.) shows Stage 1 of a secondary ELL's learning to write in English. At this stage, ELLs write mostly in their native language because of their limited, if not zero, English proficiency. At this stage ELLs learn to spell their names, dates, and school in English first.

A close examination of their native language writing has shown clearly that the student has received writing instruction in their native language, Chinese. She is able to form not just words but also idiomatic phrases and appropriate sentences in writing in Chinese. In her effort to write in English, she uses the Chinese language and thinking skills to respond to the teacher's English writing assignment.

The writing sample in the upper right-hand box (Figure 8.1.) shows Stage 2 of ELLs' learning to write in English, and the ELL's writing has progressed to a mixture of both Chinese and English. Comparing to Stage 1, here the student's writing contains more English words, though still, there are no complete sentences in English yet. A close examination of those English words and Chinese words shows that the student's ability to produce words in English at the BICS level. Words related to the CALP are still mainly written in Chinese (i.e., key verbs and adjectives used to talk about the school). What is worth noticing is that compared to the writing in Stage 1, the student has made a marked improvement. The efforts to compose in English are clearly shown here.

The writing sample in the lower left-hand box (Figure 8.1.) shows ELLs' Stage 3 writing in English. Here the student's writing is mostly done in English with fewer Chinese words in comparison to Stage 2 writing. However, the student still follows the Chinese thinking patterns and as a result, her writing shows a clear native language impact, such as "he and me inseparable" "My incapable make homework time," resulted from a direct translation from Chinese. This translated writing in English is a necessary part of ELLs' second language development. For ELLs, thinking and writing in English does not happen overnight. It often takes a lot longer to develop those skills in English than the development of listening, speaking, and reading skills. The good news is that subject matter teachers can help speed up the process of thinking and writing in English by collaborating with ESL teachers and providing language support and opportunities for those students to write.

The writing sample in the lower right-hand box (Figure 8.1.) shows Stage 4 ESL writing. Here the student's writing not only is all in English but also has shown clear signs of thinking in English, demonstrated by the paragraph development, sentence structure, and increased vocabulary power. A jump in language and thinking from a beginning ELL to an intermediate ELL is shown in the sentences such as "I like China, because in China, I have many friends"; "I don't know where their homes are"; "I wish I can speak English, because I like America, too. So, I must learn English." Even though the student's writing is still very basic, lacking a lot of key ingredients of good writing, one thing for sure is that the student is progressing both in language and thinking in English. These four writing examples give us a glimpse of ELLs' development in writing skills in English.

ELLs often learn to write personal narratives in English first, although at the secondary level they must also learn to write expository and argumentative writing simultaneously due to the need to meet graduation standards in a limited amount of time. Secondary ELLs have to beat the clock and be prepared for the challenging writing demands required on the Regents exams, ranging from document-based writing to argumentative writing. Fortunately, many subject matter teachers have already included writing instruction in their lesson plans to prepare their students for such expository and argumentative writing.

Research has found many factors coming into play for ELLs to learn to write in English. As shown in Chapter 1, Kaplan's Contrastive Rhetoric Theory argues for a possible impact of culturally varied ways of thinking and organization on ELLs' writing in English. The impact is especially pronounced in expository writing where the students must learn to follow American academic writing norms and language and thinking patterns in order to compose good academic writing (Barkaoui, 2007; Lems et al., 2010; Parks & Maguire, 1999). In this kind of writing students are asked to demonstrate, interpret, analyze, and argue the ideas presented in the reading and knowledge learned in class. For many ELLs who did not have expository writing experiences in their previous schooling back in their native countries they must also learn American academic expository writing from scratch in order to be prepared for the challenging standardized tests and academic writing tasks.

RELATIONSHIP BETWEEN READING AND WRITING

Research has documented a close correlation between reading and writing, especially at the secondary level where writing is often based on reading (Cho & Brutt-Griffer, 2015; Hedgcock & Atkinson, 1993; Lee & Schllert, 2015; Shanahan, 1997). With significant overlaps between reading and writing skill development (Shanahan, 1997), researchers call for the teacher to teach the two skills together in order to use their time efficiently in an integrated manner to facilitate ELLs' development of the two skills. Many good writers are also critical and insightful readers; and good readers are strong writers because of their constant exposures to reading and writing and using the powerful sharing between the two skills to their advantage.

In secondary subject matter classes, students are often assigned to read closely and deeply first for main arguments, writing by using supporting details/evidence, discipline-specific language and discourse structures and vocabulary. The Common Core standards emphasize (Common Core State Standards Initiative (CCSSI, 2010) such an integration to use writing to improve students' reading and using reading of more than one text to improve the writing for analysis, synthesis, and evaluation purposes (Hochman & Wexler, 2017). A close reading and writing relationship is also reflected in integrated subject matter instruction. The integrated reading and writing instruction is beneficial for ELLs in particular as they learn two skills at the same time with a clear and meaningful purpose of reading and writing.

Teaching writing to the lower level ELLs must start from where students are, even if it means some ELLs have to learn to write the alphabet or spell their names in English. Fortunately, subject matter teachers do have ESL or bilingual teachers to help break down the reading and writing assignments tailored to the English proficiency level of their ELLs. Writing instruction at those levels often centers on vocabulary learning and personal writing. Personal writing taps into those students' prior knowledge and students write about familiar topics. Below are a few writing assignment ideas for the lower level ELLs.

- Teaching clustering and outlining
- Providing language support in writing
- Double entry journal
- Translation between the mathematical symbolic language and English
- Photo/picture/graphic writing
- Subject matter vocabulary storytelling

Teaching Clustering and Outlining. For beginning ELLs, writing a grammatically and meaningful sentence in English can be a challenging task. Bereiter and Scardamalia (1987) discussed the interplay of the two domains of knowledge in composing: content knowledge (what to say) and discourse knowledge (how to say it). For ELLs, even if they have something important to say about the topic, it often takes them a tremendous effort to find appropriate words in their native language first, search for equivalent words in English next, and then combine those English words into a sentence. At this level, the time involvement and language and cognitive demands are so high that students are often left with almost no higher order concerns for the content or organization but only care about writing down words and sentences in English. Therefore, writing activities such as clustering are especially beneficial for ELLs to learn to compose.

To cluster, students either work in groups or as a whole class or individually to associate the topic of the writing with all the relevant ideas and words they can come up with. This technique can go beyond brainstorming to asking students to put their ideas into phrases and sentences (First et al., 1995). The teacher should model a few sentences using these ideas so that students can see how the words are put into sentences. Once the ideas are generated in phrases or sentences, students then work on organizing them into an outline and then sentences and a paragraph. Below is a sample of such a technique in action where an English teacher works with an ELL to compose a poem on "The Sacred" after reading Dunn's poem (1989).

The Sacred
By Stephen Dunn

After the teacher asked if anyone had
    a sacred place
and the students fidgeted and shrank
in their chairs, the most serious of them all
    said it was his car,
being in it alone, his tape deck playing
things he'd chosen, and others knew the truth
    had been spoken
and began speaking about their rooms,
their hiding places, but the car kept coming up,
    the car in motion,

music filling it, and sometimes one other person
who understood the bright altar of the dashboard
     and how far away
a car could take him from the need
to speak, or to answer, the key
     in having a key
and putting it in, and going.

ELL's Composing of His Sacred Place:
Step One: Clustering

My sacred place: my bed.

SEE:	TOUCH:
White walls	Knob on the radio
Blue blanket	
TV-MTV	
Dirty clothes under the bed	
Soccer ball	
TASTE:	**ACTION WORDS**
Coke	Relaxing in the bed
Chocolate chip cookies	Listening to music
HEAR:	
Spanish music	
Ekimosis	

Step Two: Composing
My Sacred Place

My bedroom is where I go to be alone.
The walls are white.
My blanket is blue.
Sitting on my desk is my T.V.
Under my bed are some dirty clothes.
Next to my bed rests a lonely soccer ball.
I am standing by my radio turning the knob.
     When I hear Spanish music.
My favorite band is called Ekimosis.

— by Felipe Espitia (a 7th grade ELL)

Providing Language Support. Many English proficient student writers often have a hard time just getting started. This is even more so for ELLs who are still learning the language. The way to conquer this writer's block is to provide ELLs with both vocabulary and sentence starters and sentence frames to scaffold their writing (Ferlazzo & Hull-Sypnieski, 2014; Freeman & Freeman, 2009; Grant & Fisher, 2010). Sentence starters are words and phrases used in the beginning part of the writing. Sentence frames are phrases used in the beginning, middle, or concluding part of the writing. Often sentence frames contain logical connectors or organizational links to guide and organize students' writing and mold it according to the norms of American academic writing. For ELLs those language scaffolds are especially helpful as they not only make the writing easier to start or continue but also enable them to organize their thoughts and follow discipline-specific and genre-specific writing patterns.

Below are illustrations of language support and postcard writing by using the support.

Sample sentence starters are:
This essay discusses…
The argument on …
My data show that…
Different views on this topic are …
The evidence suggests that…

Sample sentence frames are:
Although the scientists have explored…, still …
In comparison to … I conclude that …
First… second… finally…
In contrast to … the data has agreed that
The views on … range from … to …
The chief reason for …was…

ELLs' sample writing using language support based on the subject matter vocabulary and reading instruction is as follows:

Postcard Writing About Integers

Dear Aunt,

Last week in our math class we learned about whole numbers above and below zero. We can add, subtract, multiply, but not always divide integers to get another integer.

These numbers can be found on a number line (see the picture on the left). Two main types or categories of integers are positive and negative integers.

The most useful way of using integers is when we read a thermometer!

Your niece,

Yolanda—by Yolanda, a 6th grader

Postcard Writing About the Starry Night by Van Gogh

Dear Friend:

Today we went to the MoMA. We saw the painting, *Starry Night*. It's a landscape painting of the French countryside and painted by Vincent Van Gogh. I never knew about him, but I now know and like his painting.

We just learned some new words, like texture, lines, and color in our art class. The teacher asked us to describe the painting using those terms. The *Starry Night* has a lot of bright colors, such as yellow and blue. It has many swirling lines to show the storm. It is surprisingly small. The museum was very crowded and everyone was taking selfies.

Your friend,

Kevin (a 9th grade ELL)

Mimic Writing. To train ELLs to use varied vocabulary and language structure, subject matter teachers can also use mimic writing where ELLs are given sentence frames to fill and models to compose based on the reading as a model. After the reading, the teacher can design a writing assignment that requires ELLs to fill in the blanks of the original reading for creative and critical writing. Below are examples of ELLs' mimic writing after reading poem "Harlem" by Langston Hughes (1951):

Harlem
By Langston Hughes

What happens to a dream deferred?
    Does it dry up
    like a raisin in the sun?
    Or fester like a sore—
    And then run?
    Does it stink like rotten meat?
    Or crust and sugar over—
    like a syrupy sweet?

    Maybe it just sags
    like a heavy load.

    Or does it explode?

Following learning Hughes' poem and based on his model, the teacher gives her students the following fill-ins to compose their dream poems in groups:

What happens to a dream _____?
    Does it _____
    like _____?
    Does it _____
    like _____?

Below are two group poems composed by ELLs:"

What happens to a dream *lost*?
    Does it *fade*
    like *a shadow*?
    Does it *sink*
    like *a boat*?

— By a group of 9th grade ELLs

What happens to a dream *come true*?
Does it *blossom*
like *a flower*?
Or does it *fly*
like *angels' wings*?

— By a group of 9ᵗʰ grade ELLs

Exit Slip. An exit slip is commonly used in the subject matter classroom where the teacher asks students to write a quick response to a series of questions based on the lesson at the end of class. It asks students to reflect on what they have learned and report on any questions and confusions about the topic. It is an informal measure to assess how well students have grasped the lesson and pinpoint the confusions and difficulties for further instruction (Baron, 2016; Leigh, 2012). For ELLs, exit slips have an added benefit of practicing writing skills and using key vocabulary to express what they have learned and what they do not know in a timely and manageable manner (Andrews, 1997). With different language levels, subject matter teachers can provide language support to facilitate ELLs' writing. Below are sample sentence starters for lower level ELLs:

I learned in class today…
What I like most about today's lesson is…
I still don't understand…
I would like to learn more about…
Please explain more about…

Below are two samples of ELLs' exit slip writing about dilation in mathematics:

Today in class we learned about dilation. It means a shape changes size and can become either bigger or smaller size of the original shape. For example, we can enlarge a triangle to make it bigger or shrink a triangle to make it smaller. But they are still triangles in shape.

— by Felipe, a 10ᵗʰ grade ELL

In class today I translated the word "dilation" into my native language: Chinese. I found that we have two words for dilation in Chinese: One is扩张 (enlarge) and the other缩小. I know I learned this back in China. My question: Is dilation the only word in English to express both enlarging and shrinking of a shape? Why?

— By John, a 9ᵗʰ grade ELL

Double Entry Journal. Double entry journals are journals written on a loose-leaf paper divided into two columns: one column is about key concepts or excerpts taken from the reading and the other is about the student's understanding of the reading (Beeman & Urow, 2013; Tovani, 2000). Double entry journals offer the teacher an opportunity to gain insights into students' working through the reading for the teacher to identify the reader' strengths and weaknesses and for the teacher to further scaffold according to their ELLs' levels. For beginning ELLs, who tend to have trouble beginning their journals, some sentence starters should be modeled and given as a handout, such as, "This is how to…" or "The problem/question I am having with this is…" or "I can relate to … because…" Table 8.1 is an example of such a journal entry used in mathematics.

TABLE 8.1. Double Entry Journal About Mathematics Problem Solving

Mathematics Operation	Journal Writing
$5x^2 \cdot 2x^3 = (5 \cdot 2)(x^2 \cdot x^3)$ $= 10\ (x^2 \cdot x^3)$ $= 10\ (x^{2+3})$ $= 10\ x^5$	My thinking process: Since x to the second power and x to the third power are like terms, I first grouped them together $(x^2 \cdot x^3)$. Then I multiplied the numbers $(5x^2)$ and got 10. Afterwards, using the power law of exponents, I added the exponents of the x (2+3) and got 5. My final answer to the question is ten x to the fifth power. My question: What happens when the exponent is negative?

Translation Between Symbolic Language and English. Even though many ELLs may have strong subject matter knowledge foundation, say mathematics, they may still have difficulty in expressing their mathematical intelligence in English. Often times these ELLs are good at using symbolic language in mathematics or science to do calculations or manipulations of formulas and numbers; however, they are lost in translating those symbols into English or reading the word problem that often is composed in English. Without explicit reading and writing instruction and frequent language support and modeling from the teacher, the student's written skills in English may not happen automatically and quickly. One way to get even beginning ELLs to write is to translate the symbolic language to English and vice versa (DiGisi & Fleming, 2005; Dong, 2013, 2016).

TABLE 8.2. Double Entry Journal About Poetry Reading

ELA Poem Reading by Tupac Shakur (2009), MTV Books. P 3.	Journal Writing
Did you hear about the rose that grew From a crack in the concrete? Proving nature's law is wrong It learned to walk without having feet. Funny it seems, but by keeping its dreams, It learned to breathe fresh air. Long live the rose that grew from concrete When no one else ever cared.	This poem speaks to me. It's about adversity (the word I just learned). The rose grew underneath the concrete says to me that life is hard even for the beautiful rose. My coming to the U.S. is hard because I had to learn English, make new friends, and get good grades. My mom told me not to give up. I have a dream to be a doctor when I grow up. Even though my life has adversity, I won't give up. Like the rose fighting to grow from a crack in the concrete, I won't stop reaching my dream. My questions to the poet is: I want to ask the poet what he means by "proving nature's law is wrong"? What can we do make the world a better place for roses to grow?

TABLE 8.3. Translation Between Mathematical Symbolic Language and English

Mathematical Symbolic Language	English Translation
$\angle\,ABC + \angle\,DBC = 90°$	Angle ABC plus angle DBC equals ninety degrees.
$l \parallel m$	Line l is parallel to line m.
A (-2, 2)	The coordinate of point A is negative 2 positive 2.
$_4P_4 = 4!$	The permutation of four objects taken 4 at a time is 4 factorial.
$0° \le x \le 180°$	x is greater than or equal to zero degree and less than or equal to 180 degrees.

For example, mathematics teachers can ask the class to translate algebraic expressions from symbolic language into English, and vice versa, e.g., $3/x-2$ is translated into the quotient of 3 and an unknown number decreased by 2. Translation exercises like this will engage students in thinking mathematics in English. Language reflects and expresses mathematical thinking and sometimes those nuanced differences in translations can make a big difference in thinking. For example, "the difference between 3 and 9" is not $3 - 9$ but $9 - 3$; "x times (pause) $2x$ minus 1" is not the same as "x times $2x$ minus 1." As ELLs become more proficient in English, they should write their own algebraic expressions in English and pay close attention to the sentence structure as well as pronunciation rules, preposition usages, etc. The translation exercise will pay dividends in the long run. When students read word problems on standardized tests, they will have a heightened awareness of language use while thinking and doing mathematics (see Table 8.3).

Photo/Picture/Graphic Writings. A photo/picture/graphic essay is descriptive writing based on one or a series of photographs, pictures, graphics about a theme or concept (Dong, 2011; Zenkov et al., 2012). Many themes and concepts taught in the subject matter class, such as migration and acculturation, war and peace, age and family, ecology, men and women, individual and society, etc. can be illustrated and annotated through writing. The visual imagery gets second language learners to view and read for meaning first and eases their anxiety about writing an "essay." It also strengthens their conceptual understanding, expands their language abilities and creates the enjoyment of writing in English. Figure 8.2 shows an example of a visual poem about ecosystem created by ELLs.

Vocabulary Story About Subject Matter Concepts. Because secondary ELLs develop vocabulary knowledge alongside of their reading and writing skills, subject matter teachers should build a vocabulary component into writing instruction on a regular basis. Research has indicated that an integrated approach between vocabulary and writing instruction makes subject matter learning more meaningful and enables ELLs to compose more interesting writing with the words they just learned (Beeman & Urow, 2013; Kirsch, 2016; Tajer, Syal, & Marzban, 2017). Below are two examples of vocabulary stories about the concepts of inflammatory response and fermentation.

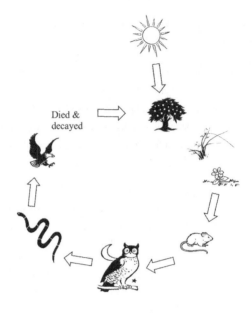

In a wild world the tree says to the sun,
"Thank you for giving me food and energy, and
Making green grass and a world so pretty."
The mouse underneath the tree thanks the tree
For giving him nuts and a nice playing ground.
The owl thanks the mouse for becoming her food
So that she can be powerful and see far and good.
The snake says, "Wait a minute, I have to thank the owl
For my feast. Otherwise, I will be starved to death."
The eagle flies in and he cannot wait for snake at once.
"Then, what happens to you?" Everyone asks the eagle.
The tree claps his hands and says
"When he dies he will be all mine."
By a group of 10th grade ELLs

FIGURE 8.2.   Visual Poem of Ecosystem

Biology Writing Assignment:

Write a story based on the scientific concept of inflammatory response and its three symptoms and underline the key words and phrases.

Last weekend when I was riding my bike, I hit a curb and went flying off my bike onto the concrete. I cut my arm pretty badly. Dirt got into my body and *bacteria* too.

My body's *inflammatory response* took over. All of my *blood flow caused my skin to be red, and hot and swollen.* My arm was also very *painful*, and I couldn't move my arm very well. My mom took me to the nearby Urgent Care clinic and doctor cleaned my wound and bandaged it. Now my arm feels much better. It isn't *swollen, red, or painful* anymore. I just have a really cool scar to show my friends!

— By Tom, a 10 grade ELL

Family and Consumer Science Writing Assignment:
Based on what you learned in class today write a story about the concept and process of fermentation process

Fermentation is cool. Bread and cheese and yogurt we eat all go through the *fermentation process* to make them so tasty and good. *Fermentation* is like when I wake up in the morning, I take a shower to *wake up (activate)* my body. I eat breakfast (like *yeast*) to give my body fuel in order to have energy for the day. When my body is fueled (*like yeast is activated*), it *produces CO_2* and I have energy throughout the day and grow taller and stronger!

— By Maria, an 8th grade ELL

Using ELLs' Background Knowledge to Design Writing Assignments. Subject matter readings and writing assignments often are set in ELLs' unfamiliar settings to require students to use American mainstream cultural knowledge to read and write (Dong, 2016; Wilburne, Marinak, & Strickland, 2011). In mathematics word problems, for example, students often encounter the problem of calculating a flat rate for babysitting, comparing different prices during the Thanksgiving sales, i.e., the discounted price, list price, regular price, sale price, and original price, investment account, federal taxes, etc. One way to tackle those cultural barriers is to set the word problem in a culturally familiar setting for ELLs composed by the teacher (see Chapter 5 for such an example). ELLs can even be asked to compose their own word problems and then solving them (Dong, 2016; Hebert & Powell, 2016). In doing so, ELLs use English to think mathematically. Two ELLs' generated math word problems are as follows:

Problem 1:
I eat fried rice back home in Thailand every day. It is different from Chinese fried rice because it is prepared with special Thai Jasmine rice. It has meat, egg, onions, garlic, and other vegetables. The rate of currency for Thailand is 1 U.S. dollar=30 Baht. Fried rice costs 360 Baht/bowl. How much is fried rice/bowl in U.S. dollars?

Solution:
1 dollar/30 Baht=x dollar/360 Baht
30 Baht • x dollar =360 Baht
x = 12 dollars (Dong, 2016, p. 537)

Problem 2:
Kimchi is a traditional Korean dish and considered Korea's national dish. My grandmother cooks great Kimchi. She prepares it using Napa cabbage, radish, scallion, red pepper, and many seasonings. It is my favorite dish! The rate of currency for Korean won is $1=1112 won. Kimchi costs 11120 won. How much do the Kimchi cost in U.S. dollars?

Solution:
1 dollar/1112 won=x dollar/11120 won
11120 won=1112 won • x dollar
x=10 dollars (Dong, 2014, p. 35)

READING AND WRITING INSTRUCTION
FOR MIDDLE AND HIGH-LEVEL ELLS

With exceptions, most ELLs at the intermediate and advanced levels of English (transitioning and expanding levels) have acquired the BICS level oral fluency in English. However, their CALP level written English still lags behind because the CALP takes more time to learn and master. At those levels of English proficiency writing, some of the reading and writing assignments in subject matter should increase cognitive challenge and textual difficulty and vocabulary power in addition to necessary scaffolds. These scaffolding strategies are:

- Subject matter learning journal
- Reader response
- Perspective writing
- Comparative writing
- Source-based writing
- Argumentative writing

Subject Matter Learning Journals. Subject matter learning journals have been frequently used by science teachers to make the lesson relevant to students' lives and to build students' habit of writing about what they learned and read (Beeman & Urow, 2013; Collins & Fulton, 2017; Lindquist & Loynachan, 2016; Urquhart, 2009). Journal writing about subject matter can train students' language and thinking skills and provide them with opportunities to use CALP, including not only vocabulary but also sentence and discourse structures. For example, a journal entry that requires students to use a conditional structure of "What if…" or "If I were…" exposes students to more complex language structure to express subject matter knowledge. Also, prompts like "Here and Now" and "There and Then" get students to practice specific language structures, such as the use of the past tense while thinking about a biological issue or historical event in a different time frame. Below is an excerpt from a 9th grade ELL's month-long journal on her observations of a tree in her yard.

> Today I realized how much it takes to really understand a tree. I have been observing this tree for a while. Before, I often thought it was silly for me to eyeball a tree every day. It seems to me it won't take a couple of minutes before I get everything down about the tree in my yard. As it turns out, it is not that simple once the teacher has given us guidelines for observations. For example, I have to use my math knowledge and skills to measure the height and the circumference of the tree. A closer examination of the tree trunk, I see damages made by insects or animals. Who are they? Where do they live? The tree leaves are interesting too. Some leaves are in fine green color and a good round shape, but others are obviously eaten by insects or birds, still others turned yellow already. What happened? Why? I have seen squirrels on the tree. As it becomes warmer and warmer, I believe there will be more animals visiting this tree. I need to keep a record of these visitors. Also, factors such as the soil,

humidity, rainfall, etc. have to make some impact on the tree also. My tree in the yard is no longer an ordinary tree anymore. Now I look forward to all the discoveries I will make to learn about it.

— By Sean, a 9th grade ELL

Table 8.4 is an 11th grade ELL's chemistry journal based on his survey and data analysis. Connecting what ELLs have learned in the classroom to real life, a subject matter journal engages them in exploring the use and meaning of the new concept.

Another example, after learning the concept of parabolas, a mathematics teacher asks students to collect everyday examples where parabolas are found in their lives and write about them. Below is an ELL's journal:

In everyday life, we can see parabolas almost everywhere. In the beginning I thought there was not going to be any parabolas. But I was wrong. I found many and even took a picture of each. For example, the inner surface of a flashlight is in the shape of parabola. On the internet it says that the parabola shape makes the light source focused, and we can see a focused beam of light. Every day I ride the school bus passing the Whitestone Bridge in the shape of parabolic curve. My question is: is the suspension bridge in this shape stronger than other bridges and why?

— A 10th grade ELL

TABLE 8.4.   Chemistry Journal

Use examples in your daily life and discuss and explain the connection between how a substance tastes and the pH scale. What do they have in common? How are those two ways (taste and scale) of finding acidity different?

My survey findings were:

Taste	Orange	Vinegar	Baking Soda	Turn Tablet
	Sour	Very Sour	Bitter	Very Bitter
Acid or base	Acid and sugar	Acid	Base	base
pH or base prediction	3	5	8	14
Actual pH scale	2	3	8	10

My family uses a lot of limes in cooking. It is very sour so I think it has pH scale of at least 5. I like to drink Spanish soda called Fanta. It's not that sour but sweet. Based on the scale, I predict its pH is 4.

I did a Google search to find actual pH levels for limes and soda. I found that the limes' pH is 2 and soda is 4. I guessed right for the soda but not limes. Now I know my taste. I wonder how the pH levels were determined. When deciding the pH scale, do scientists take into account of people's different tastes?

—by Larry, an 11th grade ELL

If the earth were only
A few feet in diameter, floating a
Few feet above a field somewhere, people
Would come from everywhere to marvel at it.
People would walk around it, marveling at its big
Pools of water, its little pools and the water flowing
Between the pools. People would marvel at the bumps
On it, and the holes in it, and they would marvel at the
Very thin layer of gas surrounding it and the water suspend
Ed in the gas. The people would marvel at all the creatures
Walking around the surface of the ball, and at the creature in
The water. The people would declare it precious because it
Was the only one, and they would protect it so that it would
Not be hurt. The ball would be the greatest wonder known
And people would come to behold it, to be healed, to
Gain knowledge, to know beauty and to wonder how it
It could be. People would love it, and defend it with
Their lives, because they would somehow know
That their lives, their own roundness, could
Be nothing without it. If the earth
Were only a few feet in
diameter

What does this poem remind you of?
Do you agree with the author? Why? Or Why not?
How can we save our planet?

FIGURE 8.4.   Reader Response to the Earth Poem

Reader Response. A reader response approach has been taken by many English language arts teachers to teach literature reading comprehension, interpretation, and appreciation. It is based on Rosenblatt's (1978) theory that when a reader interacts with the reading using his or her experience, the comprehension and motivation for reading increase. There is a special need for ELLs to experience the wonder for discoveries and expressions by using non-traditional reading and writing approaches like the reader response (Dhurandhar, 2009; Leung, 2003; Philippakos, 2017). The following is a poem written by Joe Miller (1998) that can be used to engage students visually as well as aesthetically while conversing about issues that we all care about.

Student reader response to the reading *If the Earth Were Only a Few Feet in Diameter* (Miller, 1998, Figure 8.4):

> I agree with the author. When the earth is small, everybody takes care of it. When it is huge, nobody can take care of it. Since the earth is so big, people cannot see that we are destroying the earth by killing lots of living things in order to survive. I think the earth is a beautiful place full of wonders. Its nature, animals, plants, and people are all special, and most of all it is the only planet that has water and oxygen. For future generations, I just want to say, people should take care of this earth. We should not care about ourselves only. We should take care of the animals, plants, and environment because if we lose them, we lose the earth and we lose our own lives.
>
> — *By Sam, a 9th grade Bangladeshi ELL*

Non-textbook readings in mathematics, such as newspaper, biography, or even folktales, often provoke students' thinking and crystallize concepts that they have just learned and bring out social, cultural, and human aspect of subject matter learning. Writing about the reading like this makes subject matter learning a fun and engaging activity. The following is an example of reader response writing by an ELL after reading *A Grain of Rice* by Pittman (1986):

> I first learned about this story in Chinese, back in China before coming over here. I was so glad to read the English version of the story here in the U.S. I admire Pong Lo, the young farmer, for his knowledge and determination. He outwitted the emperor and won over his daughter using his brain. Before I like to think that the high level of mathematics such as exponential function had no use in real life. The story makes me think again. The only thing that I don't like was the pictures. People in the pictures don't look like Chinese people. After reading, I still have two remaining questions: How did Pong Lo know about the emperor's daughter in the beginning? What made him so determined to marry her?
>
> — *by Adam, an 8ᵗʰ grade Chinese ELL*

Perspective Writing. Reading and writing in subject matter classes, such as English language arts and social studies often involves students writing from reading multiple sources with different views toward the topic under study. It requires the writer to take a stand on the issue by drawing on different readings (Dhurandhar, 2009; Dong, 2005, 2006, 2009; Tanaka & Gilliland, 2017). In teaching WWII history about the dropping of the atomic bomb (see the reading excerpts in Chapter 7), the social studies teacher scaffolds ELLs' reading comprehension by using a graphical presentation of possible decisions first (Table 8.5) and then providing

TABLE 8.5.   President Truman'S Decision Chart About the Atomic Bomb

Decision	Disadvantages	Advantages
Tell the Japanese that we have developed an atomic bomb and invite them to see the test in New Mexico	We have only two bombs. Suppose (what if) the first one fails to explode? Suppose the Japanese are not impressed or intimated (scared) by it?	Japan may surrender (give up). We can avoid a loss of many lives.
Drop the atomic bomb.	Thousands of Japanese will be killed, including civilians (women and children).	This should force Japan to surrender and save American lives. It can also show American military power and influence over the world.
Don't drop the atomic bomb, but continue with conventional (air) bombing.	Many lives including both American's and Japanese's will be lost. It can be a long battle with a possible invasion of Japan.	Future generations won't be held responsible for (accounted for) the devastation (sadness over a huge damage) of atomic bombs. The US won't be responsible as the first and only nation to use atomic weapons.

complex sentence structures, like "If I were …, I would …" and "As President Truman, I would…" as language frames and sentence starters to guide students' writing as following (Dong, 2005b, p. 17).

As a Japanese doctor, I would…

If I were the Japanese doctor, I would have panicked. From the first person I saw, I would have fainted. But me being a doctor, I would have tried to at least help the people that I think could have survived this horrible thing.

As President Truman, I would …

Now actually seeing how the A-bomb can be so powerful, I would try to gain as much control as I possibly could by threatening to bomb other countries. I would be in control of everything. No one would question me again. I would be a dictator. I would never question what I did that day. I won't feel bad. Did Japan feel bad when they bombed and destroyed our ships and killed our people? If I feel bad and am sorry for a country, I won't go to war or even be president. That's my job to be stronger than anyone else emotionally and mentally. (p. 17)

In teaching the topic of West Expansion and Reservation conflicts in U.S. history, a social studies teacher shows both texts and visuals to familiarize ELLs with Native American tribes and their settlement and connect that theme to ELLs' journey to America leaving their native country behind. Once prior knowledge is activated, students are more engaged in reading about the similar topic but taking place in another time and place. Then the key concepts, such as treaty, restriction, territory, promises, reservation, etc. are introduced to prepare students for the reading. Focusing on the concept of "points of view" the teacher can provide differing views presented by the reading (1) the point of view of Chief Joseph, a Native American tribal chief who led his people to fight the U.S. army on their journey to Canada to seek freedom, and (2) the point of view of General Miles, a commander who led the U.S. army in conquering Native Americans in 1877. Using a T-chart (a chart with two columns for pros and cons and to illustrate contrasting views) the teacher helps students see the differences and organize their writing. Based on the reading, the discussion, vocabulary support, and T-chart, the teacher then asks ELLs to compose a diary by assuming the persona of both Chief Joseph and General Miles as below two diary samples by the ELLs (Dong, 2006, p. 26).

Sept. 30, 1877

Dear Diary,

Today was the saddest day of my life. Too many people died. It makes me sad. We have fought for freedom to travel, freedom of working and freedom to think and talk. However, we had lost. Why didn't Americans let us go? I'm so angry that the Americans have killed my family. They could live in peace with us, if they wanted to. But they didn't. The Americans took our home, they took our freedom, and finally, they took our life. Please let us go. There isn't any reason that we have to live under their restriction. I must go to Canada, the land of free.

— *Chief Joseph*

Sept. 30, 1877

Dear Diary,

Today is the best day of my life. I captured the animal who tried to escape. I think this capture has a big contribution in the battle against Native Americans. I don't know why they tried to escape to Canada. We give them a territory, so why they are not satisfied? Our glorious nation promises them that we will let them free in this territory. We are so generous with them, but they are not satisfied. I wish that they understand who they really are and that they try not to escape again. We are more powerful than them, so they must obey our rules and our order. In history, it was always the powerful person who wins.

— General Miles

On the day of teaching the Korean War to a 10th grade ESL social studies class, John, the social studies teacher, overheard a group of his Korean and Chinese ELLs saying that it was not the way they learned about the Korean War back home during the group work. Rather than dismissing his students' view as irrelevant and fearing that he may open up something that he had limited background knowledge, John approached those students after class to learn and invite them to share what they had learned back in Korea and China the next day. Inspired by his students, John also did his own research to learn about those different historical accounts and views by reading Lindaman and Ward (2006).

With preparation and a newly found meaning, Korean and Chinese ELLs shared their views and understandings of the war with the class the next day. The class was fascinated about all this and asked many questions. Near the end of a spirited discussion, John asked the class critical thinking questions: How come there are multiple accounts of the Korean War? Based on different accounts which account do you think is more accurate and why? What does all this tell us about history? Figure 8.5 shows the graphic writing by those ELLs (Dong, 2017, p. 149).

By analyzing the narratives and perspectives given by history textbooks in South Korea, China, and the U.S., John not only created a comprehensible and meaningful learning environment for his ELLs but also engaged the whole class in exploring the perspectives and possible biases of history textbooks, thus promoting all students' development of critical-thinking skills. Excerpts from Dana Lindaman and Kyle Ward's book (2006) can be used to question the "official," "authoritative," "neutral," and "objective" account of history. All this enlivens the discussion and deepens students' understanding of the issues, topics, and concepts under study. This way, students come to view the writing and learning of history as a dynamic process, which often reveals multiple narratives and views of the past (An, 2009; Choi, Lim, & An, 2011; DeRose, 2007; Jaffee, 2016; Lin, Zhao, Ogawa, Hoge, & Kim, 2011). Sam, a Korean ELL wrote about his learning in John's class (Dong, 2017, p. 149):

Before I didn't like the social studies class because I didn't know the U.S. history and couldn't understand much of what the teacher was talking about in class or the readings. I don't know the U.S. culture, current events, and even those famous people's names. Now I like it because Mr. D. listened to what we learned back in

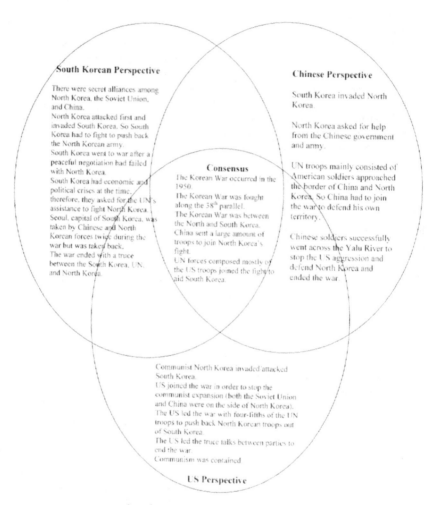

South Korean Perspective

There were secret alliances among North Korea, the Soviet Union, and China.
North Korea attacked first and invaded South Korea. So South Korea had to fight to push back the North Korean army.
South Korea went to war after a peaceful negotiation had failed with North Korea.
South Korea had economic and political crises at the time; therefore, they asked for the UN's assistance to fight North Korea.
Seoul, capital of South Korea, was taken by Chinese and North Korean forces twice during the war but was taken back.
The war ended with a truce between the South Korea, UN, and North Korea.

Chinese Perspective

South Korea invaded North Korea.

North Korea asked for help from the Chinese government and army.

UN troops mainly consisted of American soldiers approached the border of China and North Korea. So China had to join the war to defend his own territory.

Chinese soldiers successfully went across the Yalu River to stop the US aggression and defend North Korea and ended the war.

Consensus

The Korean War occurred in the 1950.
The Korean War was fought along the 38th parallel.
The Korean War was between the North and South Korea.
China sent a large amount of troops to join North Korea's fight.
UN forces composed mostly of the US troops joined the fight to aid South Korea.

Communist North Korea invaded/attacked South Korea.
US joined the war in order to stop the communist expansion (both the Soviet Union and China were on the side of North Korea).
The US led the war with four-fifths of the UN troops to push back North Korean troops out of South Korea.
The US led the truce talks between parties to end the war.
Communism was contained.

US Perspective

FIGURE 8.5.   Cross-Cultural Perspectives Toward the Korean War

Korea. I can relate to those topics and even share my learning back home with the class. That makes the social studies class enjoyable.

— *by Sam, a 10ᵗʰ grade ELL.*

In English language arts classes, writing by using different characters' voices, perspectives, and personas is a popular tool for all students to step into the character's shoes and promote aesthetic appreciation and critical thinking. For ELLs, this writing activity is important linguistically in that they can learn to use varied language structures and expressions in a meaningful way. The following is an example of such writing based on the reading of *How the Garcia Girls Lost Their Accents* by Julia Alvarez (1991):

Writing in the Voice of Yolanda

I am really scared with these men and their guns in my house. Why are they here? Last time I did something wrong and almost got my father killed as a result. My mom is acting so calm. How can she act like that when we all know why they are here?

The whole Rudy situation bothers me. On the one hand I feel like I want to live up to my "old world," parents' expectations. But on the other hand, I have to be me. I am not just Dominican, I feel American also. Who do I let Rudy treat me this way? Would my mother let my father treat her like this?

— by Olivia, a 10th grade ELL

Writing in the Voice of Sandi

Tonight, I am both excited and nervous. We are all going to dinner and Mami insists we don't mess up in front of her and Papi's friends. She always gets so nervous that we will disappoint her. Oh, well! I can't wait to put on my beautiful dress and eat in the fancy restaurant.

Well, my first "mistake" at dinner would be that I stood up to greet the Fannings when they arrived at the table. I didn't know what to do, I just followed Papi's lead. Anyway, Mami gave me the eyes, so I knew I was wrong.

Secondly, we ordered cokes. We weren't supposed to, but we couldn't resist. Hmmm! They were so good. One problem I had at dinner was with the ways Mrs. Fanning was acting. She drank so much wine, and then she kissed Papi on the lips when we went to the bathroom. I'm still shocked. Papi seemed uncomfortable, but he didn't stop her either. If Mami knew, she wouldn't be pleased. I won't say anything to her, but I knew to keep away from that Mrs. Fanning.

— by Maria, a 10th grade ELL

Comparative Writing. Many subject matter concepts can be paired up and explored further through comparative writing. The paired concepts can be both similar concepts and different concepts that students have trouble grasping to clarify their thinking (Dong, 2017; Linvill & Kendall, 2015; Waddell & Quinn, 2011). For ELLs, comparative writing also offers them a chance to practice comparative language structures and use appropriate discipline-specific vocabulary. Students can first work in pairs to create Venn Diagrams comparing and contrasting a pair of words. Then based on what they have found out, they can write to explain these points. Sample writing on the paired mathematics concepts is as follows:

Vocabulary	Comparison
Congruent	Similar
Identical/same sizes and shapes	Similar in shape
Orientation can be different	Different in size and orientation

My mathematics teacher taught us today about similar triangles. This reminds me of the time my sister and I went to Gateway India in Mumbai. Those arches are similar in shape but different in size. They are in proportion. But they are not congruent, meaning in the same size. Two side arches are smaller than the middle arch. Before I was confused about the two words: congruent and similar. My teacher told us that just remember for triangles to be congruent they must have equal measures of angles and same length in their corresponding sides. But for triangles to be similar they are similar in shape but not in size. So, their corresponding angles are the same or congruent but they have different length for their corresponding sides. Their sides are in proportion.

— by Peter, a 9ʰᵗ grade ELL

Source-Based Writing. Source-based writing, such as Document Based Question (DBQ) writing in social studies, often poses both an intellectual challenge and reading and writing challenges for all students in general, and ELLs in particular. Writing a source-based response essay requires higher order thinking skills besides language, reading and writing skills (Franquiz & Salinas, 2011; Weston-Sementelli, Allen, & McNamara, 2018; Weigle & Parker, 2012; Young & Leinhardt, 1998). Unfortunately, subject matter teachers seldom teach source-based writing skills. In the previous chapter on ESL reading instruction, I talked about how to select and modify primary source documents according to ELLs' levels and needs and provide language support to facilitate reading comprehension. After students have read and understood the texts, they need to respond to the question by not just summarizing each text but contextualizing, evaluating, and using different views presented in the reading to make a point (Mizell & Friedman, 2012). Preparing ELLs for the DBQ writing, social studies teachers should focus on the process to teach step-by-step on how to write from source readings by using the following strategies (Ogle, Klemp, & McBride, 2007):

- Read and analyze the reading in detail by taking notes, making associations, and asking questions.
- Evaluate the writer's points of view, purposes, and writing context (time and place). Provide background and conceptual support.
- Compare and contrast similarities and differences between the points of view among different primary source documents on the same topic. Use a graphic organizer if needed
- Discuss how to recount the authors' texts and make their arguments known. Highlight key differences in the writer's use of vocabulary, sentence structure, organization, etc.
- Create a thesis by writing down the key argument/position on the topic.
- Gather the details or original words from all the documents to support the thesis.

Table 8.6 is a primary source document reading (Regent's exam in U.S. history, August 2018, p. 19) and a sample analysis done by a group of ELLs using a graphic organizer adapted from Ogle, et al. (2007, p. 130) used for preparing students for a DBQ essay.

TABLE 8.6.   Primary Source Reading and Analysis

Why are we in Viet-Nam?

...Why are these realities our concern? Why are we in South Viet-Nam?

We are there because we have a promise to keep. Since 1954 every American President has offered support to the people of South Viet-Nam. We have helped to build, and we have helped to defend. Thus, over many years, we have made a national pledge to help South Viet-Nam defend its independence.

And I intend to keep that promise.

To dishonor that pledge, to abandon this small and brave nation to its enemies, and to the terror that must follow, would be an unforgivable wrong.

We are also there to strengthen word order. Around the globe, from Berlin to Thailand, are people whose well-being rests, in part, on the belief that they can count on us if they are attacked. To leave View-Nam to its fate would shake confidence of all these people in the value of an American commitment and in the value of America's word. The result would be increased unrest and instability, and even wider war...

Source: "Peace without conquest," President Lyndon B. Johnson, Address at Johns Hopkins University, April 7, 1965

Analysis for document-based response

What kind of the document did you read? The document is a speech.	**Who is the author of the document?** President Lyndon Johnson
When and where was the document created/ published? It was in the middle of the Vietnam War. The speech was given at Johns Hopkins University on April 7, 1965.	**What is the main idea of the document?** President Lyndon Johnson gave reasons for a continuation of Vietnam War and increase American's military commitment.
What is the author's point of view? President Lyndon Johnson was using the first person perspective. He argued for more military actions to defend South Vietnam and keep American promise.	**What are your difficulties in understanding the document?** We looked up the dictionary/online to understand: national pledge, word order, unrest, stability, unforgivable wrong
What questions do you have after reading the document? What happened after President Lyndon Johnson's speech? President Johnson talked about the American view but what about the view of the Vietnam people?	**What do you want to research about this topic?** We would like to hear and read the news reports about President Johnson's speech during that time. We also like to read more about the war and President Lyndon Johnson like a biography about him.

Primary source reading from Regent's in U.S. history, August, 2018, p. 19

Argumentative Writing. At the secondary level, students' writing has expanded from personal narratives to expository and argumentative essays. For many ELLs who had lived in a society where conformity, respect for the elderly, authority, and government is the way of living before coming to the U.S., learning how to think differently and argue for their points of view can be a daunting task. It requires a total change in their thinking system and identity to be willing and able to speak and write confidently and argue logically with supporting details and evidence. A sample argumentative writing prompt for the Regents exam in English language arts (*ELA Regents Exam*, June 2018, p. 10) is as follows:

Closely read each of the four texts and write a source-based argument on the topic below.

Topic: Is Graffiti Vandalism?

Your task:
Carefully read each of the four texts provided. Then, use evidence from the readings and write a well-developed argument regarding whether or not graffiti is vandalism. Clearly establish your claim, distinguish your claim from alternative or opposing claims, and use specific, relevant, and sufficient evidence from at least three of the four texts to develop your argument. Do not simply summarize each text.

Guidelines: be sure to
- Establish your claim on the topic.
- Distinguish your claim from alternative or opposing claims.
- Use specific, relevant, and from at least three of the four texts to develop your argument.
- Organize your ideas in a cohesive and coherent manner.
- Maintain a formal style of writing.
- Follow the conventions of standard written English.

In preparing ELLs for such a challenging writing task, teachers need to do more than just providing language support. They need to teach American academic writing norms for persuasion and argumentation. The following are the additional areas of writing instruction to develop ELLs' argumentative writing skills.

Interpreting the Writing Assignment. Interpreting an argumentative writing prompt involves decision making as to what position the writer takes and how ideas are going to be presented in their writing. Composing an argumentative essay requires a writer to present a position and then support it. Although this position can be either agreement or disagreement, for or against, seeing from both sides of the issue, the position has to be supported with concrete and specific details, rather than in a general and vague discussion. Furthermore, once the writer takes a position, s/he needs to stay with it, develop it, and conclude it at the end. For ELLs who have difficulty and even confusion with this type of writing, they then need to be taught how to interpret the writing assignment related to what those positions are and how to choose sides to develop their position.

Introducing the Position. American academic readers expect the writer to introduce his or her position early on in the essay and present that position clearly and follow that position throughout the essay. For writers from non-Western cultures, they may have different expectations of introducing the position when writing in their native language. For example, in Chinese and Korean as well as Russian students' reports, they all emphasized the need to make an appeal to an authority or history or religion in the introduction. A good piece of writing in Chinese is characterized by a delayed articulation of the purpose and position of the writing Dong (1998, 1999a,b). A good writing for Romance language writers is characterized by a digression from the position they initially adopt and return to their initial position at the end. For those students, subject matter teachers need to be explicit and using examples to both show and tell what, how, and why that is the way and valued academic essays in English (see Kaplan's Contrastive Rhetoric in Chapter 1).

Developing a Thesis Statement. A thesis statement is a main point or central message to argue or a position that the writer takes in the argumentative essay. It gives a clear purpose of the writing. Composing a thesis statement is often daunting for English proficient students, let alone for ELLs (Fisher & Frey, 2014; Hochman & Wexler, 2017; Ruday, 2016). Even though a writing topic is often given in the form of question or statement, turning the topic into a thesis statement requires not only the language skills both also the thinking skills to organize and synthesize the readings. Often a student writer gets stuck with a thesis statement as they begin to write. Using a graphic organizer to draw upon what they just read is the first step for them to tackle the writing assignment like this (see above DBQ reading and writing organizer). Afterwards, a student writer can use the following strategies to compose their thesis statements based on their understanding of the source texts (Hochman & Wexler, 2017; Ruday, 2016):

- Use the topic (questions or statements given about the writing task) as an anchor to try to answer or respond to it.
- Use the key word in the question or statement of the writing task, such as the effects, reasons, benefits, importance, etc. to answer it using the words, such as "because" for the causal-effect essay, "although" for points of view essay, and "in contrast to" for two opinion essay.

Using the vandalism topic as an example, the argumentative writing shown in a most recent English language arts Regent's exam, below is an illustration of how the topic: "Is graffiti vandalism?" can be used to generate a thesis statement based on the reading the four texts (give the title of each text).

Ruday (2016) gave five recommendations for teaching students how to write a good thesis statement. They are:

1. Show students examples of claim in argumentative essays.
2. Talk with students about why introducing claims is important to effective argument writing.
3. Have students analyze why claim-introducing language is important to argument writing.
4. Work with students as they introduce claims in their own pieces of argument writing.
5. Help students reflect on why their claim-introducing statement is important to their own argument writing (pp. 23–26).

Specificity and Concreteness. While American academic culture values specificity and concreteness in backing up and developing one's position in argumentative writing, students from other cultures may have different views of what is counted as a piece of good writing and how to argue and support a claim. For example, coming from a homogeneous culture which emphasized shared beliefs and values, a Greek student disclosed that writing in Greek relied heavily on vivid adjectives and verbs as raw data for the reader rather than boring the reader with details to show the reader each step of the writer's thinking process. The Asian students are taught to use the wise man's sayings such as Confucius, or the Party line as evidence for argument rather than scientific data. Below are ELLs' reflections on how to develop their essays in their native languages:

> One difference is that here in English when we write a paragraph, we have a main idea. And for that main idea, we have to give details to support the main idea. The details have to be so clear that everybody can understand [them]. But in my country [Bangladesh], my culture, sometimes, we were not encouraged to give details, we just gave some hints. And nobody had any problem understanding these hints.
>
> — by a Bangladeshi ELL

> In Russian, we usually have a very big introduction and a big conclusion. For example, if we are supposed to write about computer use in modern life, we are supposed to start like this "Mathematics was greatly appreciated by our great leaders, now it is used more in the technology such as computers." We are supposed to give a political and historical background. In the conclusion, we kind of finalize the result. I should prove the advantages of the use of the computer by saying yes, by the examples that I give in this composition, I have proven the idea that I said in the beginning.

TABLE 8.6. Thesis Statement Organizer for Argumentative Essay Writing

Topic	Is Graffiti Vandalism?
Task	Read four texts about the topic and compose an argument on whether graffiti is vandalism by stating your claim and supporting it from textual information. (From the 2018 English language arts Regent's exam, p. 10)
Point of the essay	To argue for and against and approve if graffiti is vandalism. (From Regent's exam in English language arts, June 2018, p. 10)

Thesis/claim	Based on the guidelines for writing a thesis/claim, we as a group thought process was:
	• As this is a point of view essay about for and against, the word "although" or "in contrast to" can be used to phrase the thesis and state the claim.
	• Our group came up with the following two openings for our argumentative essays:
	  • Although it has been a lot of people consider graffiti on walls and public places in the urban areas vandalism, I consider it a creative way of expression and cultural enrichment.
	Or
	  • In contrast to certain people's view that graffiti is a freedom of expression and artwork, I view it as a form of vandalism, detrimental to our environment, economy, and community. –by a group of 12th grade ELLs

— by a Russian ELL

Working with ELLs on both source-based and argumentative writing, the subject matter teacher needs to teach them how to present their argument by using supporting details and what is counted as details and evidence in academic writing.

What Counts as a Good Academic Essay in English? What counts as a good academic essay also varies from culture to culture. Below are samples of secondary ELLs' reflections on the differences in academic writing between English and their native language:

> In Japan we are modest and polite, what we call an old fashion way. We are trained to appreciate our feelings and the writers' intention of writing not directly. We try to use what we call "guessing skill." Write as not directly as we can and read as not directly as we can. All the teachers wanted here is example, example, example, and concrete, concrete, concrete. I can't understand why the reader must be told everything. Why must we be so obvious in English writing?
>
> *— by a Japanese ELL*

> In Chinese, good writing often begins with historical background information from the past to the present. For example, if you want to write: Soldiers without ambition are not good soldiers. This topic demands you to give historical examples to show your point, such as Napoleon and many Chinese historical figures to illustrate that those who did not have high goals in their lives, did not succeed at anything. Very often you don't remember the exact words such as what Napoleon said, but the teacher does not look for those details.
>
> *— by a Chinese ELL*

> Writing in Spanish, we focus more on the introduction. The introduction is much longer. We were told to write long introductions. But here they asked us for a short introduction but more details in the body.
>
> *— by a Peruvian ELL*

> I found that American system of writing an essay is very different from the system in my country. In Greek, if we write an essay, we don't write it in five paragraphs. You can use as many paragraphs as you can. Also, you don't have to give details and examples. One important criterion in distinguishing a good essay from a bad essay is by your use of vocabulary. The more complex words and long sentences you use, the better the essay.
>
> *— by a Greek ELL*

> In Korea, the teacher encouraged us to use the wise man's sayings such as what Confucius says. By doing that, the teacher would understand me. But here I feel very confused about how specific the examples have to be. For example, once I wrote about a very influential Korean Ancient philosophy called nihilism. I am a believer of that philosophy. But my teacher did not know it. I sense that it is not only that the meaning is lost in translation but also Americans do not believe in that. Words like

that make my writing very strange to the reader. But I don't know how to make my writing clear to American readers.

— by a Korean-ELL

Working with students who have already had literacy learning in their native languages, subject matter teachers need to be mindful about those differences when teaching American academic writing norms. For example, showing and proving your point, the requirement for American academic writing, is the hallmark of American academic writing. A good writer is expected not only to come up with examples but also to communicate a clear purpose of using the examples to support his or her point to the reader. A good writer fulfils the reader's expectation to take the examples further to prove her or his point. For ELLs to compose academic writing that follows American academic norms, explicit writing, cultural, and thinking instruction from all subject matter teachers is needed in addition to language instruction.

CHAPTER 9

PROMOTING ELLS' PARTICIPATION IN SUBJECT MATTER DISCUSSIONS

CLASSROOM DISCUSSIONS AND ELLS' DIFFICULTIES

Classroom discussions are a hallmark of American classroom teaching and learning (Cazden, 1988; Fisher, Frey, & Rothenberg, 2008; Zwiers & Crawford, 2011). An American teacher believes students learn through talking, responding, questioning with both the teacher and peers during the lesson. Oral communication is at the heart of those discussions. Subject matter teachers use student participation in the discussion to assess their learning and inform their teaching.

Research has suggested that classroom discussions not only facilitate students' learning about the subject matter but also develop students' language and thinking skills (Fisher et al., 2008; Zwiers & Crawford, 2011). The redundancy of ideas and talking about the concept and skills used to view different perspectives allows for opportunities for listening and speaking skills and critical-thinking skill development. Finally, through both the whole class and group/pair discussions, students develop their social skills to work with the teacher and other students. A commonly used classroom discussion exchange has a distinctive pattern of the Initiation-Response-Evaluation (IRE). This pattern includes the teacher's initiating a discussion

Teaching English Language Learners in Secondary Subject Matter Classes, pages 187–199.
Copyright © 2019 by Information Age Publishing
187

by using a question or statement, then students' responding to the teacher, and finally the teacher's evaluation of the student's response like below (Cazden, 1988).

Teacher: When we move a point or a figure on a coordinate plane, what are we doing?
Student: Translating.
Teacher: Yes!

Although research has shown serious limitations of this discussion pattern, such as restraining students' thinking, focusing more on fact-based learning, and stifling student initiation in learning, still the IRE pattern of the classroom discussion persists, especially at the secondary level where the teacher is confined by the curricular constraints and deals with a large class when the priority is to prepare students for standardized tests (Applebee, 1996; Dong, 2005a; Marshall, Smagorinsky, & Smith, 1995; Nystrand, 1997). Typical American teenagers who have been educated in American schools have had plenty of exposure to and practice of classroom discussions. By secondary school, they have acquired the ability to express their understanding and voice confusions and opinions about a topic on a regular basis in classroom discussions. To those students, learning is not an isolated and individual activity; rather, it's a social activity, involving interacting with peers and the teacher.

In comparison, classroom discussions are foreign to many ELL. For example, ELLs, especially those who come from such cultures as Chinese, Japanese, Korean, Bangladeshi, talking in front of the class is not even permitted in their previous education. Questions are not asked or allowed in class. To them, the teacher is an authority who knows all and learning is all about students listening to the teacher and following the teacher's directions and lectures. As a result, some ELLs may view class discussions and group work not as important and/or irrelevant to the learning task as the teacher lecture, thus tuning out, becoming an onlooker of those learning activities.

To compound the problem, many subject matter teachers tend to hold back on calling on ELLs in class for fear of embarrassing them in front of the whole class or losing valuable class time to rephrase the question and understand their responses. Recent research has argued that without teachers' purposeful and systematic ways of engaging ELLs in the classroom discussions, ELLs will miss out on a lot of opportunities for learning. Therefore, there is an urgent need for the subject matter teacher to develop effective ways to involve their ELLs in classroom discussions.

To begin with, subject matter teachers should communicate their goals of having classroom discussions to both the ELLs and their parents early on. ELLs also need to be trained on how to do it. In addition, subject matter teachers should be mindful of three major difficulties for ELLs in classroom discussions:

Language Difficulties. Low level ELLs who speak very little English and often do not understand what is going on in class in their initial schooling in the U.S. Some of them are in Silent Period, others might respond to simple commands or questions, often nonverbally. Over time, they begin to imitate the oral language of the teacher and those around them and speak in one-word responses. Even for the ELLs who have progressed into the intermediate level of English proficiency, still they may not be fluent with both oral English and have the CALP to express themselves in class.

Cultural Difficulties. Duff (2001) and Harklau (1994) argued that teacher talk in subject matter classes has a tendency of talking in a rapid-fire pace besides using the Initiation-Response-Evaluation (IRE) pattern. In addition, teachers tend to use slang, idioms, humor, and current events that often go above ELLs' language levels and beyond their knowledge about American culture. For example, ELLs probably will not understand let alone participate in the discussion of how the vending machine is compared to the concept of function in mathematics, the historical context of the Civil War, and the relevance of an American sporting event to the concept of irony.

Prior Knowledge Difficulties. Discussing subject matter with ELLs in class, teachers' expectations of what response is counted as a good response or a relevant response need to be examined and adjusted as well. Take a look at the following question and response between the teacher and an ELL in an 8th grade U.S. history class (Dong, 2017, p. 1):

Teacher:	Today, we are going to learn about the Civil War. What can you tell me about the Civil War?
Juan:	(an ELL from El Salvador) I know, I know. It was fought in South America.
Teacher:	Anyone else?

The social studies teacher here obviously did not expect Juan's response. It was not a response that she was looking for: the Civil War was fought in the American south. So, she moves on to the next student seeking the response she is looking for. After class, the teacher revealed that she was surprised to hear that Juan did not have any prior knowledge about the topic as an 8th grader. "What do I do with students like this?" the teacher asked.

However, taking another look at Juan's response shows that he does have prior knowledge about the Civil War in El Salvador, his home country, which should be recognized, relevant, and integrated into the discussion. Involving ELLs into the classroom discussion requires subject matter teachers to welcome possible different prior knowledge brought by their ELLs and encourage them to share and use it to learn new knowledge. Despite the fact that not all ELLs' prior knowledge or experiences can be readily linked to the learning topics and concepts, even the seemingly irrelevant and inappropriate prior knowledge, like the one Juan mentioned in the excerpt should be useful and valuable points for theme comparisons and deep understanding.

Subject matter teachers should also expand their teaching repertoire by learning about their ELLs' native country and culture and prior learning to inform their instruction and make the classroom discussion relevant, motivational, and meaningful to ELLs (see Chapters 3 and 4 for reviews of ELLs' previous schooling).

Effective Classroom Discussion Strategies for ELLs

Below I discuss strategies with examples that subject matter teachers can use to include ELLs in their classroom discussions. They are

- Model the desired behavior and speech.
- Modify teacher talk, questions, and directions.
- Provide ELLs with ample opportunities to interact with their peers.
- Teach academic and disciplinary vocabulary during the discussion.

Model the Desired Behavior and Speech. Model what the students are expected of as a participant in a classroom discussion (Doabler, Nelson, & Clarke, 2016; Fisher et al., 2008). Good modeling is not just for ELLs but also for English proficient students to be respectful and considerate to their peers' contribution to the classroom discussion. Use a written guide, think-alouds, and visuals to show the students the classroom discussion routines, the types of teacher questions and their purposes and functions, turn-taking rituals, importance of listening to each other's ideas besides talking about their own, appropriate attitude and behavior and even body language in a group setting, etc. Use sentence starters to scaffold ELLs for language support, such as I'm confused about … I wonder… I agree/ disagree… What do you mean by… I like… I have a question about…

Modify Teacher Talk. To ease comprehension difficulty, subject matter teachers should also examine their lesson plans beforehand for comprehensible input in their questions, directions, and minilessons. In Chapter 7 on ESL reading instruction I cited Jameson's ideas of modifying reading materials for ELLs (Jameson, 1998). Those ideas can be applied to teacher talk and modified directions as well. For the ELLs with a low level of English proficiency, the teacher should also provide a written handout for them with native language support and visuals as well as oral modifications. Table 9.1 gives examples of such modifications by ELLs' English language "proficiency levels."

TABLE 9.1. Adjusted Teacher Questions and Expectations by ELLs' Levels

English Proficiency Levels	Adjusted Questions	Expected Student Responses
Entering ELLs	Show we… Which of these… Is it … or …	nodding, pointing, showing using their native language
Emerging ELLs	What happened here? What do you like… What do you think… How do you like …	Respond in one or two words make a choice orally simple phrase response with errors

When asking questions, subject matter teachers should slow down their speech and use gestures and visuals as much as they can to facilitate comprehension. Try to avoid asking multiple questions all at once in one breath, leading to incomprehension and confusion. Also, the questions should be tailored to ELLs' levels. For example, a yes or no question though not good for higher-order thinking, is good for low level ELLs to get them engaged and make their participation feasible. Once the ELLs have progressed into a higher level, then they can handle what, how, and why questions and open-ended questions with language support.

Give Enough Wait Time. More wait time is needed for ELLs, more so when asking open-ended and challenging questions. Research on wait time, the pause between the teacher's question and student response, has shown that there is a positive correlation between more time given by the teacher (in seconds) and more responses and thoughtful responses from the students (Stahl, 1987). Given the complex questions asked and limited language proficiency, subject matter teachers can even allow ELLs to write down the question and their responses before speaking so they have a planned response and are not as nervous as speaking spontaneously.

Keep in mind that ELLs need quite some time to (1) comprehend what the teacher asks orally, (2) translate the teacher's question into their native language, (3) figures out the way to respond to the teacher question in their native language, (4) translate that response back into appropriate English, and 5) mentally rephrase the response in English to be sure before speaking up. This back and forth mental processing in two languages and juggling different tasks to find the right response takes time, energy, and focus away from ELLs (Dong, 2016). Often by the time when they are ready to participate, the discussion has already moved on to a new topic.

Modify Directions. Secondary subject matter teachers often give long and complicated oral directions for group work or seat work, involving several steps and a series of questions for the learning task in class. In a large class with an increased noise level and mixed level students, those directions are often announced in a hurry, likely to overwhelm ELLs. Therefore, modified and short directions are needed. Also, if the task involves quite a few steps, a written version should be given along with the oral directions. Below are examples of the original and modified directions used by subject matter teachers across the subject matter areas (Dong, 2005a, pp. 3–4):

Regular Directions Given in a Family and Consumer Science Class
- Ok, please sit down. You have a lab to complete today. You have 42 minutes to do this micro-brittle, which shows you the chemical changes when the heated sugar is mixed with the baking soda. Get out your recipe and get into your kitchen and let's get going because we will not have enough time to cool this stuff off.

Modified Directions for ELLs
- You will have 42 minutes to complete a lab today.
- The lab is about the micro-brittle.

- You will investigate the chemical changes when the heated sugar is mixed with the baking soda.
- Get out your recipe, go into your kitchen, and begin your lab.

Regular Directions Given in an ELA Class

Now, what I want you to do is read the chapter "Being Mean." In this chapter the author uses a lot of those special words to help us create images. In your groups, I want you to write down all the examples of imagery that you find. Use your post-it notes to mark your place and write on. I would like you to come up with at least three examples.

Modified Directions for ELLs

- First break up into groups.
- Read the chapter "Being Mean" in your group.
- During the reading, look for specific words that help us create images.
- Then write down three images that you find in your reading.
- Use your post-it notes to mark your image during the reading.
- Finally, write your images on the post-it notes as well.

Regular Directions Given in Social Studies Class

Ok, break yourselves off into groups of 5. I want you to pretend that you are groups of archeologists whose job is find physical remains of the Lewis and Clark expedition. I want each group to develop a list of questions. Take a few minutes to think about what questions you would want to answer.

Modified Directions for ELLs

- Divide yourself into groups of five.
- Pretend that you are groups of archeologists.
- Your job is to find physical remains of the Lewis and Clark expedition.
- Each group will develop a list of five questions.
- The questions are what archeologists may ask before they search for the remains.

Initiate a Class Discussion With What ELLs Know. Start a discussion using what ELLs know. In English language arts and social studies classes, teachers can always find a discussion topic or theme familiar to their ELLs' cultural backgrounds and experiences. Even in science and mathematics classes discussions can be tailored to ELLs' culturally familiar examples as shown in previous chapters. The following is an excerpt taken from a 9th grade English language arts class containing both ELLs and English proficient students. The English teacher launched a discussion on bilingual education related to Negi, the protagonist in *When I Was Puerto Rican* (Santiago, 2006), being placed in an ESL class to learn English only. With such a relatable topic, her ELLs dived into the discussion immediately, and their responses became insightful and informative for all students.

Teacher:	I believe bilingual education is appropriate.
Karen	(ELL): I remember when I came to the U.S., and I was put into a bilingual class and there were Chinese kids in there who had to listen to the Spanish and English instructions. They never taught in Chinese.
Jessica	(ELL): If Negi takes bilingual classes, she'll learn at her level and she'll learn both languages. She'll have more of an advantage because if they put her in an all English class, she won't know nothing.
Joel	(ELL): They should put kids in an all English-speaking class.
Teacher:	Why?
Joel	(ELL): Because when I came to this country, they put me into an English class, but they put my brother into a bilingual class. I learned English within about three months. He still doesn't know very much English. [Reaction from other students -"wow"]
Evelin	(ELL): But if you put a kid that doesn't know English into an English class, he'll just sit there lost.
Vicky	(English proficient): But if he sits there quiet, he can observe and learn.
Adam	(English proficient): Couldn't they have a separate place to learn English?
Jonathan	(English proficient): Yeah -It's called school! [Laughter]
Teacher:	How would you feel if you were Negi?
Jessica	(ELL): Uncomfortable. It would be so hard.

As shown in the above excerpt, ELLs have a lot to say about the topic by drawing on their personal experiences. Their responses are not one-word answers but elaborated responses, showing they cared about the topic and have opinions about the issue under discussion. Having a good knowledge about her ELLs, the teacher did a good job in letting ELLs take the lead in the discussion, challenging students' thinking along the way.

Even for low level ELLs, when the topic is familiar to them with language support, they are capable of discussing the topic at hand. Below is a 7th grade Bengali-English bilingual social studies discussion to respond to the teacher's questions: Where did the "first" Americans come from? How did they get here? (Dong, 2017, p. 147)

Teacher:	Who can share their response the questions?
S1:	I would like to share my idea. I think people came from Europe with ship [sic].
Teacher:	Does anyone have a different answer?
S2:	Maybe they swimmed here [sic]?
Teacher:	You mean swam here?
S2:	Yeah, swam.
Student 3	(in Bengali): But কিভাবে তারা আমেরিকা সব পথ সাঁতার কাটতে পারে (English translation: How could they swim all the way to America)? যে অসম্ভব (English translation: That is impossible.)

Teacher: Could you explain more? Why is it impossible? You can speak in Bengali.

S3:   এটা খুব দূরে এবং মহাসাগর এবং মহাদেশে অতিক্রম

          (English translation: It's too far and cross the ocean and continent) (p. 5)

Teacher: Good. Let's look at some posters to show how they arrived in America.

Note how the social studies teacher created an inviting learning environment where different responses and reasons were entertained and explained. Allowing beginning ELLs to use their native language to discuss the topic, the teacher increased the depth of the conversation as students questioned each other's responses and offered rationales for their answers in Bengali, their native language (DeRose, 2007; Gay, 2010; Ladson-Billings, 1995; Rodriguez, Salinas, Gubermanj, 2005; Salinas, Franquiz, & Guberman, 2006). The social studies teacher also modeled correct language use for the word "swam" when hearing the ELL say "swimmed." After the class, the teacher reflected on his adjustment of expectations for ELLs to participate in class (Dong, 2017, p. 147):

> Our school follows the New York State social studies middle school curriculum. I'm now in the unit on the early settlers of Americas, which covers the main theories on how early people came to this country. Those theories are pretty much European oriented, which can be difficult for my students to understand. To make the topic relevant and meaningful to my students, I asked them to write about their journeys to America and compare them to those of early Americans by posing questions. I found that my students who are new immigrants enjoying this unit very much because they can relate to the topic and delve a little deeper into the subject.

Provide ELLs With Ample Opportunities to Interact With Their Peers. Cooperative learning, such as pair work, group discussions, is a common American classroom practice and has additional benefits of promoting ELLs' language development and social interaction. Even for ELLs who are in Silent Period, observing how peers converse in a group to solve a problem can be a natural and meaningful language learning experience (DeCapua, Smathers, & Tang, 2007; Early & Marshall, 2008; Fisher et al., 2008; Gibbons, 2003; Osterling, 2001). To adjust the cooperative learning task to ELLs' levels, subject matter teachers should allow ELLs at the lower level to pair up with their native speaking peers and use their native language to discuss the task at hand. At the beginning levels, ELLs fare better and participate more with their native speaking peers if they are allowed to speak in their native language.

Some subject matter teachers may question the use of ELLs' native language; however, for ELLs at the beginning level of English proficiency, it makes sense for them to use their native language to communicate their thoughts rather than remaining silent. Group members who speak that language can translate the response into English for the teacher to know and for the ELLs to hear the English version of their responses and pick up one or two words in English. As we discussed in Chapter 1, secondary ELLs do not have the luxury of time to wait for their English skills (BICS and CALP) to develop, rather, they need to learn and participate in the subject matter simultaneously while learning to speak, read, and write in English. By allowing them to speak in their native language lowers their affective filters and makes them feel a sense of belonging. Recent ESL and bilingual education research has illustrated positive results in ELLs' using native language in speaking and writing for their overall development of secondary language (Cook, 2001; De Smet, Mettewie, & Garland, 2018; Garcia et al., 2017; Yaghobian, Samuel, & Mahmoudi, 2017).

Once ELLs are progressing in their English skills, they should be grouped with the ELLs who speak different native languages or English proficient peers to foster their ability to talk in English. Also, their roles in a group work should be rotated with other group members, such as taking on a role of a questioner or presenter, rather than only playing the roles of an artist or a poster holder.

With a well-designed, challenging, meaningful, and interesting learning task, students are eager to talk through their ideas and make decisions on how to solve the problem (Lemke, 1987a,b). Even ELLs who are constantly silent in the whole class discussion may open up to group talks. It is during these talks that students get to practice their listening and speaking skills, such as posing a question, clarifying a word, commenting on each other's performance, joking, demanding, etc. The following is an example of such a conversational episode where students learn how sickle cell disease is inherited, a topic of genetics, by randomly choosing two beans from the mix of the red and white beans representing sickle and normal cell alleles repeatedly. The sickle cell alleles, represented by red beans decreased as the population reproduced itself from one generation to another.

Student 1	(English proficient): I got AA. (meaning two white beans)
Student 2	(ELL): Yeah, I got SS. (meaning two red beans)
Student 3	(English proficient): Oh, cool, she got SS. What did you get?
Student 4	(ELL): SS.
Student 3	(English proficient): Put them back.
Student 1	(English proficient): You screw up! You cannot put these beans back. These are with sickle diseases. They are dead already. What did you get? (the one did not close his eyes in picking)
Student 3	(English proficient): AA.
Student 4	(ELL): All right, let's count them.
Student 3	(English proficient): (to the teacher) We got 15 AAs, 2 SSs, and 4 ASs.
Teacher:	Why are there always more white beans than red beans in this population?
Student 3	(English proficient): Because we have more white beans.
Teacher:	(to student 2) Why do we have more white beans?
Student 2	(ELL): Because white is dominant.
Teacher:	(to student 2) Why is it dominant?
Student 2	(ELL): Because they don't have disease and they are going to live longer.

Teacher: That's it! That's it! Does everybody hear that? If you have two SSs, the
              individuals are going to die and not pass their genes on. So, the number
              of SSs is going to decrease in the population.

Research has found that some subject matter teachers interact with English
proficient students differently than with ELLs (Duff, 2001; Verplaetse, 1998,
2000). Once they are aware of different language abilities, they do modifications
and make adjustments in class. However, sometimes the teacher unknowingly
underestimates and reduces ELLs' interaction opportunities and limits those interactions to direction giving and low-level questions. In the above group discussion
mixed with both English proficient students and ELLs, fully aware of her ELLs'
abilities, the science teacher did not go easy on the ELLs by only asking them
procedural questions or answering the questions on their behalf for fear of embarrassing them or slowing down the discussion. Rather, she challenged both English
proficient students and ELLs by asking why questions and follow-up questions to
Student 2. When she is challenged and given the opportunity, Student 2 responded
intelligently, showing her solid grasp of the subject matter knowledge about the
sickle cell disease.

Teach Academic and Disciplinary Vocabulary During the Discussion. As
discussed in Chapter 1, subject matter teachers should not wait until ELLs are
proficient in BICS level English before exposing them to the CALP level English. Research has found that subject matter discussion provides a rich and meaningful context for language learning and conceptual learning of subject matter
learning (Alxander-Shea, 2011; Bialystok, 2008; Bruna et al., 2007; Dong, 2002,
2013, 2016, 2017; Mickan, 2007; Rupley & Slough, 2010; Snow, 2008; Winsor,
2007–2008). Boyd and Kong (2017) found that during the classroom discussion,
teachers' consistent use of reasoning words, such as logical connectors and organizational links fostered the development of ELLs' thinking skills and in turn,
those students learned to use those words to express their knowledge about the
subject matter. Below is a CALP level vocabulary-centered discussion in biology
by Mark, a biology teacher.

Feathers Verse Fur. Mark discusses the concept of adaptation in biology with
a class of 9th grade ELLs. It is typical of Mark to use the discussion for students
to discover scientific concepts rather than simply giving out definitions for them
to memorize. This high expectation for students to explore concepts by talking
was established early on in all his classes, regardless of what students' level of
English. His questions are often focused and cognitively challenging. The only
difference is that in his ESL biology class, Mark's questions are simpler, more
specific, and contextualized with rich visuals and multi-media support. He trains
his students how to respond to teacher questions and informs both the students
and their parents of the importance and accountability of participating in class
discussions early in the semester. Because of all this there is increased class participation from all his students, including ELLs.

Teacher:	Take a look at this picture. What is this?
Sam:	A polar bear.
Teacher:	Do you know any bears besides polar bears?
Philip:	Black bears.
Teacher:	Where do black bears live?
Philip:	In the jungle.
Teacher:	Where do polar bears live?
Rachel:	In a very cold place.
Megan:	In the Arctic.
Teacher:	Right, in the arctic. Why are the different kinds of bears found in different parts of the world? Why aren't all bears found in the same place of the world?
Li Ann:	Because the weather is not the same.
Teacher:	Why is that?
Li Ann:	Polar bears can only live in the cold place.
Teacher:	How so?
Yong:	Because look at the picture here, the ice and the snow.
Kadisha:	Black bears cannot survive in that cold.
Teacher:	What does a polar bear do to survive the cold?
Kamal:	They have fur, white fur. Black bears do not have that thick fur, and their fur is black.
Teacher:	Interesting, how come a polar bear's fur is white?
Sam:	They have to hide to blend in?
Teacher:	You are saying that they use the white fur to defend themselves?
Dan:	The white color is also transparent to sunlight and keeps them warm.
Teacher:	OK, so the polar bear's fur and the color of the fur are for some special adaptation purposes. Let's look at this picture. What is going on here?
Patricia:	The duck is swimming in the river.
Teacher:	What kind of environment does a duck live in?
Carlos:	It's warm and close to the water.
Fidel:	Ducks have fur too.
Teacher:	Is that fur?
Kamal:	I don't think so. How can it have fur if it lives in a warm climate?
Dan:	I know what it calls.
Zoila:	It's feather not fur.
Teacher:	Why does it have feathers?
Zoila:	Feathers help it move, swim.
Teacher:	How does the fur function?
Dmitri:	Fur keeps bears warm.
Teacher:	So why do ducks have feathers and polar bears have fur?
Sam:	Because they have different functions.
Dmitri:	I know, because they have to adapt to their environments.

In this discussion, fully aware that his students come from countries where polar bears have probably not been seen before, Mark asks the question, "Do you know any bears?" to activate students' prior knowledge. Notice that Mark occasionally gives explicit feedback and he never lets his students' responses go unnoticed and acknowledged. He builds upon the student's response by asking follow-up questions. These questions play a role of both acknowledging students' responses and inviting them to think further. In doing so, he opens the floor for his students to discuss the topic like young scientists.

One characteristic of Mark's follow-up questions is his repetition of key phrases or words uttered by the students and incorporation of these utterances into subsequent questions. By doing so, Mark makes sure that the whole class hears his loud and clear voice and stays focused on the topic at hand. Mark's repetition further adds language exposure to the students. The students gain experience hearing how the words are used in discussing science.

When Mark spots that students have arrived at the critical part of the discussion, he paraphrases these responses to highlight key concepts like "you are saying that they use the white fur to defend themselves." "So, the polar bear's fur and the color of the fur are for some special adaptation purposes." This way Mark keeps the class focused on the topic and helps students crystallize the concept as the discussion progresses.

Another interesting point is Mark's treatment of the students' confusion about the words *feathers* and *fur*. Even when the students' responses are incorrect such as when they were confused about the words *feathers* and *fur*, Mark, instead of saying no or giving out word definitions or asking students to look into their dictionaries, ask such questions as "is that fur?" "Why does it have feathers?" and "How does the fur function?" to issue an invitation for more discussion on the meaning and function of these words. He lets the students figure out the difference between the two words as well as the scientific concept themselves. In doing so, Mark not only expands students' scientific knowledge but also stretches their language abilities.

Imperialism. Jean, a social studies teacher is also big on encouraging ELLs to participate in class and thinking using CALP level words rather than giving out definitions for students to memorize. Jean reveals that talking about how the concept is derived and related to student life makes a big difference in student understanding and retention. Often in Jean's class, students also ask questions to drive the discussion. Below is an excerpt of Jean's 10th grade world history class discussion on imperialism. The class is composed of both ELLs and English proficient students.

Gonzales:	(ELL) Miss, what is invasion?
Teacher:	Good question. What is invasion?
Mandy:	(English proficient) One country takes over other countries.
Teacher:	That's a good answer, but what do you mean by "take over"?
Mandy:	(English proficient) When a country invades another.
Teacher:	Interesting. What is invasion then?
Juan:	(ELL) Invasion is when a country goes into another country without that country saying ok.
Teacher:	OK. So, you mean the permission?

Class:	Yes.
Teacher:	What is it called when a country goes into another without the "permission"?
Steve:	(English proficient) They just take over.
Teacher:	So, what do we mean by "take over" in this context?
Martin:	(ELL) There is a word when a strong country takes over a weaker one.
Teacher:	Ok, so now we know it has to do with strong countries taking over the weaker ones. Why would a strong nation try to take over a weaker one?
Martin:	(ELL) Maybe the weaker country has something that the stronger country wants?
Gonzales:	(ELL) I know! I learned it in history back in my country. I'm from the Dominican Republic. Back then I learned my country was taken over by a bunch of European countries. They are strong and they see something valuable so they decide to simply take it from the weaker one using force.
Teacher:	Great answer. What do we call this?
Mandy:	(English proficient) Imperialism.

In the above discussion, instead of settling for an easy answer, "take over," Jean pushed and guided her students to think more and find the meaning of academic words themselves. In doing so, both ELLs and English proficient students went on a journey of inquiry to arrive at the concept of imperialism and its key elements. A close examination of the discussion shows that both ELLs and English proficient students took turns to share the floor and contribute. Based on her research findings, Duff (2011) reported that in a class with ELLs mixed with English proficient students there is a tendency for English proficient students to take over the discussion, ignoring or even laughing at ELLs' often accented oral English.

In Jean's class early on in the semester she established a rule of respecting each other, not discriminating ELLs for their accented English or their different prior knowledge. In the above dialogue, when English proficient students used the idiomatic usage of "take over," Jean did not settle for it, instead, she asked for an explanation using academic English, such as "permission" and challenging her students to think not only what *imperialism* is but also why it exists. Jean really listens to her student responses and firmly believes that all students are capable of learning and has something important to say. Because of Jean's consistent efforts and belief, Gonzales, an ELL was able and willing to share his prior knowledge to inform the class on the topic. All this has connected to their unique backgrounds and experiences to the concept, thus enriching and deepening the learning.

CHAPTER 10

PREPARING ELLS FOR EVALUATION AND STANDARDIZED TESTS

With the Regents exam looming over our heads, the pressure is to create dramatic improvement in all our students' abilities in order to pass the Regents. Still, facing some students who do not even speak English fluently, how do you prepare them for an exam, such as the Regents?

— a 10th grade English teacher

This English teacher's concern is also many subject matter teachers' concern. Teaching secondary ELLs, the subject matter teacher faces the challenge of facilitating their development in both English and subject matter knowledge at the same time and preparing them to meet the graduation standards. In this chapter, I discuss what and how subject matter teachers can do to prepare those students for those standardized tests, such as the Regents Exams.

While native English-speaking students struggle to meet the tough graduation standards, ELL students have double jeopardy in that they have to perform in academic content areas using the new language in which they are not yet fluent. In the past, schools and subject matter departments negotiated this dilemma by excluding ELL students from Regents exams or giving them a simpler version

Teaching English Language Learners in Secondary Subject Matter Classes, pages 201–215.
Copyright © 2019 by Information Age Publishing

of the test, such as Regents Competency Tests (RCTs) used in New York State. However, with the increasing graduation standards in recent years, ELLs can no longer be exempted from the Regents exams except for a short delay (one year) in taking the Regents for newcomer ELLs to catch up before taking those exams. To graduate in New York State, students must pass five Regents exams, including English language arts, Math, Science, Global History/Geography, and U.S. History/Government in order to earn their high school diplomas or local diplomas.

STANDARDIZED TEST ACCOMMODATIONS FOR ELLS

In New York State, there are well-established accommodation policies for ELLs on the Regents exams (New York State Department of Education, 2015, p. 12). Those policies are:

Time Extension: Schools may extend the test time for English-Language-Learners. Principals may use any reasonable extensions, such as "time and a half" (the required testing time plus one half of that amount of time), in accordance with their best judgment about the needs of the English-Language-Learner. Principals should consult with each student's classroom teacher in making these determinations.

Separate Location: Schools are encouraged to provide optimal testing environments and facilities for all students. They may administer State exams to English-Language-Learners individually or in small groups in a separate location.

Third Reading of Listening Selection: Proctors may read the listening passages a third time to English-Language-Learners who are taking the Regents Comprehensive Examination in English. This accommodation is not permitted on State examinations in foreign languages.

Bilingual Dictionaries and Glossaries: English-Language-Learners may use bilingual dictionaries and glossaries when taking State examinations in all subjects except foreign languages. The bilingual dictionaries and glossaries may provide only direct translations of words. Bilingual dictionaries or glossaries that provide definitions or explanations are not permitted. Go to http://www.p12.nysed.gov/biling/bilinged/bilingual_glossaries.htm for bilingual glossaries in 12 languages cross academic disciplines. https://steinhardt.nyu.edu/metrocenter/resources/glossaries

Simultaneous Use of English and Alternative Language Editions: For those State examinations for which the Department provides direct written translations, English-Language-Learners may use both an English and an alternative language edition of the test simultaneously.

However, they should be instructed to record all of their responses in only one of the two editions. The alternative language edition used by the student should be so indicated on the student's answer document. See translated versions of Living Environment Regents Exams in Chinese, Haitian Creole, Korean, Russian, and Spanish: http://www.nysedregents.org/livingenvironment/TranslatedEditions.html

Oral Translation for Lower Incidence Languages: Schools may provide English-Language-Learners with an oral translation of a State examination when there is no translated edition provided by the Department. This accommodation is permitted for State examinations in all subjects except English language arts and foreign languages. All translations must be oral, direct translations of the English editions; written translations are not allowed. No clarifications or explanations may be provided. Translators should receive copies of the English editions of the tests one hour prior to administration.

Written Responses in Native Language: English-Language-Learners making use of alternative language editions or of oral translations of State examinations may write their responses to the open-ended questions in their native language. Scoring the tests is the responsibility of the school. However, the Department's Office of Bilingual Education and Foreign Language Studies and the RBE-RNs can assist schools in locating persons who can translate the students' responses into English to facilitate scoring of the answer papers.

Former Limited-English-Proficient/English-Language-Learner (ELL) Students

Schools also may provide the testing accommodations listed on the previous page under the heading "English-Language-Learners (ELL)" only to former ELLs who were identified as English language proficient based on their scores on one of the two most recent administrations of the New York State English as a Second Language Achievement Test (NYSESLAT), either Spring 2011 or Spring 2012. These accommodations may not be provided to former ELLs who were identified as English language proficient prior to the 2010 NYSESLAT administration.

In addition, there are seven major bilingual subject matter classes offered in varied schools, including Arabic, Bengali, Chinese, Korean, Haitian Creole, Spanish, and Urdu (New York City Department of Education, 2016). These bilingual subject matter classes are taught using both English and ELLs' native language to teach sciences, mathematics, global histories, and U.S. government and history. For the past 14 years, New York State Regents exams have been administered in translated editions in Chinese, Haitian Creole, Korean, Russian, and Spanish. ELLs who speak those languages and have taken TBE subject matter classes in mathematics (i.e., algebra, geometry), sciences (i.e., biology, chemistry, earth sciences), and social studies (i.e., global history, and U.S. history), have an option of taking Regents Exams in their native languages (New York State Department of Education, 2009).

Students who apply for taking the bilingual version of Regents exams must have taken bilingual subject matter classes. As I discussed in Chapter 2, there are two main bilingual subject matter classes offered in New York City public schools. One is the Dual language program (DL) often offered in lower grade levels in elementary and middle schools. The other is the Transitional Bilingual Education (TBE) program offered in high school. According to New York State ESL/Bilingual guidelines, if the school has a sufficient number of ELLs speaking the same native language (25), or there is a subject matter teacher who is certified to teach in the ELLs' native language, and then those ELLs will have the TBE classes. In addition, parents need to give permission for their children to be placed in the TBE class. If not, their children will receive the English only instruction, such as the ENL classes. For schools and subject matter classes where there is an insufficient number of ELLs who speak different native languages to be taught in one ENL class, those students are placed in the mainstream subject matter classes mixed with English proficient students.

Recent ELLs' Passing Rate on the Regents' Exams. As discussed in Chapter 1, it often takes an average 5–7 years for ELLs to catch up with the grade level English proficient peers in CALP. Giving those students accommodations, providing bilingual versions of the test, and allowing one-year extension for newcomer ELLs may still not be enough for ELLs to pass the standardized tests. A review of recent New York State Regents Exams has shown that ELLs had a low passing rate across academic disciplines. According to Taylor's report (2017), while the graduation rate for New York City has increased from 67.2% in 2015 to 69.6% in 2016, an overall graduate rate for ELLs, decreased from 33.3% in 2015 to 26.6% in 2016.

As shown in Table 10.1, ELLs are seriously lagging behind in graduation rate across all subject matter areas. Why is this the case? An obvious reason is ELLs' limited English proficiency. Although the standardized tests claim to test students' subject matter knowledge, it is often difficult, if not impossible, to evaluate subject matter knowledge without some understanding of the language used to describe, explain, argue, and express that knowledge. A closer examination of these tests shows that these tests are designed for students who are not only native or fluent English speaking but who also share the mainstream American cultural values, traditions, and practices. However, for ELL students who have different cultural backgrounds and experiences that the test makers have in mind, cultural biases in addition to language difficulties often interfere with the content knowledge evaluation, which is intended to test, thus producing invalid results (Brescia & Fortune, 1988; Butler & Stevens, 2001; McKeon, 1994; Mohan, 1986; Nelson-Barber & Trumbull, 2007; WestEd, 2010).

TABLE 10.1. New York City High School Completers' Regent's Exam Passing Rate in 2016

Subject Matter Area Regent's	English Proficient Students' Passing Rate	ELLs' Passing Rate
English language arts	83%	31%
Mathematics	82%	49%
Global history	72%	23%
U.S. history	75%	29%
Science	79%	31%

PREPARE ELLS FOR STANDARDIZED TESTS

Two big barriers for ELLs to overcome on the standard tests are cultural biases and language difficulties embedded in standardized tests. Cultural bias refers to a test question that "requires special cultural knowledge that is available only to particular cultural groups" (Mohan, 1979, p. 177). According to Mohan, it is important to separate content knowledge and cultural and language knowledge in testing and evaluation in order to achieve validity. "Language tests should test language, and content tests should test content" (Mohan, 1986, p. 122).

Researchers have investigated cultural barriers and language difficulties through comparing performances by different student populations. Examining the Native American students' performance on standardized tests, researchers noted the low performance of those students may not be a lack of content knowledge but because those students do not share the cultural knowledge that test designers had in mind. In addition, test designers did not make their tests understood by linguistically and culturally diverse students. The intertwining nature of the content knowledge, cultural knowledge, and language knowledge on standardized test can put ELL students at a big disadvantage (Nelson-Barber & Trumbull, 2007).

Language Difficulties and Cultural Biases on the Regents' Exams. Take a look at the following selected Regents exam questions across academic subject matter areas:

Regent's Exam in Mathematics Algebra 1 (August 2017, p. 6)
16. Mario's $15,000 car depreciates in value at a rate of 19% per year. The value, V, after t years can be modeled by the function $V= 15,000(0.81)t$. Which function is equivalent to the original function?

(1) $V= 15,000(0.9)^{9t}$
(3) $V= 15,000(0.9)^{t/9}$
(2) $V= 15,000(0.9)2t$
(4) $V= 15,000(0.9)^{t/2}$

Taking the cultural and linguistic responsive perspectives, a group of mathematics teachers analyzed this test item below:

Analysis
This algebraic test question requires the students to have an in-depth knowledge about the U.S. culture in car selling and buying and assumes that everyone has that experience. However, for a new immigrant student whose family may not even own or rent a car, they begin the test at a disadvantage. The word "depreciates" can be a difficult term both language-wise and cultural- wise.

A close examination of the question reveals a few additional language issues for ELLs, such as the CALP level words such as value, rate, function, modeled, equivalent, etc. An examination of the mathematics Regents exam questions like this makes us more aware of the urgent need for us to teach mathematical language alongside with mathematical knowledge on the daily basis.

To modify the test item for ELLs, we rewrote the question as follows:

Mario's $15,000 car goes down in value (price) for 19% every year. After t years, its value (price) is V=15,000 (0.81)t. Which equation is the same as the above? —by a group of pre-service mathematics teachers

Even when test question is set in a neutral context not culture specific, the language difficulty can be overwhelming for English proficient students, let along for ELLs. Take a look at the most recent Regent's exam in algebra:

Regent's Exam in Algebra: August 2018 p. 9
The data obtained from a random sample of track athlete showed that as the foot size of the athlete decreased, the average running speed increased. Which statement is best supported by the data?

a. smaller foot sizes cause track athletes to run slower.
b. The sample of track athletes shows a causal relationship between foot size and running speed.
c. The sample of track athletes shows a correlation between foot size and running speed.
d. There is no correlation between foot size and running speed in track athletes.

In order to comprehend and answer this question, mathematics knowledge is not enough anymore. Rather knowledge about the English language becomes paramount for the ELL test takers to wrestle with first.

Analysis
This question is filled with complex language. The sentence structure is especially challenging for ELLs. The sentence structure used here is unnecessarily confusing. Instead of saying that "as the foot size of athletes decreased, the average running speed decreased" the question can say "a smaller foot size usually means slower running speed."

In addition, answers b and c are almost the same answers except for the tricky phrases such as "causal relationship" vs. "correlation" that makes answer C correct. It requires students to know not only mathematics but more importantly the English academic language used to express mathematics. Unfortunately, for many ELLs I observed, their linguistic power is still too limited to decipher those Tiers II and III CALP level phrases. All this is a wake-up call for me and shows me that as a future mathematics teacher I do have the responsibility to prepare ELLs for the language, especially those Tiers 2 and 3 level words and sentence structures. -By a pre-service mathematics teacher

Political cartoons, primary sources, though commonly used in the social studies class and on the Regents' exams, pose tremendous difficulties for ELLs due to the fact that those students lack American cultural, historical knowledge. A group of social studies pre-service teachers examine those test items using the cross-cultural and ESL lenses like below.

Source: Herblock, *Washington Post*, 1998

43 Which statement most accurately reflects the point of view of the cartoonist?

    (1) New technology has made modern life less convenient.

    (2) Computers have made medical records more secure.

    (3) Use of computers might compromise personal privacy.

    (4) Government records should be stored on computers.

FIGURE 10.1   Regents Exam in U.S. History and Government

Take a look at another Regents U.S. History and Government question (Figure 10.1)

Analysis

This cartoon requires students to use their insider's cultural knowledge about the U.S. cultural traditions and values to identify the concept of privacy in modern society. However, for ELLs who come from countries where privacy is not valued or there is no equivalent concept in their language, such as Chinese, they probably will not be able to understand the cultural meaning embedded here, thus unable to pick the correct answer.

We often believe that a picture speaks a thousand words, therefore, using cartoons should be easier for comprehension. However, political cartoons like this require the cultural insider's knowledge, so it is not easy to comprehend unless you have that cultural knowledge.

Language wise, the use of disciplinary vocabulary rather than every day words creates further difficulty for ELLs, such as "statement," "reflect," "cartoonist," "financial records," etc. Therefore, as future social studies teachers, we must teach ELLs this part of the US culture and use comparisons of different cultures to promote critical thinking on those key cultural concepts.

— by a group of pre-service social studies teachers

Another group of social studies teachers questioned some of the commonly used visual imagery used in the political cartoon and reflected on the impact of language and cultural learning in the social studies learning and testing, as shown in Figure 10.2.

Analysis

In the above cartoon, an arm is holding out a mug with a $ sign on it, obviously asking these people for money. But who is this person? Anyone who has lived in America and is familiar with this country's history and government will easily identify this arm as being the arm of "Uncle Sam"- also known as the U.S. government. So, the government is reaching out for money from the people for taxes. A foreign-born student will not be able to interpret the symbolism of the arm reaching out.

American-born students have also been exposed to American History in the making through television, through the news, through newspapers, and through discussions of current events in school as part of their social studies and language arts classes. For example, they may be familiar with certain Supreme Court cases, certain laws that have been enacted, and the election process in this country, because of their exposure at an earlier age. Also, American-born students have read literature that relates to the history of this country. For instance, *Huckleberry Finn* is a book read by almost every American student and it familiarizes everyone with the era of slavery. Such books and even movies (for example, *Gone with the Wind, Birth of a Nation, Glory, Pocahontas*, etc.

38.The main obstacle to solving the problem shown in the cartoon was the
1. failure of Congress to respond to public opinion
2. Government's inability to fund social programs
3. inefficiency of the Government's tax-collection system
4. demands of a variety of special interest groups

FIGURE 10.2.   Regents Exam in U.S. History Government: August, 2000, p. 6.

When a student enters junior year of high school, he/she takes a course in American History. During the first semester of the senior year, a student will take U.S. Government. These two courses are designed to inform students about American History as well as government. They have also had civics instruction in lower grades.

For an ELL who has not been acculturated and has not received education in this country, this test question will put them at a disadvantage. Therefore, it is a culturally biased question.

— by a group of pre-service social studies teacher

Cultural bias is not limited to the setting and topic but also related to the perspective and perceived correct answer that the test designer has in mind. For example, even though when ELLs encounter a test question for which they think that they have knowledge and think that they get it right, still their answer may not be what the test designer has in mind, and their answers are still wrong because test questions are biased to begin with like the question below (Nelson-Barber & Trumbull, 2007; WestEd, 2010).

Regent's Exam in U.S. History and Government (August 2000, p. 5)
Question 33: Why Truman decided to drop the atomic bomb on Japan?
1. End the war while limiting American lives
2. Punish the Japanese people by destroying their country
3. Increase Japan's potential as a future aggressor
4. Divert forces to fight Germany

Analysis
The correct answer is (1) to end the war while limiting American lives, but a student from Japan may choose (2) to punish the Japanese people by destroying their country. The student's answer is legitimate because that is how he/she learned the history of his/her country. Therefore, the key to this question is problematic. When testing students whose cultural and educational backgrounds differ from those students who share the same cultural and educational backgrounds as what the test designers have in mind, we should take into account non-native speaking students' backgrounds and include all possible correct answers.

— by a group of pre-service social studies teachers

Besides cultural difficulties ELLs also face the complex reading often well above their English proficiency levels on standardized tests. For example, reading a primary source document in social studies requires the student to close read a document for inference and interpretation. ELLs' difficulties with reading comprehension are compounded by their lack of exposure to those documents in their earlier grades as well as diverse reading and writing genres and language demands required on the Regent's exam. Take a look at the following example:

Regent's Exam in U.S. History and Government (August, 2017, p. 3)
An elective despotism, was not the government we fought for; but one which should not only be founded on free principles, but in which the powers of government

should be so divided and balanced among several bodies of magistracy [governance], as that no one could transcend their legal limits, without being effectually checked and restrained by the others.—James Madison, Federalist No. 48, 1788

Which principle of the United States Constitution is supported by this passage?
(1) Representative government
(2) Writ of habeas corpus
(3) Separation of powers
(4) Due process of law

Analysis

Facing the challenging primary source reading like above it can be difficult for English proficient students, let along ELLs. We now see a must for the social studies teacher to teach how to read the primary source document rather than simply assigning it to the students, assuming that they can understand it. Many ELLs come to the social studies class at different point or grade level, and they often do not have a good grasp of the U.S. cultural and historical knowledge in addition to language skills to get the gist of the reading. Many difficult words embedded in the above reading are "despotism," "magistracy," "governance," "transcend," "restrained," etc. Also, the whole reading is one long and complex sentence with multiple clauses, very daunting for all readers, and ELLs in particular.

In addition, the answer choices for the readings are loaded with complex social studies vocabulary, such as "separation of powers," "due process," etc. Madison's writing is a difficult read. Even with the bilingual dictionary, ELLs still may not grasp the main idea of the reading due to their limited English language proficiency.

We decided to break down the whole reading and modify it like this when teaching primary source readings to ELLs:

We fight for a government with free principles. This government should have a balance of power so that no one branch can have all the power. A good government is the government that all branches share the power and checked and monitor each other.
            — by a group of pre-service social studies teachers

Although some of the language difficulties can be reduced by allowing the student to use dictionaries or use their native language or to take extra time, still, the results were not always promising (Taylor, 2017). Mohan (1979) compared and contrasted the levels of inference demanded in standardized reading tests, including semantic inference, an inference made by drawing a conclusion from the reader's world knowledge and factual inference an inference made by drawing a conclusion from the reading material. In testing ELL students' content knowledge, if the demand for semantic inference is too great, then the test is for cultural knowledge rather than for content knowledge.

Dong (1999a,b) called for the reform on essay tests on college undergraduate students. She questioned the problematic use of agree/disagree essay format and its implication for ELL students' writing performance. Cited from the research literature and anecdotal examples from students from diverse language, cultural and educational backgrounds, she argued for taking into account of culture in standardized tests on the part of the test designers.

A Test of Subject Matter Knowledge or a Test of Language and Literacy Skills? As the Common Core Learning standards have been integrated into the subject matter curricula, there is a growing emphasis on language and literacy skills built into subject matter standardized tests, such as Regents science and mathematics in recent years. Although the rationale behind the Common Core based Regents exams is to identify students' college readiness and weed out students who are not, the over-complicated and wordy questions put ELLs at a disadvantage, especially those ELLs who may be strong in mathematics and science but weak in language skills. For ELLs who are still learning the BICS level English with limited CALP as well as literacy skills, the Common Core Regents set more barriers for those students to comprehend the test questions in the first place. Even the Common Core English Language Arts Regents has increased the breath and quantity of the reading materials and demands on the test taker's grasp of the metaphorical and figurative language as well as critical thinking skills, becoming even more daunting for ELLs.

Lakoff and Johnson (1980) argued that figurative and metaphorical language is often cultural bound. The rich contexts of the reading and in-depth cultural knowledge required for those reading materials overwhelm the ELLs even with the accommodations. Mohan (1979) argued that if a content test calls for the test taker's high level of language and literacy, then the test is not a content test but a literacy or language test. According to him, a content test should only be valid when the linguistic and cultural knowledge plays a neutral, supporting role rather than a central role often hindering ELLs from comprehending what the text and questions are all about.

Banks (2012) examined the reading items on the standardized language arts tests and found that inferential reading test items are more susceptible to cultural bias than literal reading test items because of the deep cultural background knowledge required to do those inferential and interpretative thinking. Comparing diverse students from various non-mainstream cultures such as Latino American, African American, and Native American cultures, she noted that unlike literal reading test items there is a significant bias that favors white Americans and mainstream popular culture in test designs especially for those inferential and interpretative thinking questions. She argued for the standardized test designers and writers to be familiarized with non-mainstream cultural interpretations and traditions in their design not to penalize the test takers for their lack of cultural background knowledge.

SUGGESTIONS FOR REDUCING CULTURAL BIASES ON STANDARDIZED TESTS

Butler and Stevens (2001) proposed several accommodations for ELLs in taking standardized tests like Regents exams. They call for a bias review team in test design to identify and remove those problematic test questions (Kim & Zabelina, 2015). Despite the above strategies used to accommodate ELL students' needs, more has to be done when a large number of ELL students cannot pass the standardized exams. Reform in standardized testing is needed. With a significant number of ELLs in public schools in states such as New York, California, Texas, and Florida, an involvement of ESL/Bilingual professionals in the high-stakes test design and review for cultural bias and language accessibility are necessary. Norm procedures have to make sure to include ELLs. Is it fair to use a universal test to evaluate all students, including ELLs? Can a test designed to evaluate students from one culture be used to evaluate students from different cultures? If not, then we need to think about designing a different version of the test using modified language and reduced cultural bias for ELLs. Finally, the answer and the rubric used in these tests have to be re-examined to see whether they are appropriate for ELLs. For example, can we judge an ELL's response based solely on what we consider to be appropriate as shown in some social studies test items?

In addition, subject matter teachers must be aware of the bias issue and language and literacy demands on the Regents exam in their respective subject matter. They need to design their daily lessons to include relevant background knowledge and cultural insights. That way their ELLs will progress both culturally as well rather than waiting for the test prep at the end of the semester or school year.

Alternative Evaluation for ELLs. Evaluating ELLs, more than one measures are needed to ensure validity of the evaluation and give those students more chances to perform. Research has shown a great promise in using performance assessment in recent years. Performance assessment evaluates students' learning in contexts and over time by assigning students to perform a series of learning tasks that require them to weave different knowledge sets and skills into a meaningful and coherent whole and reflect on their work using reading, writing, listening, and speaking (French, 2017; Khattri, Kahe, & Reeve, 1995; Wiggins, 1992).

Performance assessment focuses on the process and goes beyond the knowledge telling and the passive learning model and enables the teacher to teach and assess creatively and students to demonstrate their learning over time. It is especially enticing in that it offers a comprehensive view of these students' language learning and academic learning in context. Therefore, the teacher can trace students' progress and identify their strengths and growth over time. Standardized tests are often used as an after-the-fact one shot device unable to accurately evaluate the performance of the learner when the learner's language skills are still developing.

In the late 1990s, some high schools in New York City adopted the Regents Biology Variance Curriculum which used a thematic approach to biology learning that focused on the conceptual development and inquiry in learning biology. Both native and non-native English-speaking students in the selected New York City high schools were required to compile biology portfolios that included four research and creative biology projects and to complete response essays during the school year besides taking the Regents biology exam by the end of the year. Students' final course grade was a combination of the three, the portfolio, the response essays, and the Regents Biology Test. This curriculum, according to both the science chairs and the teachers, though still very limited, was better than the previous curriculum in that it gave more chances and an on-going process for students, especially non-native English-speaking students, to succeed than relying on the Regents biology exam alone in the end.

These projects tapped into students' cultural backgrounds and engaged them in a unique and meaningful way. Rather than being an object of assessment, students were active participants in these tasks. The projects offered rich opportunities to observe students in a broader context where students were doing science, reflecting on one's learning, conducting scientific inquiries, and making connections between biology learned in school and biology in real life. These performance assessment strategies should be included as part of the formal assessment. The following are some excerpts from these students' biology portfolio projects.

Portfolio Exhibit 1: An Albanian Student's Interview Reflection

For this science interview project, I interviewed my father an Albanian doctor specialized in cardiology. He has been working for 30 years at the medical field in my country. However, because of the war, we had to leave our country and move to the U.S. last year. Now he is no longer a doctor, but I still have immense respect for him. I interviewed him because it was my desire to recognize his interesting career, which is dedicated to human service.

When I asked my father about his career, he told that he attended the Medical High School and graduated from the University of Medicine of Tirana, Albania. After the medical school, he worked as a country doctor for two years and then he was employed as a cardiologist at Berat Hospital. He has published a lot of scientific articles and many books. Besides being a doctor, he worked as an adjunct professor at University of Medicine and a member of Albanian Cardiology Association. He was honored with the highest award: Doctor of Medical Science for his achievement.

When I asked, "What was the most difficult time in his career as a doctor?" my father told me that was the time when he was a country doctor, a doctor away from the big city. He said that he didn't have enough experience and sometimes he didn't have the necessary medication for the patients, also being far away from other doctors made his work very difficult.

I wanted to be a doctor like my father when I was small. Over the years my father has told me many things about being a doctor. He helped me with my biology study. However, he thinks most quality for one to be a doctor is to understand a human being, his feelings and needs. To him, that understanding is most important. My father also told me that to be a good doctor you need to have a good heart and an excellent communication skill with the patients besides a strong foundation in science. My father told me to learn to see the relationships between the medical science and other sciences, such as physics, chemistry, and mathematics. With the fast development of technology, a doctor needs to be able to use the new technology to treat patients.

At the end of this investigation I asked myself if I wanted to enter this career. My early childhood dream has been to be a doctor. Raised in a family where my father is a doctor and looking to him and admiring him for what he was doing, I always wonder what else I can do that is better than being a doctor. After finishing this interview, I found that I learned a lot from my father and knew more about why I wanted to be a doctor.

— by an 11ᵗʰ grade Albanian ELL

Portfolio Exhibit 2: An Excerpt from a Korean Student's Journal on Her Experiment on Photosynthesis

Day 12

The plant, Accent Carmine Impatiens, in the shoebox in the corner of my room is almost dying due to lack of light. The unborn baby flower is dead. Some of the leaves are already fallen apart. I could see the difference now between the second plant and this one. The second plant at the window with sunlight is still green and healthy. Most of its leaves are green and its branches are growing taller. I give both plants water. The second plant looks very nice and the leaves are wide like yesterday's leaves. By now I could answer my own questions between the two plants that I experimented...

— by a 7ᵗʰ grade Korean ELL

Portfolio Exhibit 3: A Columbian Student's Reflection on Science Reading on Pfiesteria

I recently read an interesting article named "The cell from hell: Pfiesteria strikes again—in the Chesapeake Bay" written by Mary Hager and Larry Reibstein and published in *News Week*. After reading the article I learned that from the beginning of organisms on earth, there has been a struggle between these organisms for food. Many of these organisms used to change their homes and stay out of trouble in order to survive. As we learned in our biology class, often strong organisms survive and weak ones die. Most recently, scientists discovered a micro-organism in water called Pfiesteria. Even though it is a tiny organism, it has unusual survival ability. It can reproduce rapidly and it kills hundreds and thousands of fish. This organism was first discovered by a botanist, Dr. Joann Brukholder in 1991. However, there has no research done to investigate the impact of Pfiesteria on humans. Some scientists even wonder whether fish killed was because of Pfiesteria or the polluted water.

I like this article because writers give us different points of views about Pfiesteria. It shows that in biology we are constantly learning new things and finding the unknown. My question is why they named this organism Pfiesteria? What are some of the ways that the scientists can investigate the real cause for the fish's death? As I live close to the East River, I know there are many things to consider in order to be certain that Pfiesteria is the killer. I would like to keep reading about this topic and find out more about it.

— by a 9ᵗʰ grade Columbian ELL

Portfolio Exhibit 4: A Bangladeshi Student Writing About His Museum Visit
My visit to the American Museum of Natural History in Manhattan last Friday was a big adventure for me. Since coming to over to America I have not had a chance to tour Manhattan myself. My father got me a subway map and I marked the place on the map before I left home. It took me an hour and a half by train to get there.

There were a lot of exhibits in the museum. I chose "Ocean Life" because I liked the ocean most. The exhibit was on the first floor. Once I walked into the entrance of the exhibit, I was in the middle of the ocean world. The introduction gave me an idea of what a fish was: an aquatic vertebrate animal, usually possessing gills in the adult stage and having limbs in the forms of fins. I was fascinated to learn that unlike other commonly recognized groups of animals, the fish is a heterogeneous assemblage of groups that cannot be recognized by any defining trait. So, the word fish can refer to an individual fish or a group of fish. The exhibit was divided into four sections. They were: diversity and evolution, anatomy, breathing, reproduction of the fish... (The student then goes to each section describing and explaining the exhibits in detail.)

The exhibit is closely connected with the biology we are learning now. Viewing the exhibit makes what we learn in biology more real to me. I was glad that I learned about the use of the word fish. The most interesting thing I found is the fish's external fertilization and development. The exhibit said that a single cod could produce about three million eggs.

I have a few questions after my museum trip:

What happens to these three million eggs once they are produced? Do other fish eat them before they are fertilized? What is the birth rate for these eggs? I have taken a lot of notes and am thinking to investigate the fish in my fish tank at home.

— by a 10th grade Bangladeshi ELL

CONCLUSION

Right after the first day of my graduate class, Language, Literacy, and Culture in Education, Lee a high school English teacher shared with me something special. Lee took my multicultural literature class the previous semester and did her final project on engaging her class of reluctant and struggling readers in reading Langston Hughes' "Mother to Son." Lee told me with excitement that one of her ELLs, who never wrote anything in the whole semester, wrote such a beautiful poem about his mother that Lee mailed it home to his mother. Lee did not imagine that the mother sent her a big bouquet of flower days later with a card, thanking her for what she did for her son, who wrote such a beautiful poem in English. Deeply touched by the parent's gesture, Lee talked about how rewarding teaching ELLs can be.

Working with ELLs can be a really challenging, but rewarding and exhilarating experience for many teachers. I feel a certain kinship with those ELLs after listening to their stories and watching their struggles with English. I too was an ESL learner coming to The University of Georgia to work on my graduate degree from Mainland China many years ago. Fortunately, I was with a group of open and supportive faculty members and fellow graduate students characterized by their "southern hospitality." To this day I still remember especially the faculty members who viewed my foreignness as a resource rather than a burden, who saw my bilingual and bi-cultural status as a strength rather than a weakness, and who did not benignly neglect me but included me in the class discussions, challenged

Teaching English Language Learners in Secondary Subject Matter Classes, pages 217–218.

and supported me to grow both linguistically and culturally. Their willingness to listen to my voice of silence, to spend time learning about my native culture, and their persistence in helping with my second language learning serves as models for me to pursue my career in teacher education in working with English as second language learners in subject matter classes.

This book is no way providing "solve all" recipes for subject matter teachers. It is my hope that the book opens ways of teachers' thinking about those often-silenced students in their subject matter classes. I also hope the strategies and ideas discussed and illustrated in the book serve as points of departure for those teachers to get on a journey of using ELLs' native language, cultural, and literacy learning backgrounds to teach subject matter knowledge and integrating language instruction into their subject matter instruction in order for those students to succeed academically and socially as they develop their English proficiency. My best wishes to all teachers on that journey!

BIBLIOGRAPHY

Abadiano, H., & Turner, J. (2003). Thinking it through: Re-examining our beliefs about assessment for diverse students. *The NERA Journal, 39*(1), 58–63.

Acton, W. R., & Felix, J. W. (1986). Acculturation and mind. In J. M. Valdes (Ed.) *Culture bound: Bridging the cultural gap in language teaching* (pp. 20–32). Cambridge, UK: Cambridge University Press.

Adamson, H. D. (1993). *Academic competence: Theory and classroom practice: Preparing ESL students for content classes*. New York, NY: Longman.

Adamson, J., & Coulson, D. (2015). Translanguaging in English academic writing preparation. *International Journal of pedagogies and learning, 10*(1), 24–37.

Alexander-Shea, A. (2011). Redefining vocabulary: The new learning strategy for social studies. *The Social Studies, 102*(1), 95–103.

Alvarez, J. (1991). *How the Garcia girls lost their accents.* New York, NY: A Plume Book.

Amuedo-Dorantes, C., & Pozo, S. (2010). Accounting for remittance and migration effects on children's schooling. *World Development, 38*(12), 1747–1759.

An, S. (2009). Learning US history in an age of globalization and transnational migration. *Journal of Curriculum Studies, 41*(6), 763–787.

Andrews, S. E. (1997). Writing to learn in content area reading class. *Journal of Adolescent & Adult Literacy, 41*(2), 141–142.

Applebee, A. N. (1996). *Curriculum as conversation: Transforming traditions of teaching and learning*. Chicago, IL: The University of Chicago Press.

August, D., Carol, M., Dressler, C., & Snow, C. (2005). The critical role of vocabulary development for English language learners. *Learning Disabilities Research & Practice, 20*(1), 50–57.

Teaching English Language Learners in Secondary Subject Matter Classes, pages 219–237.

Copyright © 2019 by Information Age Publishing

August, D., McCardle, P., Shanahan, T. (2014). Developing literacy in English language learners: Findings from a review of the experimental research. *School Psychology Review, 43*(4), 490–498.

Avalos, M., Plasencia, A. Chavez, C., & Rascon, J. (2007). Modified guided Reading: Gateway to English as a second language and literacy learning. *The Reading Teacher, 61*(4), 318–329.

Ballenger, C. (2008). Case study: Using two languages to learn science. In A. S. Rosebery & B. Warren (Eds.), *Teaching science to English language learners: Building on students' strengths* (pp. 119–124). Arlington, VA: NSTA Press.

Bangladesh: Curriculum planning, development and reform for primary and secondary education. (1998). In *UNESCO statistical yearbook.* Paris. Retrieved from http://www.ibe.unesco.org/curriculum/Asia%20Networkpdf/ndrepbd.pdf

Bangladesh education system. (n.d.). In *The Library of Congress Country studies: CIA world fact book.* Retrieved from http://www.photius.com/countries/bangladesh/society/bangladesh_society_education_system.html

Bangladeshi culture. (n.d.). In Wikipedia. Retrieved from https://en.wikipedia.org/wiki/Culture_of_Bangladesh

Banks, K. (2012). Are inferential reading items more susceptible to cultural bias than literal reading items? *Applied Measurement in Education, 25*(3), 220–245.

Barkaoui, K. (2007). Teaching writing to second language learners: Insights from theory and research. *TESL Reporter, 40*(1), 35–48.

Baron, L. M. (2016). Formative assessment at work in the classroom. *Mathematics Teachers, 110*(1), 46–52.

Barwell, R. (2009). Mathematical word problems and bilingual learners in England. In R. Barwell (Ed.), *Multilingualism in mathematics classrooms: Global perspectives* (pp. 63–77). UK: Multilingual Matters.

Bedggood, G., & Benady, I. (2010). *Dominican Republic: Cultural smart! The essential guide customs & culture.* Chicago, IL: Kuperard Publishing.

Beeman, K., & Urow, C. (2013). *Teaching for biliteracy: Strengthening bridges between languages.* Philadelphia, PA: Caslon Publishing.

Beene, T. (2017). *Teaching social studies to ELLs.* San Clemente, CA: Canter Press.

Bengali language. (n.d.). In *Wikipedia.* Retrieved from https://en.wikipedia.org/wiki/Bengali_language

Bereiter, C., & Scadamalia, M. (1987). *The psychology of written composition.* Hillsdale, NJ: Lawrence Erlbaum Associates.

Bialystok, E. (2008). Essay: Learning a second language. In A. S. Rosebery & S. Warren (Eds.), *Teaching science to English language learners: Building on students' strengths* (pp. 107–118). Arlington, VA: NSTA.

Biggs, J. (1999). Western misperceptions of the Confucian-heritage learning culture. In D. A. Watkins & J. B. Biggs (Eds.), *The Chinese learner: Cultural, psychological, and contextual influences* (pp. 45–67). Hong Kong, China. Comparative Education Research Centre.

Blackwell, A. J., & McLaughlin, T. F. (2005). Using guided notes, choral responding, and response cards to increase student performance. *International Journal of Special Education, 20*(2), 1–5.

Boorstin, D. J., & Kelley, M. (1989). *A History of The United States.* Englewood Cliffs, NJ: Prentice-Hall.

Boyd, M., & Kong, Y. (2017). Reasoning words as linguistic features of exploratory talk: Classroom use and what it can tell us. *Discourse Processes, 54*(1), 62–81.

Boyd-Batstone, P. (2013). *Helping English language learners meet the Common Core: Assessment and instructional strategies K–12.* New York, NY: Routledge.

Boyles, N. (2012–2013). Closing in on close reading. *Educational Leadership, 70*(4), 36–41.

Brescia, W., & Fortune, J. C. (1988). *Standardized testing of American Indian students.* ERIC Digest, ED 296 813.

Brockway, C. S., Gardner, L., & Howe, J. (1985). *General science.* Newton, MA: Allyn & Bacon.

Brown, H. D. (1987). Learning a second culture. In H. D. Brown's *Principles of language learning and teaching* (pp. 129–144). Englewood, NJ: Prentice-Hall.

Brown, R. (1973). *A first language: The early stages.* Cambridge, MA: Harvard University Press.

Brown, S. (2016). Story nights: An apprenticeship into literacy through bilingual story reading. *Teaching Education, 27*(3), 286–304.

Bruna, K. R., Vann, R., & Escudero, M. P. (2007). What's language got to do with it? A case study of academic language instruction in a high school "English Learner Science" class. *Journal of English for Academic Purposes, 6*(1), 36–54.

Buley-Meissner, M. L. (1990). Teaching American literature in China: Learning how students read and respond. *English Education, 22*(3), 192–199.

Burdett, L. (1998). *Romeo and Juliet for kids.* Buffalo, NY: Firefly Books.

Butler, F. A., & Stevens, R. (2001). Standardized assessment of the content knowledge of English language learners K–12: Current trends and old dilemmas. *Language Testing, 18*(4), 409–427.

Calderon, M. (2007). *Teaching reading to English language learners, grades 6–12.* Thousand Oaks, CA: Corwin Press.

Campbell, E., & Cuba, M. (2015). Analyzing the role of visual cues in developing predictive-making skills of third-and-ninth grade English language learners. *CATESOL Journals, 27*(1), 53–93.

Carrasquillo, A. L., & Rodriguez, V. (1996). *Language minority students in the mainstream classroom.* Clevedon, Great Britain: Multilingual Matters Ltd.

Carroll, J. B. (Ed.) (1956). *Language, thought, and reality: Selected writings of Benjamin Lee Whorf.* Cambridge, MA: MIT Press.

Carson, J. (1992). Becoming biliterate. *Journal of Second Language Writing, 1*(1), 37–60.

Cazden, C. B. (1988). *Classroom discourse: The language of teaching and learning.* Portsmouth, NH: Heinemann.

Chamot, A. U., & O'Malley, J. M. (1994). *The CALLA handbook: Implementing the cognitive academic language learning approach.* Reading, MA: Addition-Wesley.

Chang, L., Xu, L, Perfetti, C. A., Zhang, J., & Chen, H. (2014). Supporting orthographic learning at the beginning stage of learning to read Chinese as a second language. *International Journal of Disability, Development and Education, 61*(3), 288–305.

Chauncey, M. (2011). Beyond reading comprehension and summary: Learning to read and write in history by focusing on evidence, perspective, and interpretation. *Curriculum Inquiry, 41*(2), 212–249.

Chinese language. (n.d.). In *Wikipedia.* Retrieved from https://en.wikipedia.org/wiki/Chinese_language

Cho, H., Brutt-Griffer, J. (2015). Integrated reading and writing: A case of Korean English language learners. *Reading in a Foreign Language, 27*(2), 242–261.

Choi, Y. (2013). Teaching social studies for newcomer English language learners: Toward culturally relevant pedagogy. *Multicultural Perspectives, 15*(1), 12–18.

Choi, Y., Lim, J. H., & An, S. (2011). Marginalized students' uneasy learning: Korean immigrant students' experiences of learning social studies. *Social Studies Research and Practice, 6*(1), 1–17.

Chowdbury, F. D. (2004). The socio-cultural context of child marriage in a Bangladeshi village. *International Journal of Social Welfare, 13*(3), 244–253.

Cisneros, S. (1991). *The house on Mango Street*. New York, NY: Vintage Books.

Clancy, M. E., & Hruska, B. L. (2005). Developing language objectives for English language learners in physical education lessons. *Journal of Physical Education, Recreation & Dance, 76*(4), 30–35.

Collier, V. P. (1987). Age and rate of acquisition of second language for academic purposes. *TESOL Quarterly, 21*(4), 617–641.

Collier, V. P. (1989). How long? A synthesis of research on academic achievement in a second language. *TESOL Quarterly, 23* (3), 509–531.

Collins, L. W., & Fulton, L. (2017). Promising practices for supporting students with disabilities through writing in science. *Teaching Exceptional Children, 49*(3), 194–203.

Commissioner's Regulation Part 154. (2015). *English language learners (ELLs) screening, identification, placement, review, and exit criteria*. Albany, NY: New York State Department of Education.

Common Core State Standards Initiative (CCSSI). (2010). Washington, DC: National Governors Association Center for Best Practices and the Council of Chief State School Officers. Retrieved from https://www.common-core-state-standards-init.html

Cook, V. (2001). Using the first language in the classroom. *Canadian Modern Language Review, 57*(3), 402–423.

Cooke, S. (2013). Literacy in Bangladesh: Reading between the lines. In *The Daily Star*, Sept. 8. Albany, NY. Retrieved from https://www.thedailystar.net/news/literacy-in-bangladesh

Cooks, J., & Sunseri, A. (2013–2014). Leveling the playing field: The efficacy of thinking maps on English language learner students' writing. *The CATESOL Journal, 25*(1), 24–40.

Culture of Mexico. (n. d.). In *Wikipedia*. Retrieved from https://en.wikipedia.org/wiki/Culture_of_Mexico" after Cooks' reference.

Cummins, J. (1979a). Cognitive/academic language proficiency, linguistic interdependence, and optimum age question and some other matters. *Working Papers on Bilingualism, 19*, 121–192.

Cummins, J. (1979b). Linguistic interdependence and the educational development of bilingual children. *Review of Educational Research, 49*(2), 222–251.

Cummins, J. (1984). *Bilingualism and special education: Issues in assessment and pedagogy*. Clevedon, UK: Multilingual Matters.

Cummins, J. (1986). Empowering minority students: A framework for intervention. *Harvard Educational Review, 56*(1), 18–36.

Curdt-Christiansen, X. L. (2008). Reading the world through words: Cultural themes in heritage Chinese language textbooks. *Language and Education, 22*(2), 95–113.

Davison, C. (2006). Collaboration between ESL and content teachers: How do we know when we are doing it right? *The International Journal of Bilingual Education and Bilingualism, 9*(4), 454–475.

DeCapua, A., Smathers, W., & Tang, L. F. (2007). Schooling interrupted. *Educational Leadership, 64*(6), 40–46.

DeRose, J. (2007). Comparing international textbooks to develop historical thinking. *Social Education, 71*(1), 36–39.

Derwing, T. M., DeCorby, E., & Ichikawa, J. (1999). Some factors that affect the success of ESL high school students. *The Canadian Modern Language Review, 55*(4), 533–547.

De Smet, A., Mettewie, L., & Galand, B. (2018). Classroom anxiety and enjoyment in CLIL and non-CLIL: Does the target language matter? *Studies in Second Language Learning and Teaching, 8*(1), 47–71.

Dhurandhar, A. (2009). Writing the other: An exercise in empathy. *Journal of Learning through the Arts. 5*(1), Article 3.

DiGisi, L. L., & Fleming, D. (2005). Literacy specialists in math class! Closing the achievement gap on state math assessments. *Voices from the Middle, 13*(1), 48–52.

Doabler, C. T., Nelson, N. J., Clarke, B. (2016). Adapting evidence-based practices to meet the needs of English learners with mathematics difficulties. *Teaching Exceptional Children, 28*(6), 301–310.

Dominican Republic. (n.d.). In *Wikipedia*. Retrieved from https://en.wikipedia.org/wiki/Dominican_Republic"

Dong, Y. R. (1998). From writing in their native language to writing in English: What students bring to our writing classrooms? *College ESL, 8*(2), 87–105.

Dong, Y. R. (1999a). The need to understand ESL students' native language writing experiences. *Teaching English in the Two-Year College, 26*(3), 277–285.

Dong, Y. R. (1999b). The impact of native language literacy on ESL college freshmen's writing of argumentative essays. *Journal of Teaching Writing, 17*(1 & 2), 88–117.

Dong, Y. R. (2002). Integrating language and content: How three biology teachers work with non-native English-speaking students. *International Journal of Bilingual Education and Bilingualism. 5*(1), 40–57.

Dong, Y. R. (2004a). Don't keep them in the dark: Teaching metaphorical language to English language learners. English Journal, 93(4), 29–35.

Dong, Y. R. (2004b). Preparing secondary subject area teachers to teach linguistically and culturally diverse students. *The Clearing House, 77*(5), 202–208.

Dong, Y. R. (2005a). Promoting ELL students' participation in mainstream subject matter classes. *Thresholds in Education, 16* (1 & 2), 33–40.

Dong, Y. R. (2005b). Getting at the content. *Educational Leadership, 62*(4), 14–19.

Dong, Y. R. (2006). Learning to think in English. *Educational Leadership, 64*(2), 22–27.

Dong, Y. R. (2009). Linking to prior learning. *Educational Leadership, 66*(7), 26–31.

Dong, Y. R. (2011). *Unlocking the power of academic words with secondary English language learners*. Gainsville, FL: Maupin House Publishing, Inc.

Dong, Y. R. (2013). Powerful learning tools for ELLs. *The Science Teacher, 80*(4), 51–57.

Dong, Y. R. (2013–2014). The bridge of knowledge. *Educational Leadership, 71*(4), 30–36.

Dong, Y. R. (2016). Creating a responsive learning community for ELLs in mathematics classrooms. *Mathematics Teacher, 109*(7), 534–540.

Dong, Y. R. (2017). Tapping into English language learners' (ELLs') prior knowledge in social studies instruction. *The Social Studies, 108*(4), 1–9.

Doolan, S., & Fitzsimmons-Doolan, S. (2016). Facilitating L2 writers' interpretation of source texts. *TESOL Journal, 7*(3), 716–745.

Duff, P. A. (2001). Language, literacy, content, and (pop) culture: Challenges for ESL students in mainstream courses. *Canadian Modern Language Review, 58*(1), 103–32.

Dunn, S. (1989). The sacred. In Stephen Dunn, *Between angels: Poems by Stephen Dunn* (p. 55). New York, NY: Alfred A. Knopf. Reprinted with permission.

Durband, A. (1985). *Romeo and Juliet: Shakespeare made easy.* Portland, ME: Barron's Educational Series.

Early, M., & Marshall, S. (2008). Adolescent ESL students' interpretation and appreciation of literary texts: A case study of multimodality. *The Canadian Modern Language Review, 64*(3), 377–397.

Ebe, A. E. (2010). Culturally relevant texts and reading assessment for English language learners. *Reading Horizons, 50*(3), 193–210.

Education in Bangladesh. (n.d.). In *Wikipedia.* Retrieved from https://en.wikipedia.org/wiki/Education_in_Bangladesh

Education in China. (n.d.). In *Wikipedia.* Retrieved from https://en.wikipedia.org/wiki/Education_in_China

Education in Mexico. (n.d.). In *Wikipedia.* In Retrieved from https://en.wikipedia.org/wiki/Education_in_Mexico

Education in The Dominican Republic. (n.d.). In *Wikipedia.* Retrieved from https://en.wikipedia.org/wiki/Education_in_the_Dominican_Republic

Education system Bangladesh. (2012). In *EP-Nuffic International Education.* Retrieved from https://www.nuffic.nl/en/publications/find-a-publication/education-system-bangladesh.pdf

Education system in the Dominican Republic. (n.d.). In *Foreign Credits.* Retrieved from https://www.classbase.com/countries/Dominican-Republic/Education-System

Edwards, V. (2015). "'Doing school': Cross cultural encounters. *TESOL in Context, 25*(1), 4–15.

Ellis, R. (1993). *Naturally simplified input, comprehension, and second language acquisition.* ERIC Database. ED 371 577.

Esquinca, A. (2011). Bilingual college writers' collaborative writing of word problems. *Linguistics and Education, 22*(2), 150–167.

Esty, W. W., & Teppo, A. R. (1994). A general-education course emphasizing mathematical language and reasoning. *Focus on Learning Problems in Mathematics, 16*(1), 13–35.

Fairbairn, S., & Jones-Vo S. (2010). *Differentiating instruction and assessment for English language learners.* Philadelphia, PA: Caslon Publishing.

Falk, F., & Linder, R. (2009). Reading and writing connections using media: Addressing the literacy needs of students in intermediate and middle level classrooms. *The Language and Literacy Spectrum, 19*, 29–38.

Ferlazzo, L., & Hull-Sypnieski, K. (2014). Teaching argument writing to ELLs. *Educational Leadership, 71*(7), 46–52.

Figueredo, L. (2006). Using the known to chart the unknown: A review of first-language influence on the development of English-as-a-second-language spelling skill. *Reading and Writing, 19*(8), 873–905.

First, C. G., MacMillan, B., & Levy, C. (1995). Writing process versatility. *Intervention in School and Clinic, 31*(1), 21–27.

Fisher, D., & Frey, N. (2014). *Close reading and writing from sources.* Newark, DE: International Reading Association.

Fisher, D., Frey, N., & Lapp, D. (2012). Building and activating students' background knowledge: It's what they already know that counts. *Middle School Journal, 43*(3), 22–31.

Fisher, D., Frey, N., & Rothenberg, C. (2008). *Content-area conversations: How to plan discussion-based lessons for diverse language learners.* Alexandria, VA: ASCD.

Folse, K. S. (2004). *Vocabulary myth: Applying second language research to classroom teaching.* Ann Arbor, MI: University of Michigan Press.

Foucault, D. C., & Schneider, B. H. (2009). Parenting values and parenting stress among impoverished village and middle-class small city mothers in the Dominican Republic. *International Journal of Behavioral Development, 33*(5), 440–450.

Franquiz, M., & Salias, C. S. (2011). Newcomers developing English literacy through historical thinking and digitized primary sources. *Journal of Second Language Writing, 20*(3), 196–210.

Freeman, L. (2015). Using close reading as a course theme in a multilingual disciplinary classroom. *Reading in a Foreign Language, 27*(3), 262–271.

Freeman, Y., & Freeman, D. (2006). *Teaching reading and writing in Spanish and English in bilingual and dual language classrooms.* Portsmouth, NH: Heinemann.

Freeman, Y., & Freeman, D. (2009). *Academic language for English language learners and struggling readers.* Portsmouth, NH: Heinemann.

French, D. (2017). Future is performance assessment. *Voices in Urban Education, 46*, 6–12.

French, L. A., & Manzanarez, M. (2002). Mexico's education system. In *World Education Encyclopedia.* Retrieved from https://www.academia.edu/21052902/Mexico_Education_System

Fu, D. L. (1995). *"My trouble is my English: Asian students and the American dream.* Portsmouth, NH: Boynton/Cook Publishers

Fu, D. L. (1998). Unlock their lonely hearts. *Voices from the Middle, 6*(1), 3–10.

Garcia, M. (1997). *The adventures of Connie and Diego.* New York, NY: Lee & Low Books/Children's Book Press.

Garcia, O., Johnson, S. I., & Seltzer, K. (2017). *The translanguaging classroom: Leveraging student bilingualism for learning.* Philadelphia, PA: Caslon Publishing.

Garrod, A., & Davis, J. (1999). *Crossing customs: International students write on U.S. college life and culture.* New York, NY: Falmer Press.

Gay, G. (2010). *Culturally responsive teaching: Theory, research, & practice.* New York, NY: Teachers College Press.

Gaytan, F. X., Carhill, A., & Suarez-Orozzo, C. (2007). Understanding and responding to the needs of newcomer immigrant youth and families. *The Prevention Researcher, 14*(4), 10–13.

Gee, J. P. (2008). Essay: What is academic language? In A. S. Rosebery & S. Warren (Eds.), *Teaching science to English language learners: Building on students' strengths* (pp. 57–70). Arlington, VA: NSTA.

Genesee, F. (1976). The role of intelligence in second language learning. *Language Learning, 26* (3), 267–280.

Genesee, F. (1993). All teachers are second language teachers. *The Canadian Modern Language Review, 50*(1), 47–53.

Gerofsky, S. (1996). A linguistic and narrative view of work problems in mathematics education. *For the Learning of Mathematics, 16*(2), 36–45.

Gewertz, C. (2012). History lessons blend content knowledge, literacy. *Education Digest: Essential Readings Condensed for Quick Review, 78*(4), 11–16.

Gibbons, P. (2003). Mediating language learning: Teacher interactions with ESL students in a content-based classroom. *TESOL Quarterly, 37*(2), 247–273.

Golding, W. (2013). *Lord of the flies*. Hemdon, VA: A & A Publishers.

Goodman, Y. M., Watson, D., & Burke, C. (1987). *Reading miscue inventory: Alternative procedures*. New York, NY: Richard C. Owen.

Grant, M. C., & Fisher, D. (2010). *Reading and writing in science: Tools to develop disciplinary literacy*. Thousand Oaks, CA: Corwin.

Graziano, K., & Navarrete, L. A. (2012). Co-teaching in a teacher education classroom: Collaboration, compromise, and creativity. *Issues in Teacher Education, 21*(1), 109–126.

Hache de Yunen, A. M., & Montenegro, L. (1993). Transplanting literacy methods across cultures: A case study in the Dominican Republic. *The Reading Teacher, 47*(3), 264–266.

Hall, A. (2006). Keeping La Llorona alive in the shadow of Cortes: What an examination of literacy in two Medican schools can teach US educators. *Bilingual Research Journal, 30*(2), 385–406.

Harklau, L. (1994). ESL versus mainstream classes: Contrasting L2 learning environments. *TESOL Quarterly, 28*(2), 241–272.

Harrison, G. L., & Krol, L. (2007). Relationship between L1 and L2 word-level reading and phonological processing in adults learning English as a second language. *Journal of Research in Reading, 30*(4), 379–393.

Hasegawa, T., Gundykunst, W. B. (1998). Silence in Japan and the United States. *Journal of Cross-cultural Psychology, 29*(5), 668–684.

Haynes, J., & Zacarian, D. (2010). *Teaching English language learners across the content areas*. Alexandria, VA: ASCD.

Heath, S. B., & Sobol, D. (2013). When literacy brings too many risks: A successful lesson in failure. In J. Kalman & B. Street (Eds.), *Literacy and numeracy in Latin America: Local perspectives and beyond* (pp. 127–140). New York, NY: Routledge.

Hebert, M. A., & Powell, S. R. (2016). Examination fourth-grade mathematics writing: Features of organization, mathematics vocabulary, and mathematical representations. *Reading and Writing, 29*, 1511–1537.

Hedgcock, J., & Atkinson, D. (1993). Differing reading-writing relationships in L1 and L2 literacy development? *TESOL Quarterly, 27*(2), 329–333.

Herrara, V. A. (1996). *Education in Mexico: Historical and contemporary educational systems*. Education Resources Information Center, ED 393 634.

Herrera, R. L. (2015). Mexican secondary school students' perception of learning the history of Mexico in English. *Teachers' Professional Development, 17*(1), 105–120.

Herrero, El. A. (2006). Using Dominican oral literature and discourse to support literacy learning among low-achieving students from the Dominican Republic. *The International Journal of Bilingual Education and Bilingualism, 9*(2), 219–238.

Hersey, J. (1946). *Hiroshima*. New York, NY: Alfred A. Knopf.

Hochman, J., & Wexler, N. (2017). *The writing revolution: A guide to advancing thinking through writing in all subjects and grades.* San Francisco, CA: Jossey-Bass.

Hoffert, S. B. (2009). Mathematics: The universal language? *Mathematics Teacher, 103*(2), 130–139.

Honigsfeld, A., & Dove, M. (2008). Co-teaching in the ESL classroom. *Delta Kappa Gamma Bulletin, 74*(2), 8–14.

How are K–12 schools different in Mexico compared to the US? (n.d.). In *TeAchnology.* Retrieved from http://www.teach-nology.com/teachers/employment/esl/mexico/

Howard, E. (2007). A day in the life of a Mexican student. In *Journey North.* Retrieved from https://www.learner.org/jnorth/tm/monarch/sl/49/Day_in_the_Life.pdf

Hudson-Ross, S., & Dong, Y. R. (1990). Literacy learning as a reflection of language and culture: Chinese elementary school education. *The Reading Teacher, 44*(2), 110–123.

Hughes, L. (1951). *Harlem.* Retrieved from: https://www.poetryfoundation.org

Ibrahim, E. H. E., Sarudin, I., & Muhamad, A. J. (2016). The relationship between vocabulary size and reading comprehension of ESL learners. *English Language Teaching, 9*(2), 116–123.

Irizarry, J. G. (2007). Ethnic and urban intersections in the classroom: Latino students, hybrid identities, and culturally responsive pedagogy. *Multicultural Perspective, 9*(3), 21–28.

Irizarry, J. G. (2011). Ethics and urban intersections in the classroom: Latino students, hybrid identities, and culturally responsive pedagogy. *Multicultural Perspectives, 9*(3), 21–28.

Jaffee, A. T. (2016). Community, voice, and inquiry: Teaching global history for English language learners. *The Social Studies, 107*(3), 1–13.

James, M. (2002). *Schooling in Mexico: A brief guide for US educators.* Education Resources Information Center, ED 470 948.

Jameson, J. H. (1998). Simplifying the language of authentic materials. *TESOL Matters, 8*(3), 13.

Jimenez, E., & Lockheed, M. E. (1995). *Public and private secondary education in developing countries: A comparative study.* World Bank, Washington DC. SO 026 579.

Johnson, J. S., & Newport, E. L. (1989). Critical period effects in second language learning: The influence of maturational state of the acquisition of English as a second language. *Cognitive Psychology, 21*(1), 60–99.

Jones, J. F. (1999). From silence to talk: Cross-cultural ideas on students' participation in academic group discussions. *English for Specific Purposes, 18*(3), 243–259.

Kaplan, R. B. (1966). Cultural thought patterns in inter-cultural education. *Language Learning, 16*(1), 1–20.

Kenner, C., Al-Azami, S., Gregory, E., & Ruby, M. (2008). Bilingual poetry: Expanding the cognitive and cultural dimensions of children's learning. *Literacy, 42*(2), 92–100.

Khattri, N., Kahe, M. B., & Reeve, A. L. (1995). How performance assessments affect teaching and learning. *Educational Leadership, 53*(3), 80–83.

Kim, H. K., & Zabelina, D. (2015). Cultural bias in assessment: Can creativity assessment help? *International Journal of Critical Pedagogy, 6*(2), 129–147.

Kirsch, C. (2016). Using storytelling to teach vocabulary in language lessons: Does it work? *The Language Learning Journal, 44*(1), 33–51.

Kostka, I., & Maliborska, V. (2016). Using Turnitin to provide feedback on L2 writers' texts. *TESL-EJ, 20*(2), 1–22.

Krashen, S. (1981). The case of narrow reading. *TESOL Newsletters, 15*(6), 23.

Krashen, S. (1982). *Principles and practice in second language acquisition*. Oxford:, UK Pergamon.

Krashen, S. (1985). *The input hypothesis: Issues and implications*. London, UK: Longman.

Kunihira, S., & Asher, S. (1965). *The strategy of the total physical response: An application to learning Japanese*. ERIC database, ED 011–108

Ladson-Billings, G. (1995). But that's just good teaching! The case for culturally relevant pedagogy. *Theory into Practice, 34*(3), 159–165.

Lakoff, G., & Johnson, M. (1980). *Metaphors we live by*. Chicago, IL: Chicago University Press.

Lapp, D., Grant, M. C., Modd, B., & Johnson, K. (2013). Students' close reading of science texts: What's now? What's next? *The Reading Teacher, 67*(2), 109–119.

Laufer, B., & Aviad-Levitzky, T. (2017). What type of vocabulary knowledge predicts reading comprehension: Word meaning recall or Word meaning recognition? *The Modern Language Journal, 101*(4), 729–741.

Lee, H. (1960). *To kill a mockingbird*. Philadelphia, PA: J.B. Lippincott Company.

Lee, J. S. (2010). Culturally relevant pedagogy for immigrant children and English language learners. *National Society for the Study of Education Yearbook, 109*(2), 153–173.

Lee, J., & Schllert, D. L. (2015). Exploring the reading-writing connection: A yearlong classroom-based experimental study of middle school students developing literacy in a new language. *Reading Research Quarterly, 51*(2), 143–164.

Lee, M. E. (2014). Shifting to the World Englishes paradigm by way of translingual approach: Code-meshing as a necessary means of transforming composition pedagogy. *TESOL Journal, 5*(2), 312–329.

Leigh, S. R. (2012). The classroom is alive with the sound of thinking: The power of the exit slip. *International Journal of Teaching and Learning in Higher Education, 24*(2), 189–196.

Leki, I. (1992). *Understanding ESL writers: A guide for teachers*. Portsmouth, NH: Boyton/Cook Publishers.

Lemke, J. L. (1987a). Making text talk. *Theory into Practice, 28*(2), 136–141.

Lemke, J. L. (1987b). *Talking science: Content, conflict, and semantics*. ERIC Database. ED 282 402.

Lems, K., Miller, L. D., & Soro, T. M. (2010). *Teaching reading to English language learners: Insights from linguistics*. New York, NY: Guilford Press.

Lenneberg, E. (1967). *Biological foundations of language*. New York, NY: John Wiley.

Leung, C. (2003). Bicultural perspectives and reader responses: Four American readers respond to Jean Fritz's "Homesick." *Canadian Modern Language Review, 60*(1), 27–54.

Lightbown, P. (2012). Intensive L2 instruction in Canada: Why not immersion? In C. Munoz (Ed.), *Intensive exposure experiences in second language learning* (pp. 25–44). Bristol, UK: Multilingual Matters.

Lightbown, P., & Spada, N. (2013). *How languages are learned*. (4th ed.). Oxford, UK: Oxford University Press.

Lin, L., Zhao, Y., Ogawa, M., Hoge, J., & Kim, B. Y. (2011). Whose history? An analysis of the Korean War in history textbooks from the United States, South Korea, Japan, and China. *The Social Studies, 100*(5), 222–232.

Lindaman, D., & Ward, H. (2006). *History: How textbooks from around the world portray U.S. history.* New York, NY: The New Press.

Lindquist, B., & Loynachan, C. (2016). Learning science in a second language. *Science and Children, 54*(3), 47–51.

Linvill, D. L., & Kindall, B. (2015). Teaching metatheory through Venn Diagramming, *Communication Teacher, 29*(5), 135–140.

List of countries by literacy rate. (2017). In *Wikipedia*. Retrieved from https://en.wikipedia.org/wiki/List_of_countries_by_literacy_rate

Liu, Y. (2005). A pedagogy for digraphia: An analysis of the impact of Pinyin on literacy teaching in China and its implications for curricular and pedagogical innovations in a wider community. *Language and Education, 19*(5), 400–414.

Long Island Regional Bilingual Education Resource Network (2014). *Co-teaching and collaboration for teachers of ELLs.* Retrieved from: https://www.esboces.org

Lopez-Bonilla, G. (2015). Curricular reforms in Mexico: Challenges for developing disciplinary literacy in upper secondary education. *Journal of Adolescent & Adult Literacy. 58*(7), 541–545.

Lucas, T., & Villegas, A. M. (2010). The missing piece in teacher education: The preparation of linguistically responsive teachers. *National Society for the Study of Education Yearbook, 109*(2), 297–318.

Luna, J. (2015). Bengali students need teachers who speak their language. In *WNYC.* Retrieved from http://www.wnyc.org/story/wanted-teachers-who-speak-bengali/

Mahadi, A. (2017). School enrollment high but dropouts even higher. *Dhaka Tribune, Sept. 8th*, 1.

Manning, K. (2014). *Dominican Republic revamps failing education system.* Retrieved from http://www.dw.com/en/dominican-republic-revamps-failing-education-system/a-17625149

Manyak, P. (2007). Character trait vocabulary: A school wide approach. *The Reading Teacher, 60*(6), 574–577.

Marino, M. (2011). World history and teacher education: Challenges and possibilities. *The Social Studies 102*(1), 3–8.

Marshall, J. D., Smagorinsky, P., & Smith, M. W. (1995). *The language of interpretation: Patterns of discourse in discussions of literature.* Urbana, IL: NCTE.

Martinez-Miron, E., & Rebolledo-Mendez, G. (2015). Cultural aspects related to motivation to learn in a Mexican context. *AIED 2015 Workshop Proceedings, 7*, 44–48.

Martiniello, M. (2008). Language and the performance of English-language learners in math word problems. *Harvard Educational Review, 78*(2), 333–368.

Matalene, C. (1985). Contrastive rhetoric: An American writing teacher in China. *College English, 47*(8), 789–808.

McKeon, D. (1994). When meeting "common" standards is uncommonly difficult. *Educational Leadership, 51*(8), 45–49.

Mckeown, M. G. (1993). Creating effective definitions for young word learners. *Reading Research Quarterly, 28*(1), 16–31.

Mckeown, M. G., Beck, I. L., & Worthy, M. J. (1993). Grappling with text ideas: Questioning the author. *The Reading Teacher, 46*(7), 560–566.

Mexico: Closing the gap in Mexico's upper secondary education system. (2007). *World Bank Washington DC.* Retrieved from http://documents.worldbank.org/curated/en/946531468045049013/Mexico-Closing-the-gap-in-Mexicos-upper-secondary-education-system

Meyer, L. M. (2000). Barriers to meaningful instruction for English learners. *Theory and Practice, 39*(4), 228–236.

Meyers, S. V. (2009). So you don't tricked: Counter-narratives of literacy in a rural Mexican community. *Community Literacy Journal, 3*(2), 19–35.

Meyers, S. V. (2011). They didn't tell me anything: Women's literacies and resistance in rural Mexico. *Gender in Education, 23*(7), 857–871.

Nath, S. R. (2012). Factors influencing primary students' learning achievement in Bangladesh. *Research in Education, 88,* 50–63.

Miah, M. B. (2006). *Current situation of basic education in Bangladesh.* Conference presentation, Mymensingh, Teacher's Training College. Mymensingh, Bangladesh. Retrieved from http://www.criced.tsukuba.ac.jp/pdf/06_Bangladesh_Badal.pdf

Michener, C. J., Proctor, C. P., & Silverman, R. D. (2018). Features of instructional talk predictive of reading comprehension. *Reading and Writing: An Interdisciplinary Journal, 31*(3), 725–756.

Mickan, P. (2007). Doing science and home economics: Curriculum socialization of new arrivals in Australia. *Language and Education, 21*(2), 107–123.

Miller, A. (1976). *Death of a salesman.* New York, NY: Penguin.

Miller, J. (1998). *If the earth were a few feet in diameter.* Seymour, CT: The Greenwich Workshop Press.

Miller, G. A., & Gilda, P. M. (1985). How to misread a dictionary. *AILA Bulletin.* Pisa, IT: AILA.

Miller, R. (2001). A 20-year update on reading instruction and primary school education: Mexican teachers' viewpoints. *The Reading Teacher, 54*(7), 704–716.

Mirza, G. H., Mahmud, K. (2012). Reading habits of the students with Bengali medium background at the English medium private universities in Bangladesh. *Higher Education Studies, 2*(2), 100–106.

Mizell, M. D., & Friedman, A. (2012). Tools for thinking: How the analysis of primary sources influence students' critical thinking. In McCoy, L. P. (Ed.). *Studies in teaching: 2012 research digest* (pp. 85–90). Winston-Salem, NC: Wake Forest University Press.

Mohan, B. (1979). Cultural bias in reading comprehension tests. In A. Y. Carlos (Ed.), *TESOL '79: The Learner in Focus* (pp. 171–177). Washington DC: TESOL.

Mohan, B. (1986). *Language and content.* Reading, MA: Addison-Wesley.

Moll, L. C., Amanti, C., Neff, D., & Gonzalez, N. (1992). Funds of knowledge for teaching: Using a qualitative approach to connect homes and classrooms. *Theory into Practice, 31*(1), 132–141.

Monte-Sano, C. (2011). Beyond reading comprehension and summary: Learning to read and write history by focusing on evidence, perspective, and interpretation. *Curriculum Inquiry, 41*(2), 212–249.

Morgan, D. N., & Rasinski, T. V. (2012). The power and potential of primary sources. *The Reading Teacher, 65*(8), 584–594.

Morris, M. J. (1993). *Shakespeare made easy.* Portland, ME: J Weston Walch.

Moss, B., Lapp, D., & O'Shea, M. (2011). Tiered texts: Supporting knowledge and language learning for English learners and struggling readers. *English Journal, 100*(5), 54–60.

Mount-Cors, M. F. (2013). Bridging the differences: Cultural background of Mexican students entering US schools. In *Learn NC*. Retrieved from http://www.learnnc.org/lp/editions/brdglangbarriers/4486

Nagy, W., & Townsend, D. (2012). Words as tools: Learning academic vocabulary as language acquisition. *Reading Research Quarterly, 47*(1), 91–108.

Naslund-Hadley, E., Varela, A. L., & Hepworth, K. A. (2014). What goes on inside Latin American math and science classrooms: A video study of teaching practices. *Global Education Review, 1*(3), 110–128.

Nation, I. S. P. (2001). *Learning vocabulary in another language.* Cambridge University Press.

Nation, I. S. P. (2006). How large a vocabulary is needed for reading and listening? *The Canadian Modern Language Review, 63*(1), 59–82.

Nation, I. S. P. (2008). *Teaching vocabulary: Strategies and techniques.* Boston, MA: Heinle.

Nation, I. S. P., & Deweerdt, J. P. (2001). A defense of simplification. *Prospect, 16*(3), 55–67.

Nation, P. (2015). Principles guiding vocabulary learning through extensive reading. *Reading in a Foreign Language, 27*(1), 136–145.

National Center for Education Statistics. (2018). *English language learners.* Retrieved from: https://nces.ed.gov/fastfacts

NCES (National Center for Education Statistics). (2019). *English language learners in public schools.* Retrieved from: https://nces.ed.gov/programs/coe/indicator_cgf.asp

Nelson-Barber, S., & Trumbull, E. (2007). Making assessment practices valid for indigenous American students. *Journal of American Indian Education, 46*(3), 132–147.

Nesbit, E. (1997). *Beautiful stories from Shakespeare for children.* New York, NY: Smithmark Publication.

New York City Department of Education. (2016). *English language learners and student support: School year 2015–2016 demographic report.* New York, NY.

New York City Department of Education. (2017). *English language learner policy and reference guide: 2017–2018.* New York, NY: New York City Department of Education.

New York City Department of Education. (2018). *English language learner demographics report for the 2016–17 school year.* New York, NY: New York City Department of Education.

New York State Department of Education. (2009). *Bilingual glossaries.* Retrieved from http://www.p12.nysed.gov/biling/bilinged/bilingual_glossaries.htm

New York State Department of Education. (2015). 2015 Edition. School administrator's manual: Secondary level examinations. Albany, NY.

New York State Department of Education. (2016). *NYC public schools.* https://data.nysed.gov/

New York State Department of Education. (2017). *2017 NYSESLAT.* Albany, NY: New York State Department of Education.

New York State Department of Education. (2018). *Guide to the NYSITELL 2018 Edition.* Albany, NY: New York State Department of Education.

Noguchi, J. (1998). *Easifying ESP texts for EFL science majors*. Education Resources Information Center, Washington DC. FL 025 577.

Novak, J. D., & Gorwin, B. (1984). *Learning how to learn*. Cambridge, UK: Cambridge University Press.

Nystrand, M. (1997). *Opening dialogue: Understanding the dynamics of language and learning in the English classroom*. New York, NY: Teachers College Press.

Ogle, D., Klemp, R., & McBride, B. (2007). *Building literacy in social studies: Strategies for improving comprehension and critical thinking*. Alexandria, VA: ASCD.

Oliver, K. (2009). An investigation of concept mapping to improve the reading comprehension of science texts. *Journal of Science Education Technology, 18*(5), 402–414.

On, L. W. (1999). The cultural context for Chinese learner: Conceptions of learning in the Confucian tradition. In D. A. Watkins & J. B. Biggs (Eds.), *The Chinese learner: Cultural, psychological, and contextual influences* (pp. 25–41). Hong Kong, China. Comparative Education Research Centre.

Onishi, N. (2008). For English studies, Koreans say goodbye to dad. *The New York Times*, Asia Pacific.

Ortmeier-Hooper, C. (2013). *The ELL writer: Moving beyond basics in the secondary classroom*. New York, NY: Teachers College Press.

Ortega, D. P., & Minchala, O. E. (2017). Assessing students in an authentic and ongoing manner in the English classroom. *Theory and Practice in Language Studies, 7*(3), 159–165.

Osterling, J. (2001). Waking the sleeping giant: Engaging and capitalizing on the sociocultural strengths of Latino community. *Bilingual Research Journal, 25*(1), 59–88.

Parks, S., & Maguire, M. H. (1999). Coping with on-the-job writing in ESL: A constructivist-semiotic perspective. *Language Learning, 49*(1), 143–175.

Pawan, F., & Craig, D. A. (2011). ESL and content teacher responses to discussions on English language learners' instruction. *TESOL Journal, 2*(3), 293–311.

Peizman, F., & Gadda, G. (1994). *With different eyes: Insights into teaching language minority students across the disciplines*. Reading, MA: Addison-Wesley.

Philippakos, Z. A. (2017). The use of responses to reading as a vehicle to opinion writing in the primary grades. *The Language and Literacy Spectrum, 27*(1), Article 1.

Piaget, J. (1947). *The psychology of intelligence*. New York, NY: Harcourt, Brace.

Piaget, J. (1972). Intellectual evolution from adolescence to adulthood. *Human Development, 15*(1), 1–12.

Pignatiello, J., Siggens, R. F., Chiappari, F. D., & Madama, J. (1998). *Essentials of biology*. Austin, TX: Holt, Rinehart and Winston,.

Pittman, H. C. (1996). *A grain of rice*. New York, NY: Bantam Doubleday Dell Books for Young Readers.

Porter, C. (2009). Words, words, words: Reading Shakespeare with English language learners. *English Journal, 99*(1), 44–49.

Price, D. W. W. (1998). A model for reading and writing about primary sources: The case of introductory psychology. *Teaching of Psychology, 17*(1), 48–53.

Prodhan, M. (2016). The present situation of education system in Bangladesh and scope for improvement. *Journal of Education and Social Sciences, 4*, 122–132.

Rahman, M., Hamzah, M. I. M., Meerah, T. S. M., & Rahman, M. (2010). Historical development of secondary education in Bangladesh: Colonial period to 21st century. *International Education Studies, 3*(1), 114–125.

Rahman, U. (2014). *Bangladesh-culture smart! The essential guide to customs & culture.* London, UK: Kuperard.

Ramirez, P., & Jaffee, A. T. (2016). Culturally responsive active citizenship education for newcomer students: A cross-state case study of two teachers in Arizona and New York. *International Journal of Multicultural Education, 18*(1), 45–67.

Rayan, S. (2012). Islamic philosophy of education. *International Journal of Humanities and Social Sciences, 2*(19), 150–156.

Reese, L. (2012). Storytelling in Mexican homes: Connections between oral and literacy practices. *Bilingual Research Journal, 35*(3), 277–293.

Regalla, M. (2012). Language objectives: More than just vocabulary. *TESOL Journal, 3*(2), 210–230.

Richard-Amato, P. A., & Snow, M. A. (1992). *The multicultural classroom: Readings for content-area teachers.* Reading, MA: Addison-Wesley Publishing Company.

Richter, C. (2004). *The light in the forest.* New York, NY: Vintage Books.

Rodriguez, H. M., Salinas, C., & Guberman, S. (2005). Creating opportunities for historical thinking with bilingual students. *Social Studies and the Young Learner, 8*(2), 9–13.

Rodriguez, T. A. (2001). From the known to the unknown: Using cognates to teach English to Spanish-speaking literates. *The Reading Teacher, 54*(8), 744–746.

Rosado, L. A., Hellawell, M., & Zamora, E. B. (2011). *An analysis of the education systems in Mexico and the United States from pre-kinder to 12 grade.* Education Resources Information Center, Washington, DC. ED 520 900.

Rosenblatt, L. (1978). *The reader, the text, the poem: The transactional theory of the literary work.* Carbondale, IL: Southern Illinois University Press.

Ross-Hudson, S. & Dong, Y. R. (1990). Literacy learning as a reflection of language and culture: Chinese elementary education. *Language Arts, 44*(2), 110–123.

Rubinstein-Avila, E. (2003). Facing reality: English language learners in middle school classes. *English Education, 35*(2), 122–136.

Rubinstein-Avila, E. (2006). Connecting with Latino learners. *Educational Leadership, 63*(5), 38–43.

Ruday, S. (2016). *The argument writing toolkit: using mentor texts in grades 6–8.* New York, NY: Routledge.

Rupley, W. H., & Slough, S. (2010). Building prior knowledge and vocabulary in science in the intermediate grades: Creating hooks for learning. *Literacy Research and Instruction, 49*(2), 99–112.

Salinas, C., Franquiz, M. E., & Reidel, M. (2008). Teaching world geography to late-arrival immigrant students: Highlighting practice and content. *The Social Studies, 99*(1), 71–76.

Salinas, C., Franquiz, M. E., & Guberman, S. (2006). Introducing historical thinking to second language learners: Exploring what students know and what they want to know. *The Social Studies, 97*(5), 203–207.

Samuel, M. (1995). Using versions of literary texts to improve comprehension. *TESOL Journal, 4*(3), 21–23.

Santiago, E. (2006). *When I was Puerto Rican: A memoir.* Cambridge, MA: Da Capo Press.

Sarkar, M., & Corrigan, D. (2014). Bangladeshi science teachers' perspectives of scientific literacy and teaching practices. *International Journal of Science and Mathematics Education, 12*(5), 1117–1141.

Scales, P. C. Benson, P. L., & Dershem, L. (2013). Building developmental assets to empower adolescent girls in rural Bangladesh: Evaluation of project Kishoree Kontha. *Journal of Research on Adolescence, 23*(1), 171–184.

Schraer, W. D., & Stoltze, H. J. (1995). *Biology: The study of life.* Upper Saddle River, NJ: Prentice Hall.

Schleppegrell, M., & Achugar, M., & Oteiza, T. (2004). The grammar of history: Enhancing content-based instruction through a functional focus on language. *TESOL Quarterly, 38*(1), 67–93.

Schleppegrell, M., & Oliveira, L. C. (2006). An integrated language and content approach for history teachers. *Journal of English for Academic Purposes, 5*(3), 254–268.

Schmitt, N., & Carter, R. (2000). The lexical advantage of narrow reading for second language learners. *TESOL Journal, 9*(1), 4–9.

Schogar, I. A. (2014). General characteristics of Islamic philosophy of education: How it is relevant to society of globalizing world. *Oasis International Conference on Islamic Education.* Kuala Lumpur Malaysia. Retrieved from https://conferencealerts.com/show-event?id=13543

Schraer, W., & Stoltze, H. J. (1995). *Biology: The study of life* (6th ed.). Upper Saddle River, NJ: Pearson Prentice- Hall.

Schumann, J. (1978). Second language acquisition: The pidginization hypothesis. In E. Hatch (Ed.), *Second language acquisition* (pp. 181–190). Rowley, MA: Newbury House.

Secondary Education. (2015). *National encyclopedia of Bangladesh.* Retrieved from http://en.banglapedia.org/index.php?title=Secondary_Education

Selinker, L. (1972). Interlanguage. *International Review of Applied Linguistics, 10*(3), 209–231.

Shalett, S. (1945, August 7). First atomic bomb dropped on Japan. *The New York Times,* 1.

Shanahan, T. (1997). Reading-writing relationships, thematic units, inquiry learning... In pursuit of effective integrated literacy instruction. *The Reading Teacher, 51*(1), 12–19.

Shen, F. (1989). The classroom and the wider culture: Identity as a key to learning English composition. *College Composition and Communication, 40*(4), 459–466.

Shi, L. (2004). Textual borrowing in second-language writing. *Written Communication, 21*(2), 171–200.

Shin, S., & Koh, M. (2005). Korean education in cultural context. Essays in Education, 14.

Sipra, M. A. (2013). Impact of English orthography on L2 acquisition. *English Language Teaching, 6*(3), 116–124.

Slater, T., & Mohan, B. (2010). Cooperation between science teachers and ESL teachers: A register perspective. *Theory in Practice, 49*(1), 91–98.

Slavit, G., & Slavit, D. (2007). Teaching mathematics and English to English language learners simultaneously. *Middle School Journal, 39*(4), 4–11.

Smith, P. (2014). A Dominican philosophy of education. In G. Kelly & K. Saunder (Eds.), *Dominican approaches in education* (pp. 3–18). Hindmarsh, SA: ATF Theology Publishing.

Smith, P. H., Jimenez, R. T., & Martinex-Leon, N. (2003). Other countries' literacies: What US educators can learn from Mexican schools. *The Reading Teacher, 56*(8), 772–781.

Snow, C. E., & Hoefnagel-Hohle, M. (1978). The critical period for language acquisition: Evidence from second language learning. *Child Development, 49*(4), 1114–1128.

Snow, C. (2008). Essay: What is the vocabulary in science? In A. S. Rosebery & S. Warren (Eds.), *Teaching science to English language learners: Building on students' strengths* (pp. 71–84). Alexandria, VA: NSTA.

Snow, M. A., Met, M., & Genesee, F. (1989). A conceptual framework for the integration of language and content in second/foreign language instruction. *TESOL Quarterly, 23*(2), 201–217.

Sorensen, C. W. (1994). Success and education in South Korea. *Comparative Education Review, 38*(10), 10–35.

Spanish. (n.d.). In *Omniglot: The online encyclopedia of writing systems and languages.* Retrieved from http://www.omniglot.com/writing/spanish.htm

Spanish language. (n.d.). In *Wikipedia.* https://en.wikipedia.org/wiki/Spanish_language

Stahl, R. J. (1987). *Using "think-time and "wait-time" skillfully in the classroom.* Education Resources Information Center, Washington, DC. ERIC Digest. ER370885.

Sullivan, P. N. (1996). Sociocultural influences on classroom interactional styles. *TESOL Journal, 6*(1), 32–34.

Sultana, Q. N. (2012). Philosophy of education: An Islamic perspective. *Philosophy and Progress, LI–LII,* 10–36.

Swain, M. (1996). Integrating language and content in immersion classrooms: Research perspectives. *The Canadian Modern Language Review, 52*(4), 529–548.

Tajeri, M., Syal, P., & Marzban, S. (2017). Enhancing vocabulary and writing skills through digital storytelling in higher education. *Journal of Educational Technology, 14*(3), 40–47.

Tanaka, J., & Gilliland, B. (2017). Critical thinking instruction in English for academic purposes writing courses: A dialectial thinking approach. *TESOL Journal, 8*(3), 657–674.

Tang, F., & Dunkelblau, H. (1998). Chinese students in the U.S.: Myths and reality. *ESL Magazine, 1*(6), 26–29.

Tapan, M. S. M. (2010). Science education in Bangladesh. In Y. J. Lee (Ed.), *World of science education: Science education research in Asia* (pp. 16–34). Rotterdam, Netherlands: Sense.

Tasdemir, H., & Yidirim, T. (2017). Collaborative teaching from English language instructors' perspectives. *Journal of Language and Linguistic Studies, 13*(2), 632–642.

Taylor, K. (2017). Graduation rate in New York State hits a new high: 79.4%. *New York Times* A16.

Teemant, A., Bernhardt, E., & Rodriguez-Munoz, M. (1996). Collaborating with content area teachers: What we need to share. *TESOL Journal, 5*(4), 16–20.

Thornbury, S. (2002). *How to teach vocabulary.* London, UK: Pearson Education Limited.

Tovani, C. (2000). *I read it, but I don't get it: Comprehension strategies for adolescent readers.* Portland, ME: Stenhouse Publishers.

Truman, H. S. (1945). *Radio report to the American people on the Potsdam Conference.* August 9, 1945. Retrieved from https://www.trumanlibrary.org/publicpapers/?pid=104.

Turner, J. (2017). Getting to know your learners. *CENGAGE: National Geographic Learning.* June, 21, PD 20-22.

Urquhard, V. (2009). *Using writing in mathematics to deepen student learning.* Education Resources Information Center, Washington, DC. ERIC Database ED 544 239.

Verplaetse, L. S. (1998). How content teachers interact with English language learners. *TESOL Journal, 7*(5), 24–28.

Verplaetse, L. S. (2000). Mr. Wonderful: Portrait of dialogic teacher. In J. K. Hall & L. S. Verplaetse (Eds.), *Second and foreign language learning through classroom interaction* (pp. 221–242). Mahwah, NJ: Lawrence Erlbaum.

Vygotsky, L. S. (1978). *Mind in society*. Cambridge, MA: Harvard University Press.

Waddell, G., & Quinn, R. J. (2011). Two applications of Venn Diagrams. *Teaching Statistics, 33*(2), 45–48.

Walker, S., Edwards, V., & Blacksell, R. (1996). Designing bilingual books for children. *Visible Language, 30*(3), 269–283.

Walters, S. (2011). Provision, purpose and pedagogy in a Bengali supplementary school. *Language Learning Journal, 39*(2), 163–175.

Wang, A. (2015). The difference between Chinese and American education. In *Epoch Times*. Oct. Retrieved from http://www.theepochtimes.com/n3/1483758-the-difference-between-chinese-and-american-education/

Wang, W., Wang, J., Lang, Y., & Mayer, V. (1996). Science education in the People's Republic of China. *Science Education, 80*(2), 203–222.

Watkins-Goffman, L., & Cummings, V. (1997). Bridging the gap between native language and second language literacy instruction: A naturalistic study. *Bilingual Research Journal, 21*(4), 381–394.

Weisman, E. M., & Hansen, L. E. (2007). Strategies for teaching social studies to English-language learners at the elementary level. *The Social Studies, 98*(3), 180–184.

Welie, C., Schoonen, R., Kuiken, F., & Bergh, H. (2017). Expository text comprehension in secondary school: For which readers does knowledge of connectives contribute the most? *Journal of Research in Reading, 40*(S1), 42–65.

WestEd. (2010). Education Digest (2011). Culture and assessment: Discovering what students really know. *R&D Alert, 11*(2), 6–9.

Weston-Sementelli, J. L., Allen, L. K., & McNamara, D. S. (2018). Comprehension and writing strategy training improves performance on content-specific source-based writing tasks. *International Journal of Artificial Intelligence in Education, 28*(1), 106–137.

Weigle, S. C., & Parker, K. (2012). Source text borrowing in an integrated reading/writing assessment. *Journal of Second Language Writing, 21* (2), 118–133.

Wharton, E. (2018). *Ethan Frome*. Scotts Valley, CA: CreateSpace Independent Publishing Platform.

Wiggins, G. (1992). Creating tests worth taking. *Educational Leadership, 49*(8), 26–33.

Wilburne, J. M., Marinak, B. A., & Strickland, M. J. (2011). Addressing cultural bias. *Mathematics Teaching in the Middle School, 16*(8), 461–465.

Winsor, M. S. (2007–2008). Bridging the language barrier in mathematics. *Mathematics Teacher, 101*(5), 372–378.

Wolfe, P. (2004). "The owl cried": Reading abstract literacy concepts with adolescent ESL students. *Journal of Adolescent & Adult Literacy, 47*(6), 402–413.

Woodall, B. R. (2002). Language-switching: Using the first language while writing in a second language. *Journal of Second Language Writing, 11*(1), 7–28.

Woude, M. V. D. (1998). Korean students in the United States. *ESL Magazine, 1*(1), 28–30.

Wylie, E. (2016). Puritan sonnet. In *Crumbs from the feast of the mind*. Retrieved from http://poetryandcrumbs.blogspot.com/2016/12/puritan-sonnet-by-elinor-wylie.html

Yaghobian, F., Samuel, M., & Mahmoudi, M. (2017). Learner's use of first language in EFL collaborative learning: A sociocultural view. *Malaysian Online Journal of Educational Sciecnesm, 5*(4), 36–55.

Young, K. M., & Leinhardt, G. (1998). Writing from primary documents: A way of knowing in history. *Written Communication, 15*(1), 25–68.

Yum, J. O. (1988). The impact of Confucianism on interpersonal relationships and communication patterns in East Asia. *Communication Monographs, 55*(4), 374–388.

Zahar, R., Cobb, T., & Spada, N. (2001). Acquiring vocabulary through Redding: Effects of frequency and contextual richness. *The Canadian Modern Language Review, 57*(4), 541–572.

Zarate, M. E. (2007). *Understanding Latino parental involvement in education: Perceptions, expectations, and recommendations*. Ivine, CA: University of Southern California, TRPI.

Zenkov, K., Ewaida, M., Ne, A., & Lynch, M. (2012). Seeing how to ask first: Photo elicitation motivates English language learners to write. *Middle School Journal, 44*(2), 6–13.

Zhao, Y. (2002). Work often comes first for Bangladeshi students. *New York Times, July 10*, N.Y./Region.

Zhou, W., Shu, H., Miller, K., & Yan, M. (2018). Reliance on orthography and phonology in reading in Chinese: A developmental study. *Journal of Research in Reading, 41*(2), 370–391.

Zimmermann, K. A. (2015). Mexican culture: Customs & traditions. In *Live Science Contributor, Feb. 10*. Retrieved from: https://www.livescience.com/38647-mexican-culture.html

Zwiers, J., & Crawford, M. (2011). *Academic conversations: Classroom talk that fosters critical thinking and content understandings*. Portland, ME: Stenhouse Publishers.

INDEX

Teaching English Language Learners in Secondary Subject Matter Classes, pages 239–242.
Copyright © 2019 by Information Age Publishing
239

Mon - Radoncic

Period 6 - 3rd Grade

Period 8 - 6th Grade

Tues flores
Period 2 - 8th Grade

Wed →Flores
Period 7 - 1st Grade

Period 8 - 6th Grade
→Radoncic

Made in United States
North Haven, CT
30 January 2024

thurs

48131783R00141

Fri
Period 7 - 8 →Flores
7th Grade